# When Sonia Met Boris

# When Sonia Met Boris

## An Oral History of Jewish Life under Stalin

ANNA SHTERNSHIS

OXFORD
UNIVERSITY PRESS

**OXFORD**
UNIVERSITY PRESS

Oxford University Press is a department of the University of Oxford. It furthers
the University's objective of excellence in research, scholarship, and education
by publishing worldwide. Oxford is a registered trade mark of Oxford University
Press in the UK and certain other countries.

Published in the United States of America by Oxford University Press
198 Madison Avenue, New York, NY 10016, United States of America.

© Oxford University Press 2017

Library of Congress Cataloging-in-Publication Data
Names: Shternshis, Anna, author.
Title: When Sonia met Boris : an oral history of Jewish life under Stalin / Anna Shternshis.
Description: New York : Oxford University Press, [2017] |
Includes bibliographical references and index.
Identifiers: LCCN 2016033941| ISBN 9780190223106 (hardcover) |
ISBN 9780190223120 (ebook epub)
Subjects: LCSH: Jews—Soviet Union—Interviews. | Jews—Soviet Union—Social conditions. |
Jews—Soviet Union—Economic conditions. | Jews—Employment—Soviet Union. |
Discrimination in employment—Soviet Union. | Jews—Soviet Union—Identity. | Interviews.
Classification: LCC DS134.85 .S58 2017 | DDC 305.892/4047—dc23
LC record available at https://lccn.loc.gov/2016033941

9 8 7 6 5 4 3 2 1

Printed by Edwards Brothers Malloy, United States of America

*To Bella and Arkady Shternshis, with love*

# Contents

# Acknowledgments

This book took twelve years to write, and I could not have done it without the input of my wonderful colleagues, friends, and family members. Doris Bergen helped me to think through the entire concept of the book and provided perceptive comments on the entire manuscript. Our numerous discussions of how people make decisions under duress, and how they reflect about these choices, informed almost every sentence. Zvi Gitelman, always my first-go-to colleague and mentor, helped to emphasize the fundamental direction of the project and make decisions about the uses of oral history. Lynne Viola pointed to crucial issues relating to the nature of Soviet history, and important policies that informed the lives of my interviewees. Arkady Zeltser provided amazing insights and interpretations on the Soviet Jewish experience, and helped to correct a lot of factual mistakes (all those that remain were introduced after he finished reading!). Olga Gershenson suggested that I reframe the book as a story about people, rather than trends, and also suggested looking into narrative analysis theories. David Shneer encouraged me to think broader about the nature of the Soviet Jewish experience and about meanings of identity. Ato Quayson pointed out the importance of Vladimir Propp and stressed the significance of genres in analyzing narratives, a suggestion that changed the interpretive framework. Naomi Seidman shared her deep insight on how gender is discussed in Jewish culture and thus helped me to understand the interviewees better. I thank Jeffrey Veidlinger for his suggestions about how to read and interpret Soviet oral history and for sharing, many times, his own work-in-progress. Scott Ury encouraged me to ask (and answer) bigger questions and challenge the established wisdom. Bob Weinberg gave very careful and useful suggestions about almost every page of the manuscript. Mikhail Krutikov proposed so many innovative ways to analyze the historical data from testimonies and, as usual, came up with (correct) interpretations I did not even suspect would be possible! My work with Pavel Lion (better known as Psoy Korolenko) helped me visualize the relationship between public and private spheres of Soviet Jewish life. I also thank Mordechai Altshuler, Vadim Altskan, Olena Bagno, Elissa Bemporad, Robert Brym, Oleg Budnitsky, Jonathan Dekel Chen, Israel Cohen, Diana Dimitru, Gennady Estraikh, Kiril Feferman, Laurie Fialkoff, Gabriel Finder, David Fishman, ChaeRan Freeze, Willi Goetschel, Sol Goldberg, Marat Grinberg, Anat Helman, Sam Kassow, Zohar Weiman Kellman, Jeffrey Kopstein, Gennady Kostyrchenko, Zeev Levin, Michael Marrus, Dan Michman, Andrea Most, Harriet Murav, Melanie Newton, Derek Penslar, Larissa Remmenick, James Retallack, Sveta Robeman, Yaakov Roi, Moshe Rossman, Gabriella Safran, Maxim D. Shrayer, Alison Smith, Susan Solomon, Catherine Wanner, Karen Weisman, Piotr Wrobel, Carol Zemel and many others for discussing the project, answering my questions, providing insights, clarifying inconsistencies, and above all for being great colleagues and friends. None of these individuals of course, are responsible for any mistakes or problems in the book.

I thank Anna Rodzevich, Josh Tapper, Simran Karir, and Symon Foren for being wonderful research assistants. Special thanks go to Gregory Eady, who designed the tables, and to Natasha Richichi-Fried for creating the bibliography. Thank you Janet Hyer, Dan Rosenberg, and Nick Underwood for editing and proofreading the manuscript. A very special-thank you goes to Nancy Toff, the editor of the Oral History series at Oxford University Press, whose close reading, razor-sharp advice, and advocacy for the reader improved clarity, helped me to rephrase key ideas, and transformed the manuscript into an actual book. I also thank the entire team of Oxford University Press, including Julia Turner, Elda Granata, and Steve Dodson for their professionalism and help.

Earlier versions of parts of chapters 3, 4, 5, and 6 appeared in following publications: "From the Red Cradle: Memories of Jewish Family Life in the Soviet Union" in Catherine Wanner, editor, *State Secularism and Lived Religion in Soviet Russia and Ukraine* (Oxford: Oxford University Press, 2012), 63–92; "Choosing a Spouse in the USSR: Gender Differences and the Jewish Ethnic Factor," *Jews in Russia and Eastern Europe*, Winter 2, no. 51 (2003), 5–30; and "Salo in Challah: Soviet Jew's Experience of Food in the 1920s-1950s," in *Jews and Their Foodways: Studies in Contemporary Jewry. An Annual XXVIII*, edited by Anat Helman. (Jerusalem: Oxford University Press, 2015), 10–27.

Funding for this work was made possible with the help of generous support from the Insight Grant and the Standard Research Grant from the Social Sciences and Humanities Research Council of Canada, and two grants from Rabbi Israel Miller Fund for Shoah Education, Research, and Documentation of the Material Claims Conference against Germany (grant 1413 and grant S028), both of which were received jointly with Zvi Gitelman. I conducted the field work in Philadelphia when I was a fellow at the Herbert D. Katz Centre for Advanced Judaic Studies at the University of Pennsylvania, and I am extremely grateful to the center and to David Ruderman for his support of this project.

I have benefited tremendously from working at the University of Toronto—being affiliated with the department of Germanic Languages and Literatures and enjoying support from all my colleagues there, especially Markus Stock who created a wonderful atmosphere of collegiality. Very special thanks go to Dale Gebhardt, who helped me to manage the logistics of complex projects, always striving to keep a great sense of humor in face of terrifying paperwork. Being at the Centre for Diaspora and Transnational Studies changed the way I understand Russian Jewish culture. I thank Ato Quayson, Hui Kian Kwee, Antonela Arhin, Ken McDonald, Kevin O'Neill, and the late Richard Iton, for true interdisciplinary dialogue (and fun discussions at the coffee machine!). The Anne Tanenbaum Centre for Jewish Studies has been my intellectual home at the University of Toronto for so many years. Its support for Yiddish, Russian Jewish Studies and interdisciplinary approaches has been exemplary. I thank the former directors of the center—David Novak, Derek Penslar, Hindy Najman, and especially Jeffrey Kopstein—for their personal and institutional support of this project. Sol Goldberg, Emily Springgay, and Galina Vaisman made the center the most welcoming place on campus, and I thank them for their professionalism and tireless work. The fact that I am able to finish this book while directing the Center is yet another testament to their incredible talents and dedication.

The book is based on interviews with 474 individuals who lived through very difficult times in the Soviet Union. I would have never been able to accomplish these interviews without the help of journalists, activists, social workers, and officers working with the Russian Jewish elderly in the United States, Germany, Russia , and Canada, too numerous to list here. I would like to thank Igor Akselrod, Dmitrii Morgulis, and Sofiya Lipkina (New York), Ella Shakhnikova (Berlin), Vladimir Oks (Potsdam), and Leonid Essen

(Moscow) for helping to run the project. Toronto-based journalist Alexander Gershtein helped publicize my research and introduced me personally to many interviewees. Maia Master, the editor-in-chief of the *Russian Express* newspaper in Toronto; the staff of the Jewish Russian Community Centre of Toronto; and Elena Kasimova, a journalist at *Exodus* magazine all helped finding interviewees. Special thanks goes to Zelina Iskanderova of Toronto, who first introduced me to the Russian-speaking community of Toronto. I also want to thank my friend Svetlana Dvoretsky for helping me to think about the present and the future of the Russian Jewish community. Above all, I thank each and every person who volunteered to be interviewed for this project—it is only because of your generosity, resilience, good spirits, and patience that the readers will get a glimpse of what it was really like to live under Stalin.

Over the course of twelve years, the concept of the book changed many times; eventually, it became a story of balancing work and family choices. Although I was often unhappy with how slowly the project was progressing, I now understand that I could not have written it twelve or even ten years ago. Raising my four children, Isaac, Shana, Mira, and Avi, who were all born during this period, helped me understand that essentially my interviewees had found the proverbial and ever unobtainable work-life balance which I was trying to achieve, but in very different circumstances. I thank Alicia Gabriel, who took care of my children when I was working. My husband, Daniel Rosenberg, who listened to and discussed every idea that appeared in this book, who edited every single word of it, and who put up with my long days of work, deserves very special gratitude. I thank my sister Julia Shternshis for her constant cheer and appreciation. On the cover of this book—appropriately, I think—is a wedding photograph taken in 1937, featuring my grandparents, Faina Khromaya and Isaac Zimerman. Writing this book made me appreciate my own parents, Bella and Arkady Shternshis, on an entirely different level. I dedicate this book to both of them, with love.

# Part I

Oral History and the First Generation of Soviet Jews

# 1

# When Only Memories
# Tell the Truth

Boris G., a retired surgeon from Ukraine, had just reached his 90th birthday when a local Jewish newspaper contacted him with an interview request. In preparation, he positioned his documents on the table: a record of excellent service in a medical unit of the Red Army, complete with three military awards, and a workbook from the hospital where he worked for 40 years. Boris was born in 1913 in Slavuta, a small town in the Khmelnitsky region of Central Ukraine. His grandfather, who owned a tiny beehive business, was arrested in the 1920s, when Boris was a little boy. His father, who worked as an accountant, encouraged him to get out of Slavuta and get a better life. Following his father's advice, Boris left when he turned 15 and eventually completed his medical training in Kyiv in 1937. That same year two other important things happened: he got married to his classmate Sonia, and his father was arrested on false accusations of espionage. Boris never heard from him again.

During the war, Sonia went to Central Asia, where she worked in a hospital and took care of their toddler son. Boris was drafted into the Red Army—as a military surgeon, working in a field hospital, conducting dozens of surgeries per week (sometimes per day), and saving the lives of countless soldiers. After the war, Boris worked in a hospital in Kyiv, first as a staff surgeon and eventually retiring as the chief of surgery. In 1946, he found out that his parents, his grandparents, and many family friends had been killed in Slavuta in 1941 along with the majority of both local Jews and those from neighboring towns and villages. He never found the strength to go back to Slavuta, even for a short visit, but he contributed money to help erect a monument to commemorate the victims of the war there. He arrived to Canada in the early 2000s, after spending about 10 years in Israel.

His grandchildren were born in Toronto, his children found good jobs, but Boris felt out of place—with no knowledge of English or understanding of the local community, he was sinking into a depression. It was his great-grandson Michael, a high school student, who contacted the newspaper suggesting that they should interview his grandfather, a decorated Jewish surgeon from the Soviet Union. Michael also volunteered to translate.

The journalist arrived right on time, a pleasant Canadian-born Jewish woman in her late 40s. She began by asking Boris whether he had witnessed any pogroms, because, she said, her great-grandparents too came from the Russian Empire, and they had barely survived. Boris told her that his older brother had been wounded in a pogrom in Slavuta. The family hid in a neighbor's cellar in 1918, when Boris was five years old. "What about the Holocaust?" she asked. Boris explained that he served in the Red Army as a doctor, but as soon as the journalist found out that the story of the Holocaust did not have references to Auschwitz, she seemed to lose interest.

Then they moved to the questions of faith. "Was it hard to practice Judaism under Stalin?" she asked. Boris misunderstood. He started telling her about discrimination that his children encountered when they tried to enter medical schools, about day-to-day negative remarks from neighbors. All of that happened in the 1970s, under Brezhnev. But the journalist wanted to know whether his wife lit candles for Shabbat, and whether they celebrated Passover in hiding. Boris, who had learned about religious holidays *after* he left the Soviet Union in the 1990s, had nothing to contribute. In desperation, the journalist asked whether she and his wife Sonia had a Jewish wedding when they got married in 1937. Boris misunderstood again, and showed her a photograph from his anniversary celebrating 50 years of marriage, featuring guests from all over the world and a local ultra-Orthodox rabbi.

The journalist wanted a picture from the 1930s, but Boris was at a loss about what to tell her. He and his wife registered in a civil ceremony. They did not really have a wedding, and of course, he had no photographs.

They spent an hour talking, but Boris never got to show the documents that he had prepared. He had lived his life as a Jew, he never hid that he had been a Jew, he and his family suffered from discrimination, but somehow he did not seem Jewish enough (or interesting enough) to the well-meaning but unprepared journalist. His life story never appeared in print. However, the story of the failed interview firmly entered family lore.

Boris and Sonia lived through the entire history of the Soviet Union both suffering and enjoying it, like so many of their peers. In fact, after our conversation, I decided to put them into the title of this book in an attempt to repair their failed encounter with the Canadian Jewish world and to bring together the seemingly parallel universes of the Russian Jewish civilization of Boris and Sonia and the Western society in which they currently live.

Boris's story, like the wider Soviet Jewish history of which it is a part, is not one of pure suffering.[1] Soviet Jews were both creators and victims of the Soviet regime. Like all Soviet citizens, they lived through serious tribulations—expropriation of their private property in the 1920s, famines and the Great Terror in the 1930s, and World War II—while as Jews, they also had to deal with the Holocaust and postwar discrimination. Surviving one of those episodes would normally be more than enough to change a human life, but experiencing *all* of them seems unimaginable. In addition, Soviet Jews witnessed both the formation of the Soviet Union and its collapse.[2] Every person who lived through this time has a story, but the story is usually told on that person's behalf. Often when people like Boris try to tell it, they are not heard, at least not properly. Despite the sea of literature devoted to the history of Jews in the Soviet Union, we still know very little of how an ordinary person born to a Jewish family lived through the Soviet experiment, including the period of Stalin's reign.[3]

Jeffrey Veidlinger's latest book revealed that in smaller towns, deeply seated religious beliefs dominated Jews' identities throughout the Soviet period because they never left the shtetl.[4] My book, based on 474 oral histories, examines how other Jews of the same generation, the ones who did leave their smaller villages and *shtetlekh* (small towns) in the 1930s or 1940s, understood the Soviet experience. These are Soviet-educated individuals, like Boris and Sonia, who held low- to mid-rank white-collar jobs in large, medium, and small urban centers in the Soviet Union and who represent the majority of the Soviet Jewish population.[5]

In the Soviet Union, personal lives were deeply affected by the political, social, and economic policies of the state. It has been known for some time that Soviet people tend to remember their lives in terms of public, rather than personal, milestones.[6] But are these events the same for all Soviet citizens? Can we talk about Soviet Jewish memory, and Soviet Jewish narrative, and if so, what is it?

By 1917, there were approximately 6 million Jews in the former territories of the Tsarist Empire. In 1923, after new borders were drawn, there were 2,431,000 Jews in Soviet-held territories. By 1926, Jews numbered 2,680,823.[7] Prior to that, the civil war that followed the Russian Revolution of 1917 left many Jewish shtetlekh devastated. More than 50,000 Jews were killed in pogroms, including Boris's brother, and half a million were left homeless.[8] In the 1920s, many Jews, especially younger men like Boris, migrated from smaller towns to larger ones, and then from Ukraine to Russia. The famine of 1932 and 1933 catalyzed large population movements as well. In fact, the early Soviet period witnessed one of the largest internal Jewish migrations in Europe, with hundreds of thousands of Jews flocking to Moscow, Leningrad, Kyiv, and other large Soviet cities. At least 300,000 Jews (almost 20 percent of Ukrainian Jewry) moved from smaller towns to the large urban centers between 1926 and 1939.

From the outset, Soviet government policies that attacked religious beliefs, expropriated possessions, and fiercely fought against the "old order" transformed the traditional Jewish community. Soon after the Bolsheviks came to power in 1917, they established organizations designed to "Sovietize" Jews, economically and culturally.[9] Meanwhile, many Jews in Ukraine suffered severely in the mid-1920s.[10] In fact, 30 percent of them were arrested on accusation of being capitalists, usually for possession of a modest amount of private property, just like Boris's grandfather.[11] These families, as well as families of religious activists, became *lishentsy* (persons deprived of rights). Until 1936, when the law was abolished, children from families of *lishentsy* needed to publicly denounce their parents in order to be eligible for admission into institutions of higher education. By 1937, the Great Terror— the mass arrests that swept the Soviet Union and took millions, including Boris's father, into its prison system or, worse, killed them—affected many Jews as well. Although the Great Terror was not directed at Jews because they were Jews, a large, still unknown number of them were assassinated or jailed during this time.[12]

In the 1939 census, 3,020,000 people declared themselves Jewish, 89 percent of them living in large urban centers.[13] The annexation of the Baltic states and parts of Poland and Romania over the following two years brought the Jewish population to just above 5 million.[14] During the war, of the 27 million Soviet people killed, about 2.7 million were Soviet Jews.[15] Of that number, more than 140,000 were killed in combat (out of

460,000–480,000 who served in the Soviet army).[16] The rest died in Nazi and, later, Allied-occupied Europe. But 1.8 million Jews, including approximately 200,000 Polish Jews, survived the war in the Soviet interior, to which some were exiled, evacuated, or escaped.[17] About 180,000 Jews survived the occupation, mostly in Romanian-occupied Transnistria.[18]

The war not only took lives, it changed Soviet Jews' socioeconomic status. Artisans, craftsmen, agricultural workers, people without higher education, and the elderly died in larger numbers than did engineers, scientists, doctors, and other skilled professionals who were evacuated by the Soviet government as part of the major Soviet relocation project, or, like Boris, who served in the Red Army.[19]

By 1945, 2.3 million Jews survived in the Soviet Union.[20] From 1948 to 1953, unofficial government policies began to restrict Jewish rights; the Soviet persecution machine began targeting activists, people who actively sought to develop ethnic cultural institutions.[21] These policies culminated in the arrest and execution of the members of the Jewish Anti-Fascist Committee, a Soviet organization designed to help the Soviet war effort from 1941 to 1945.[22] In addition, the insinuation that Jews plotted to poison Stalin led to the arrest and persecution of many prominent doctors, the majority of them Jews—an affair that became known as the Doctors' Plot of 1953.[23] During this time, the "fifth line," a 1932 ordinance that recorded nationality (ethnicity) in Soviet internal documents, clearly identifying Jews as such, began to play an important role in denying Jews employment. This period, 1948–53, is known as "the black years of Soviet Jewry" because of the large number of Jews that were arrested and harassed.[24]

After Stalin's death in 1953, the social and political climate in the country changed again. Accusations against Jewish doctors were dismissed; arrested Jewish cultural activists and Yiddish writers were released. However, government institutions did not combat growing anti-Jewish discriminatory practices.[25] Jewish cultural life was never restored during Khrushchev's rule, 1953–64. However, it became easier for Jews to enter institutions of higher education, especially in technical disciplines. Once again, certain restrictions, although never official, applied to Jewish career choices and, therefore, to social status.[26]

This book studies the spheres of family and work, defined as broadly as possible. Studying marriage patterns, family dynamics, anecdotes about memorable home celebrations, and stories of raising children and choosing professional occupations sheds light on the mechanism of control imposed by the totalitarian state on individual choices, as well as ways of adjusting, accepting, or resisting these policies. Before the Revolution, Jewish migration usually entailed a change of residence but not a change of job.[27] After the Revolution, resettlement meant a different life, bringing about the transformation of social, economic, and cultural aspects. One illustration is the influx of Jewish young people into universities and scientific institutions: approximately 13 percent of all students and scientists in the USSR were Jewish by the end of the 1930s. Jews accounted for 15 percent of adults with higher education, 10 times the rate of the general population and three times that of other urban dwellers.[28] The book examines the personal decisions behind these numbers, and for the later period, stories of personal discrimination. How did the policy against cosmopolitanism of 1948–53 actually work? How did it affect Jewish workers and students, as well as youth in various industries? What career choices resulted from these policies? What does the situation in regard to Jewish employment tell us about how the Soviet system actually functioned on an everyday basis? Above all, would a Jew and a non-Jew from the same location and within the same socioeconomic background make similar choices in choosing careers and marital partners? Once we know the answer, we get closer to knowing how Jews lived in the county ruled by Joseph Stalin.

# 2

# Who Gets to Tell the Story

## Oral Histories of the First Soviet Jewish Generation

People who live through historical events and people who study those events often have different views on what was significant and why. Hardly any historian of Soviet Jewry, for example, will dismiss the importance of the Molotov-Ribbentrop Nonaggression Pact of 1939, the creation of the State of Israel in 1948, or Israel's Six Day War of 1967 in analyzing the milestones of Soviet Jewish life. However, Jews who lived through these events in the Soviet Union frequently need to be prompted to speak about them. Because of these discrepancies, many historians tend to dismiss oral histories as "unreliable" at best and "useless" at worst.

Indeed, oral histories should not be used as the only source for understanding the past; neither should newspapers, secret government memos, or memoirs. Each source tells its own story, and each of these stories has to be analyzed in accordance with its nature. Some important events in Soviet Jewish history simply cannot, however, be understood properly *without* oral histories.

This book is based on in-depth interviews obtained from 474 Ashkenazi Jews who were born in the Russian Empire or the Soviet Union between 1906 and 1928.[1] After the collapse of the Soviet Union, most of these people left the country and settled in Israel, the United States, Canada, Germany, and other countries in the Western Hemisphere.[2] The interviews were therefore conducted in the United States (New York and Philadelphia), Canada (Toronto), Germany (Berlin and Potsdam), and Russia (Moscow). Most of the interviewees volunteered to meet and tell their life stories.[3] A slight preference was given to Yiddish speakers, but overall anyone who identi-fied as a Jew and was born in the Soviet Union before 1928—and who, of course, wanted to participate in the project—was interviewed.[4]

The project started with the goal of fleshing out the history of Jewish life in the Soviet Union before the war. Eventually, it evolved into a broader inquiry into the daily life of Soviet Jews before, during, and after World War II, with one underlying question of how being Jewish impacted one's life in the Soviet Union. Open-ended questions, which left room for devia-tions, associations, and retracing of steps, allowed people to follow their trains of thought.

Many people needed to share their life story in order to find a context from which they could remember "things Jewish." Most interviewees did not associate the word "Jewish" with culture or religion. Instead, they wanted to talk about five periods in their lives: the Great Terror in 1937–39, World War II, the period right after the war between 1945 and 1953, their children's struggles in the 1970s, and their immigration or (for those who stayed) the collapse of the Soviet Union in the 1990s. More than half of all people interviewed (and the absolute majority of those from Ukraine) spoke about barely surviving the Famine of 1932. Many were forced to leave their homes, others lost parental support (because their parents had been arrested), and some experienced starvation and disease. About three out of five interviewees mentioned that their parents had been arrested in the 1930s, and most also spoke of their parents and grandparents having been arrested for possession of private property in the late 1920s (in accordance with the OGPU [Secret Police][5] directive to arrest private traders, issued on January 4, 1928).[6]

Approximately 20 percent of the interviewees themselves had been either arrested and imprisoned briefly during 1937–39 or had lost fam-ily members to arrest and exile. Usually, this trauma defined the narra-tive of their future lives, even if they were released from prison in 1941. Historians do not consider the Great Terror as an attack against Jews,[7] yet the interviewees unanimously present the recollections of it as an attack on Jewish life and essential to their Jewish identity.[8] None of the partici-pants of the project wanted to talk about the actual experience of surviving in the Soviet punitive system. Therefore, despite the importance of these episodes in their lives, they do not play a significant role in constructing their life stories.

During World War II, some interviewees served in the army, while others were evacuated to the Soviet interior, joined partisan units, hid with non-Jews, or lived in ghettos. The war was understandably the most important historical event that each of these people had witnessed and was a central feature in many testimonies. It also had a profound impact on marital and career choices.

The immediate postwar period (1945–53) provided the most stories. Many people described discrimination at workplace and school, restrictions in continuing higher education, and exposure to mockery in both the official press and their daily encounters. Many remembered attempting to hide their ethnicity by changing their names and bribing officials to change their documents. All this took place at the same time that they were grieving over family members and friends who had perished during the war. Unconditional loyalty to the state, which had prevailed within the Jewish community during the 1930s, was replaced with disappointment in the Soviet government and its policies of unwritten Jewish discrimination. In the 1940s, being Jewish started to signify misfortune and seen without any positive aspects.

During this time, Jews began to keep more secrets than other Soviet citizens. Those who survived the war in German- or Romanian-occupied territories[9] were automatically considered suspicious and were subjected to interrogations until they could prove that they had not collaborated with the German army.[10] Many survivors of Soviet-based camps and ghettos lied in their documents, saying they had been evacuated, in order to avoid troubles with the law. Often, their children did not know the truth about their wartime past. As unofficial restrictions on Jewish occupations and life began in the late 1940s, many Jews tried to hide their origins by rewriting the "nationality" indicator in their passports—they did everything possible to make sure that they and their children would not live with the stigma of being Jewish. Not a single aspect of Jewish life under Stalin can be understood without knowing how much Soviet Jews kept silent and secret within both their professional and personal worlds.

Finally, all interviewees lived through the collapse of the Soviet Union. The majority of them emigrated during this period. Many said this had been the hardest thing that they ever had to do—which is noteworthy, since they had survived famine, the war, and Stalin. The collapse of the Soviet Union was also a time when being Jewish was very important in their lives. For those who stayed in Russia, the transformation was no less traumatic than for the immigrants—many people lost their savings, pensions, and apartments and had to rely on Jewish charitable organizations for survival.[11]

Almost everyone that I talked to used the word "Jewish" to mean "negative" or "stressful" when they discussed their experiences in the workplace, their relationships with neighbors, and other social interactions. In describing the process of finding their spouses, however, they almost universally used the word "Jewish" as a synonym for "good," "smart," and "worthy."

## What Narrators Did before They Retired

The interviewees were highly educated: more than half had the equivalent of a college degree, and almost all had completed high school; 98 percent finished seven years of schooling and 85 percent ten years, 60 percent received higher education in an institute or university, 25 percent went through vocational schools (*technikum*), 15 percent earned a degree of *kandidat nauk* (doctoral degree equivalent), and a few earned a *doktor nauk* (postdoctoral degree). Even people without a higher degree usually worked as highly skilled professionals. This means that my interviewees represent a more educated segment of the population compared to the average member of Soviet society in the 1930s to1950s, and they are more educated than Soviet Jews as a whole during the same period.[12]

Given that the interviewees were chosen without an effort to hear from as many professions as possible, some professions are not represented at all. For unexplained reasons, not a single dentist was interviewed (despite the fact that their number is significant, both among the Jews of this generation and the immigrants among them).[13] Similarly, very few nurses or pharmacists were interviewed. While Jews were widely represented in the "gray area" of the Soviet economy, such as the production and distribution of clothes and shoes produced outside of government-controlled factories, not a single person admitted to being directly involved in such activities. At the same time, almost every interviewee discussed how they dealt with the gray economy for obtaining goods and services.[14]

Not all aspects of interviewee's careers ended up being discussed during the interviews or in this book. Because the theme was how being Jewish affected their professional lives, people focused on choosing a profession and a type of education, getting their first job, their first successes and failures, and instances of extraordinary importance, such as unexpected promotions, firings, breakthroughs, or setbacks. They ignored those aspects of their lives which they did not associate with being Jewish—such as choices of vacation spots, entertainment, intergenerational relationships and more.

One group of interviewees stood out. These were professionals in the sphere of Yiddish culture, including former actors of the Moscow State Jewish Theater (Gosset) and of Jewish theaters in Kyiv, Odessa, and Minsk; four Yiddish writers and journalists; one teacher from a Soviet Yiddish school; and six performers of Yiddish music. The youngest and last of the cohort of Soviet Yiddish cultural activists from the Stalin era, they presented the unique perspective of people who were actively involved in building the content of Soviet Jewish culture and who also witnessed its demise. The trajectories of their lives, as well as their understanding of what it means to be a Jew, are quite different from those of the rest of the narrators, which justified a separate section for their experiences. In fact, their testimonies suggest that there was no such thing as one mode of Jewish daily life in Stalin's Soviet Union, but rather several approaches to navigating it.

## Successful Optimists with a Long Lifespan: Personal Characteristics of Interviewees

All the interviewees experienced a number of traumas during their lives,[15] and lingering trauma can result in intrusive thoughts and depression.[16] But for a variety of reasons, post-Soviet Jewish elderly immigrants tend not to seek the help of mental health professionals.[17] In a spontaneous and unintended way, some people treated the interview process as an improvised therapy opportunity. Though I was not able to provide any help or advice, I listened intently, showed interest, and asked follow-up questions. After reading through the interview transcripts, it became evident that many of the interviewees created a "life-review" narrative.

Coined by the geriatrician Robert Butler in 1963, the term "life review" refers to the process of recalling events in order to make sense of one's past.[18] Butler writes:

> People may recall unresolved conflicts that happened many years before. By reexamining what has happened, they may be able to come to terms with their conflicts.... Through these efforts, such reminiscence can give

new significance and meaning to life and prepare the person for death by lessening anger, fear and anxiety. In late life, people have a particularly vivid imagination and memory of the past. Often, they can recall with sudden and remarkable clarity early life events. They may experience a renewed ability to free-associate and to bring up material from the unconscious. . . . Sometimes, the life story is told to anyone who will listen. . . . Life reviews are extremely complex, often contradictory, and frequently filled with irony, comedy, and tragedy.[19]

Applying life review lenses to understanding the collected narratives helps to make sense of how people describe their lives. As mentioned, the interviewees had often lost their parents and grandparents to unnatural deaths due to repressions, military conflicts, famine, pandemics, and other tribulations. Many had lost their spouses and, worst of all, children. Finally, the majority went through a very painful immigration at an advanced age, a process firmly linked to profound psychological traumas.[20] During interviews, many people downplayed conflicts, probably in attempts to provide closure to the unresolved issues, to heal themselves, and to find peace with their decisions and past.[21]

The interviewees were generally very resilient people. All of them enjoyed above-average longevity—some were interviewed after they reached the age of eighty, and many were in their nineties. Psychologists link longevity with heredity, gender, socioeconomic status, nutrition, social support, medical care, and personality and behavioral characteristics.[22] Some suggest that as much as 75 percent of one's longevity may be due to nongenetic attributes, including psychological and behavioral factors,[23] especially the ability to handle troubling events with the confidence that the future holds a positive outcome.[24] Studies have also found that a positive self-perception in aging is definitely linked to longevity, especially when the group studied is stigmatized.[25]

These studies are directly relevant to my interviewees, who, despite belonging to a marginalized immigrant population, all led relatively active lives. Many participated in cultural events and attempted to study foreign languages (usually the language of their new country), computers, or pottery. In fact, I first encountered some of my best narrators (the ones with an enviable memory and a gift for storytelling) when they attended my own lectures organized by the local community centers. For example, Esfir A. (born in Orsha, Belorussia, 1908), whom I met in Potsdam at a community workshop on Soviet Jewish history in 2001, asked me to elaborate on "reasons for antisemitism" and wanted to know of historical examples of successful and unsuccessful ways Jews dealt with antisemitism around the world. When we sat down a few days later for an interview, I learned that Esfir had had an unusually difficult life. She had lost her first husband early in the war, and her second husband in the 1980s; her newborn son died in her arms in 1941 from complications of being delivered on the run; and her thirty-something-year-old daughter died in the 1970s from an aggressive melanoma. This left Esfir to take care of her young grandchildren. Yet she was smiling, confident, curious, active, and surrounded by friends and family.

Another example of an active life is the story of a former surgeon Semyon Sh. (born in 1918 in Kuty, Ukraine), who continued to keep up with medical research in his specialty (otolaryngology) long after he had retired and immigrated to Brooklyn, New York. So is the story of Viktor P. (born in 1916 in Piliava, Ukraine), a former rocket engineer, who spent a great deal of time learning about the origins of his name, his shtetl, and his family and created an impressive file of data on the topic.

Overall, the narrators represent individuals with healthy attitudes, the ability to adapt to radically changing circumstances and to make peace with the consequences of trauma and loss. In addition, they demonstrated better than average health—the majority lived on their own at the time of the interviews—and a better than average financial position.

These characteristics are vital in understanding the types of stories received as well as why they are told. The sample collected here is limited: educated Yiddish speakers leading healthy and happy lives are overrepresented, whereas many others are not represented at all. Unluckily for psychologists, who might potentially want to study these interviews, their narratives are not comprehensive, nor were they facilitated by a psychologist. Unfortunately for Soviet historians, the interviews lack details that are not relevant beyond Jewish experiences. But luckily for scholars interested in Jewish perceptions of Soviet policies, and the process of formation and transformation of Jewish life under Stalin, the testimonies do not speak of anything else.

## The Present Shaping the Past: Today's Country in Yesterday's Life

Immigrants make up 89 percent of people interviewed, and the majority of them do not speak the language of their new home country.[26] Moreover, the majority of them also did not choose the destination for immigration; instead, they all followed one of their grown children to a newly adopted country.[27] Nevertheless, the comparative analysis of the interviews recorded in different countries suggests, quite strongly, that the interviewees learned to adjust the story of their past to their present (country).[28] Interviews recorded in the United States, Germany, Russia, or Canada differed significantly from one another in what they consider important and, above all, how they present the life stories.[29].

People interviewed in New York and Philadelphia emphasized memories of Jewish family celebrations and expressions of solidarity with the Jewish people after 1967 and featured numerous stories of the Soviet government's antisemitism. Many of them attended numerous programs in synagogues and Jewish community centers and appreciated the developed infrastructure of these Jewish cultural institutions.[30] They also probably learned how to present their life story through the context appropriate in those community organizations. Most of the US-based interviewees immigrated in the late 1980s and the very early 1990s, some of the earliest of the "Great exodus" of Russian Jews. Their stories associated with the Soviet past are influenced, much more so than anyone else's, by the early perestroika rhetoric of condemnation of the Soviet past and the emphasis on lies of Soviet propaganda, especially when it came to the portrayal of the United States. The story of being Jewish in these narratives is the story of resistance to the Soviet regime, even if that included benefiting from Soviet policies or narratives of success.

Like US-based interviewees, Canadian ones were also exposed to numerous programs in Russian-language Jewish community centers and Chabad-Lubavitch-run synagogues. But unlike their American counterparts, who were registered as refugees on their own merit, Canadian interviewees were usually sponsored by their children or grandchildren who had previously immigrated through a skilled-labor program aimed at young professionals under the age of 35.[31] These people usually did not have Canadian pensions and thus reported higher levels of dissatisfaction with their current life. Because of their low socioeconomic status, they were much more likely to accuse each other of fabricating their documents, inventing their stories of persecution and suffering, as well as other "sins" within the immigrant community. For example, of the 60 veterans of World War II interviewed in Toronto, at least 50 insisted that the majority of the people who call themselves veterans had bought their documents and medals on the black market. Astonishingly, they seem to have internalized, almost entirely, the antisemitic rhetoric of postwar Soviet society, when Jews were accused of buying their medals from bazaars in Tashkent.[32] Although such statements seemed offensive in the former Soviet Union, they now had no problem accusing their fellow immigrants of these very sins.

A second important feature of the Russian Jewish community of Toronto is that a significant part of its members, including the elderly, did not travel to Canada directly from Russia or other countries of the former Soviet Union. Rather, many immigrated initially to Israel, where they resided for an average of five to ten years.[33] Most interviewees were employed professionally in both the Soviet Union and in Israel, thus representing arguably the most cosmopolitan of all interviewees. Their stories of the Soviet past are influenced by the combination of Israeli sensibilities (with an emphasis on Jewish bravery, heroism, solidarity with Israel during the Soviet times, and the ability of Jews to stick together) and Canadian sensibilities of their immigrant life (stories about the lack of integrity among fellow immigrants), as well as notions of religious identity, the importance of which they learn from Chabad-run public lectures and other programs.

In Germany, the presentation of the Soviet past is significantly different from that in the United States and Canada. First, unlike their counterparts in the United States and Canada, narrators living in Germany do not complain about their present country. In fact, they speak favorably of Germany's European culture, the Central European climate, and the excellent medical services they receive. Moreover, unlike anywhere else, German interviewees mention the relative ease of their language adaptation. Some knowledge of the Yiddish and German languages helps them to function in stores and medical offices, and in some cases, to accustom themselves to their new lives, often before their children and even grandchildren are able to do so. Even though Berlin does not have a Russian neighborhood, Russian stores are popular, and all Jewish community centers run Russian-language programs, some specifically designed for retirees. Moreover, contemporary

Germans increasingly associate being Russian with being Jewish, as Russian Jews constitute a majority of the German Jewish community.[34]

Scholars and the general public alike seem to think that the Russian elderly living in Germany find themselves in double jeopardy: not only are they Jews who remember the Holocaust and live in the country that initiated it, but some are also actual veterans of the Soviet army that fought against Germany during World War II. Aware of these claims, narrators reported a Soviet past that addressed such negative perceptions. German-based participants were more likely to discuss the internationalist nature of their upbringing and downplay the importance of being Jewish in daily life. Second, they were more likely to emphasize a lack of Jewish solidarity and discuss how Jews from Poland or Bessarabia betrayed Soviet Jews during the war. The memory of such sentiments was most likely provoked by the current politics of the Jewish community—organizational leaders are descendants of Polish Jews, whereas the majority of the Jewish community in Berlin were born in the Soviet Union.[35]

Finally, people interviewed in Moscow provided quite a different story. All of those interviewed in Russia were somehow connected with the organized Jewish community; many received food packages from Jewish charitable organizations, attended daytime educational and entertainment programs, or at least received a free Jewish newspaper distributed by local Chabad Lubavitch. Nevertheless, Moscow-based interviewees were the only ones who needed to be prompted to discuss how being Jewish had influenced their lives (unless they were Yiddish activists, in which case no prompting was necessary). They often misunderstood the purpose of the interview by thinking that I was evaluating the work of the charity organizations that provided them with services.

Left to their own devices, these participants only mentioned 1948–53 as the time when being Jewish mattered and only in the context of being able to avoid persecutions due to their good dispositions. They were also eager to emphasize that they believed that Jewish organizations should be helping their non-Jewish neighbors as well, both because these neighbors were in equal need of help and in order not to provoke antisemitism in advertising that Jews receive special benefits for being Jewish. Very often, these narrators wrote petitions to Jewish organizations advocating on behalf of non-Jewish widows and widowers of deceased Jews, as well as their friends. The second feature of Moscow interviewees was that they were much more open to Christianity as a religious doctrine and were frequent visitors to Christian churches (in addition to Jewish community centers or synagogues).[36] Though all those interviewed for this project were not hostile to Christian beliefs, only those from Moscow actually went regularly to church. Overall, their testimonies presented a life story that fit with the accepted early-2000s version of Soviet history that permeated Russian society (Stalin and his role in history as controversial; Soviet past as partially good and partially shameful; the Great Terror condemned). It is possible that if these people had been interviewed more recently, their stories would have been adjusted to accommodate changes in the current Russian political climate, which looks more favorably at Stalin and perceives the Great Terror as a "necessary measure."[37]

The most intriguing observation to emerge from this four-country research is that, despite living in four different countries with significantly different politics of Jewishness, all the interviewees were able to use the language from their youth as a way to meaningfully represent and justify their attitudes. People currently living in the United States spoke of Jewish solidarity, replacing the "proletarian" with "Jewish" in the Soviet rhetoric of "proletarian solidarity." Those who had first immigrated to Israel before moving to Canada spoke of "Jewish heroism," once again replacing "Soviet" with "Jewish" in discussions of bravery and heroism. Those in Germany spoke of "internationalism" and "friendship of people" without changing a word from the Soviet vocabulary, though they use those expressions in a non-Soviet context. Those who lived in Russia tended not to say the word "Jewish" out loud and managed to present the story of their lives as Jews without referring to it as "Jewish."

## Oral Histories as Literary Texts

Following the lead of historian and literary scholar Irina Paperno, who combined the historical method of analyzing tendencies with the literary approach of close reading of individual texts,[38] this study applies methods of both historical and textual analysis to the oral histories.[39]

Oral histories have been shown to provide valuable information on the reception, interpretation, and internalization of Soviet ideology.[40] The very act of remembering seemed dangerous in the Soviet Union as early as the 1920s, let alone sharing or recording those memories in forms of oral histories later.[41] However, to Soviet-born people, memories seemed more reliable than documents.[42] The observation is acutely relevant in the case of Soviet

Jews, because Jewish memory and Jewish history per se were not topics of public discussion, let alone education, starting from the late 1940s.

The innovation in this study is the primary focus on testimonies as built in accordance with the genre of tales, which has to include villains, heroes, obstacles, and methods of overcoming these obstacles. Following Vladimir Propp's approach of identifying the formal characteristics of a tale, including a hero, an obstacle, a mentor, a goal, and a villain, enables a sophisticated analysis of testimonies that considered not only *what* the narrators were saying, but also *when*.[43]

Tamar Rapoport and her colleagues apply a similar approach of analyzing an immigrant narrative as the process of creating a story centered on the *normalization* of traumatic experiences, such as antisemitism, among Russian-speaking Jewish immigrants.[44] The connections can help to reconstruct the associative foundation of this genre. For example, after interviewees discussed the celebration of Jewish holidays, they would often move on to discussing repressions against their grandparents in the 1920s. Similarly, when they discussed Jewish food, they would frequently turn to stories of persecution in 1948–53.[45] However, when elaborating on the importance of choosing a Jewish spouse, they would not shift to the narrative of persecution, but instead found ways to equate being Jewish with being a good and moral person.

The location in which the interviews took place also changed, quite significantly, the genre of the testimonies. Many interviewees in the United States, for example, presented their life stories as versions of the "American Dream," in which an individual succeeds thanks to hard work, despite humble origins. Present circumstances shape the narrative of the past quite significantly among Canadian-based interviewees, too. Their stories are most often laments: tales of missed opportunities, tragic misunderstandings, and misfortunes. It seems that difficult present circumstances trigger vivid memories of injustice. German stories are filled with unexpected twists and turns, which probably relate to inherited ambiguities about their lives in Germany. Each testimony carries a narrative about mysterious powers, conveys messages centered on the idea that "nothing is what it seems," and concludes with miraculous and (very) happy endings. Finally, Russian-based interviewees presented a version of a "Soviet dream," in which modesty, hard work, and the desire to help others helped them lead honest, albeit slightly impoverished, lives.

Close scrutiny of the wording that interviewees choose to express their ideas, as well as nonverbal cues, can assist in understanding hidden meanings and associations.[46] The combination of textual analysis, attention to nonverbal cues, and verifying historical context helps to extract the fullest possible meaning from the testimonies, which might, at first glance, seem to be "scattered" and even incomprehensible.[47] Ultimately, the combination of literary analysis and historical scrutiny makes it possible to produce a diamond from unpolished rock.

This book therefore does not present an alternative or new history of Soviet Jews. Instead, it fleshes out and revises the historical record by using oral histories that were not available previously. No historian would question the value of studying Leo Tolstoy's *War and Peace* for understanding Imperial Russia, or Vasily Grossman's *Life and Fate* for the history of the Soviet Union. Narratives by Soviet Jews are just as valuable (although less famous) for our understanding of Soviet Jewish history, culture, and sensitivities.

# Part II

The Making of a Soviet
Jewish Family

# 3

# Boys Are Like a Glass, Girls Are Like Cloth

## Raising Jewish Children in the 1930s

At 11:00 A.M. sharp, in mid-August 2001, I knocked on the door of an apartment in a low-rise building close to Brighton Beach Avenue in Brooklyn. I had come to meet Klara G. (born in Uman, Ukraine, in 1914), a woman who responded to my ad in *Vechernii Niu-Iork* (Evening New York), a Russian-language newspaper geared to recent immigrants.

She invited me in, offering me a chair near a large dining table, where she had papers and photographs nicely laid out. She started with a photograph of herself as a child, then a picture of her parents that was taken in the 1920s. Klara, as a little girl, is next to them in the photo, and the resemblance was clear. She then showed me a picture of herself in a military uniform—she had served as a nurse during the war—as well as many pictures of her grandchildren winning dancing awards in New York. Then a photograph of just her parents surfaced. I asked if she had a wedding picture of her own. After some digging, she retrieved a photo. In it, a young man posing cheek to cheek with a young woman, unmistakably Klara, is smiling. Both are dressed in nice, but casual, clothes. "This is my wedding picture," she explained.

> Monya and I registered right before he had to go to Magnitogorsk; he was a Komsomol leader, and he was sent to a construction site. He was twenty; I was eighteen. I was a third-year student in a medical school; he was finishing the Construction Engineering Institute. We met near the dormitory one day, and he invited me to go for a walk. We registered [to marry] a few weeks later.[1]

Klara remembered that right after they registered, they went to her new husband's dormitory and bumped into Monya's uncle, who was a photographer. Once the uncle heard the news, he invited them to his studio and took a picture. She did not have a formal wedding ceremony or celebration. She told her parents only after the fact. They had a great relationship, she said. In general, Klara spoke fondly about her parents and especially her mother's father, who lived with them. The grandfather was quite strict and very respected. "No one would dare to eat pork in front of him," she laughed.

She then showed a picture of man in a military uniform, embracing a young woman. "This is my brother," she explained:

> He got married in 1949. The story of how they met is interesting. He came back from the front, and my mother's neighbor knew a woman—we called her Auntie Dvoyra—and she knew everyone. So she invited him over to meet the girl. He didn't want to go. He was a war veteran, a handsome man, but Auntie Dvoyra insisted. So he came in, just to say that he wouldn't be staying, then he saw his Lenochka and fell in love at first sight. They live close by, we can call them later, if you want.[2]

Klara's brother, Yasha (who I indeed met later that week), like Klara, went to a Yiddish school, and then continued into a Yiddish-language vocational school. They both lived at home until they were eighteen. Klara recalled that as a girl she was treated quite differently than her two brothers:

> My brothers often came home late, but I wasn't allowed to. Whenever I was five minutes late, my mother would beat me up. I asked my mother: "Why can [my brother] Yasha stay out late, and I can't? Why can [my brother] Petya stay out, and I can't?" She said: [in Yiddish] "Dear daughter, a man is like a glass. It can get dirty, and then you clean it, and you don't know if it was dirty. A woman is like a piece of cloth, if it gets dirty, it will be stained forever." I didn't understand her then, and yelled at her: "What glass? What are you talking about?!" I was so angry.[3]

Because Klara's social life was more controlled and restricted than her brothers', she found herself more involved with family life—helping around the house and even learning about Jewish holidays that were celebrated for the sake of her grandfather. During Passover, when her brothers were allowed to do what they wanted, Klara had to stay home to help out.

After Klara got married, she continued to cook some dishes that she learned how to make from her mother (she was very proud of her special sweet and sour meatballs):

> Everyone loved my cooking. I learned from my mother, but later I began coming up with things too. So, for example, I would add little pieces of *salo* (pig fat) into each little meatball—no one could understand why they tasted so good and so different from theirs![4]

Klara never cooked anything special for Jewish holidays. In fact, she ignored them. Monya became a Party member in 1937 (he was later an executive official) and had a high position at a research institute in Kyiv, where they had moved two years prior. They got a room in a communal apartment and lived there with their two children until 1941. Monya went to serve in the army as a tank driver, and Klara was evacuated to Fergana, Uzbekistan, where she miraculously met her sister-in-law. In 1942, Klara left her children with her sister-in-law to become an army nurse. She returned from the front in May 1945, and Monya came back in 1947. Both Klara's and Monya's parents and grandparents were killed in Uman. Monya was wounded, hard of hearing, and suffered from headaches, but he was alive. So was she, and so were their children. Many of their friends' and colleagues' families were not that lucky.

Klara constantly referred to herself as "lucky." Her husband and her children survived the war. Her husband was almost fired in 1949, but ended up simply being demoted. He was restored as a chief executive engineer in 1956. She finished at the medical institute and worked as a polyclinic doctor. During the Doctors' Plot of 1953, when many of her Jewish colleagues were fired and living in fear, she kept her spirits up and managed to keep her job and the respect of her patients.

Nothing in Klara's story took place by accident or lacked meaning. The order in which she showed me her photographs had a significance: Klara made sure I saw the photograph of her parents, labeled in Yiddish, thus confirming both her place of birth and her Jewish ethnicity. The photograph of her in a military uniform suggests that she, as a Jew, helped to combat fascism during the war. The fact that she did not prepare her wedding picture is also significant, because she, like many, if not most, women of her generation, did not consider her own wedding an important milestone in her life. In fact, the story of the picture is more the story of how it was taken rather than of the actual wedding. Sharing numerous and repetitive pictures of grandchildren was the real goal of showing family photographs to a stranger (albeit an interested one). It was an act of pride and joy—the culmination of the story of overcoming difficulties, surviving despite the odds, and, above all, "making it in America." It was a Soviet Jewish version of the American Dream: they started with nothing and achieved success through hard work, persistence, and a little bit of magical luck. Eventually, I understood that *everything* Klara told me—from the stories about her grandparents and herself to those of the grandchildren's successes—was a story of the present filtered and understood through memories of the past. "Little things," like parental punishments, wedding pictures (or the lack thereof), stories of courtships, reports of their own parental and grandparental challenges and successes, and even the recipe for her meatballs, all constitute the mosaic of living Soviet Jewish subjectivity, complete with the story of its formation, modification, and sustenance.

Klara's stories were still tales of the past, however. Specifically, her narrative documents the transformation of family structures and values that took place in the Soviet Union from shortly after the Russian Revolution through the Stalinist period. Indeed, this transformation was nothing short of remarkable: in the early 1920s, the process of creating a family began to exclude matchmakers, and weddings became rare, just to name a couple of the dramatic shifts that took place.[5] These changes resulted from modernization that was already ongoing as well as Bolshevik legislation. Compared to other aspects of modernization, such as abandoning celebrations of Jewish holidays or kosher slaughter, changes in creating (and breaking up) a Jewish family were quicker and more complete.[6]

Many elements of Klara's story appear as significant milestones in the development of Soviet Jewish daily life through the prism of individual choices and decisions. For example, Klara mentions in passing that she was expected to stay home more than her siblings because she was needed to help out with household chores. As a result, she was more familiar with Jewish traditions than her brothers were. Indeed, in the 1920s, girls were often penalized for not helping enough with household chores, whereas their brothers were not required to help around the house.[7] In the 1920s, girls who lived in Moscow were less involved in political activities due to their responsibilities at home, and because many parents felt that a woman's primary task was to learn to raise children and take care of the household.[8] A similar situation developed in the rural parts of the European USSR and across Central Asia.[9]

Pre-Soviet Jewish communal structure put more emphasis on boys' religious education, if their families could afford it. Girls were sometimes educated in secular and practical topics, and even if educated outside the home, they were still expected to be competent in maintaining the household.[10] Nevertheless, without formal religious education, neither girls nor boys of the 1920s and 1930s learned how to internalize religious values as their own. The mandatory anti-religious education in schools also helped to quickly and successfully teach Klara and her counterparts that being Jewish had nothing to do with observing the laws of Judaism.[11]

One of the jewels of Klara's narrative is her recollection of her mother telling her about the importance of staying modest, providing the analogy "boys are like a glass, and girls are like cloth." Aside from the actual message about modesty and methods of parenting, such as physical punishments, it is noteworthy that Klara reproduced her mother's words about the difference between men and women in Yiddish as opposed to Russian. She emphasized that "modesty was a Jewish virtue," and that is why, whenever she thinks about it, she does so in Yiddish.[12] It was rather common among interviewees to use folk wisdom in explaining their relations toward members of the opposite sex. People rarely quoted Russian folk proverbs on this issue, even though most people were quite versed in Russian literature and folklore. Rather, they preferred to use Yiddish expressions, which they heard from their parents (often without fully being able to understand their meanings). Often, these were the only Yiddish expressions interviewees knew. Yet they found that for describing issues related to the difference in upbringing of boys and girls in their families, the Yiddish language was more suitable than Russian.

Both women and men who grew up in the 1920s and early 1930s often report punishments associated with the Jewish way of life. Children were disciplined for eating non-kosher food at home.[13] In fact, for the majority of interviewees, the notion of kashruth is firmly associated with punishment. Maya D. (born in 1928 in Chervone, in the Zhitomir region of Ukraine) told a story documenting this. Petite and graciously moving around her small Berlin apartment, Maya was a former student of the Jewish Theater

Studio. Fashionably dressed, with a long, curly, graying head of hair, Maya was one of the most passionate interviewees I have ever met. She expressed strong opinions about Russian, German, and American politics, sex education, and especially the local Jewish community. Like many other German-based interviewees, she did not approve of much of the local community center's politics, which in her opinion, treated Russian Jews without respect. Maya strongly believed that even if people are religious, they should respect those who are not. Many times, during the interview, she made the point of outlining the "proper" and respectful way to behave: one should not punish people who do not observe kashruth, a trait apparently lacking within Berlin's Jewish community culture. To support this argument, she told the following story about her grandfather, a figure she remembers vaguely:

> In my mother's house, we always observed kashruth. Why? Because we always believed that people should respect their elders. [...]One day, however, my mother received a punch in the face from her father. She was carrying around flyers to some Ukrainian villages. There was nothing to eat there. She came home, and she threw up. And my grandfather noticed that there were pieces of *salo* [pig backfat] in her vomit. And naturally, he hit her. It was the first time he hit her, because it wasn't a custom in our house to hit children. My mother remembered [this punishment] her whole life. Kashruth was observed in the family all the time, without interruption. At least, everyone tried to eat non-kosher things when the grandparents couldn't see, or when they weren't home. It was all tactful, no one wanted to offend them.[14]

Even though Maya started with the contemporary situation, the moment she brought up punishment she remembered kashruth. To continue the free association, Maya then connected the observance of the laws of kashruth with an older generation and with conflicts between her parents and grandparents. For Maya, the story of breaking and observing the laws of kashruth is a story of family conflict, a story of old versus new, a story of respect for elders. This was something she considers a "Jewish value," though it is associated with being accommodating and tolerant to people who live according to Jewish law, as opposed to observing the law itself. In other words, the story is told as an illustration of how her parents showed respect for Maya's grandparents despite different worldviews. It also, of course, implies that the leaders of the Jewish community in Berlin are not brought up properly, and, paradoxically, do not share the Jewish values that Maya considers important.

In her story of the past, Maya chooses to talk about the details of kashruth observances in order to most effectively discuss the role of the older generation within their family structure. For her, kashruth and its rules firmly belong to the older generation's sphere.[15] Klara's use of a secret ingredient—pork fat—in her meatballs is yet another illustration of the process of fading Jewish values in the 1930s. She understands the recipe as part of the family tradition, but kashruth was something relevant only to the generation of the 1920s, a useless relic from old times, rather than an important part of one's Jewish heritage.[16]

All interviewees remembered that girls had far less freedom than boys to socialize with their friends. Restrictions on girls' freedom, especially for shtetl residents, resulted in a lower rate of their socialization among non-Jews, compared to boys.[17] Still, numerous interviewees remembered their participation in extracurricular activities at school, such as drama and singing workshops. Many women spoke about dancing. In fact, for some people, the moment in the interview during which they remembered dancing was a turning point. They began to relax, smile, and talk about their past with pleasure.

One such person was Etya G. (born in Kopaigorod, Ukraine, in 1918). When I came to interview her, she was very nervous. Recently diagnosed as legally blind, this survivor of the Kopai ghetto did not leave the house very often. With the exception of her family members, she received no visitors. She wanted to be interviewed, but she could not see me, and she did not know whether she could trust me (a common issue in interviewing the visually impaired), but once we began talking about her school years, boys, and leisure, her face lit up for the first time during our meeting and she shared a treasured memory:

> Our favorite [after school] activity was dancing. We would get together at someone's house, put a record on, and dance. We especially liked "Rio Rita," Argentine tango, and the foxtrot. We would dance all evening. Once a week, I also went dancing in a club.[18]

Interestingly, men of the same generation presented quite a different picture of Jewish girls' leisure during the prewar period. A retired construction engineer, Ilya F. (born in Voznesensk, Ukraine, in 1910), a teenager in the mid-1920s, recalled:

> When we were young, we liked to go out dancing. But there were no Jewish girls there. We danced with shiksas [non-Jewish girls]. Jewish girls weren't allowed ... We met Jewish girls at home-parties, but most Jewish girls weren't allowed to go there either. We boys went to the movies sometimes, but girls never went with us. It wasn't proper for a Jewish girl.[19]

Ilya's wife of 58 years, a retired teacher, Sima F. (born in Voznesensk, Ukraine, in 1911), was present during our conversation. When Ilya finished a sentence, she winked at me, and quietly said: "That's what they all thought, but I knew how to dance, and, in fact, we went to dance parties too." Ilya, who has trouble hearing, asked his wife to repeat what she had just told me, and she replied, "Nothing important. Continue with your story!"[20]

Although there is no evidence that the behavior of Jewish young women and girls was different from that of non-Jews, many interviewees agreed with Ilya's sentiments. During the interview, Ilya repeatedly emphasized that he was brought up as an "internationalist" and did not think about ethnicity at all. However, when it came to evaluating his choice of partner for marriage or finding a romantic partner, his judgment assumed some specifically ethnic coloration.

In sum, girls tended to spend more time at home with their parents, whereas boys took part in activities outside of their family circles. Girls were generally punished more than boys for being friends with non-Jews. Women paid more attention to the ethnicity of their spouse. That does not mean that they were more likely to choose a Jew (which is not true, according to this sample), but rather that they gave it more thought. Perhaps this attitude is a consequence of the greater influence that parents (and therefore traditional Jewish values) had on them during their adolescent years.

Differences between how boys and girls were treated at home were not as pronounced when people spoke about their own lives as when they spoke about their friends, family members, acquaintances, and, especially, about Jews and non-Jews. Actual experiences frequently did not coincide with interviewees' ideas of what they thought Jewish life was supposed to be. The example of Jewish girls and dancing is quite representative. Though many Jewish girls went to public dances during the interwar period, both men and women often said that this was not a Jewish activity (even if they themselves enjoyed it). The definition of "Jewish" and "non-Jewish" often had little to do with what Jews had actually practiced. Rather, most frequently it meant something that people considered positive. For example, "modest behavior" was labeled as a "Jewish" feature. This phenomenon could be observed not only in descriptions of childhood, but also in the process of choosing a spouse, as well as building their own families. In fact, this is perhaps the most important lesson in the determination of their ethnic identity that both boys and girls learned in their childhood. Yet the creation of a family was of course also influenced by government policies and the economic, social, and cultural changes that transformed the Soviet Jewish community in the 1920s and 1930s.

# 4

## Weddings between Errands

### Love and Family during the Soviet Jewish Golden Age

### Accidental Acts of Destiny: Courtship and Choice of Partner in the 1930s

In stories of how they met their spouses, both men and women often used the word "by accident." Courtships were usually short and casual. Above all, interviewees did not see marriage and the creation of a family as the most significant or even an important event of their life. To the contrary, they described the process of meeting their future spouse, their decision to get married, and the wedding (or marriage registration) itself in between other stories of education, career, or migration, which they considered worthy of more attention.[1] For example, Yosef V. (born in Bar, Ukraine, in 1907) met his future wife, Serafima, when he came to visit Odessa in 1932. After a short stay, Yosef went back to Moscow and later invited her to join him. Upon Serafima's arrival, the young couple got married at a ZAGS (Office of Civil Registrations) and settled down. Both sets of parents were notified several months after the event.[2] Similarly, Ilya Sh. (born in Voznesensk, Ukraine, in 1913), who met his future wife at university and married her upon graduation in 1938, did not even tell his parents about the event. He explained, "They lived far away, and I did not see how it was their business."[3]

Women talked more often than men about asking their parents for permission to marry, but even in these cases, parents' opinions were supplementary, not obligatory to follow, and narrators expected approval, not permission. Of course, not all parents agreed with their children's choices. Sometimes parents protested against the age or other characteristics of the prospective bride or groom. Others remembered conflicts related to their match's backgrounds. Olga K. (born in Kamenka, Ukraine, in 1905) said her parents did not want her to marry a Lithuanian Jew, but rather a Ukrainian one, because "Ukrainian Jews are kinder and nicer people."[4] When asked whether she followed their advice, Olga replied, "Actually, I did not. I married a non-Jew, an Austrian man, who was a Communist and escaped from Austria to live in the Soviet Union. I met him at work, and my parents loved him!"[5]

Women constituted about 39 percent of Soviet workers between 1928 and 1940, with a higher proportion of younger women among them, so it is no wonder that many Soviet urban residents met their future spouses in the workplace.[6] Olga was no exception. Others mentioned meeting their future spouses at schools, universities, or social gatherings, but no one described the participation of a matchmaker, or even an active relative, in facilitating these introductions. Independent choices of marital partners in the 1920s certainly led to the destruction of one of the most significant rules of traditional Jewish community life, marrying within one's ethnic group.[7]

Many people confirm that their future spouses' ethnicity did not play an important role in their decision to marry. Grigorii B. explained, "I wanted a good wife, a good person. I did not think about nationalities."[8] Veniamin Sh. (born in Sobolevka, Ukraine, in 1907) agreed: "I thought very little about it [the ethnicity of my wife]. This was not a factor."[9] Ilya Sh. confirmed, "I wanted a smart, interesting wife, her ethnicity did not interest me. These were times when it did not matter."[10]

But why did the ethnicity no longer matter? Such testimonies were especially common among men from urban localities who were born between 1906 and 1914. Women, on the other hand, spoke more about the difficulties and complexities that arose because of their future spouses' ethnicity. The most elaborate story on the topic came from Lilia Sh. (born in Cherkassy, Ukraine, in 1909). Lilya was, by far, the most eccentric interviewee I have ever met. Before we started the interview, she insisted on reading my palm (predicting happiness in love) and my tarot, and then speaking at length about her relationships. She spent a long time describing each of her partners, her lovers, emphasizing the importance of romantic attraction above all other necessary characteristics for a happy relationship. In her early nineties at the time of the interview, she was remarkably sharp and unapologetically authoritative. It was only towards the end of the interview, after about three hours of talking in her room at the assisted living facility in Berlin, that she told me the story of her first love:

> It was in 1926. I was seventeen, and I fell in love. It was in Odessa, I was on the beach. The weather was beautiful.... Many young men tried to court me there ... I was with my sister. One man asked me, right there on the beach: "Marry me. I fell in love with you at first sight!" I hated such advances. Then suddenly, another young man approached us. He had a big book, and he didn't pay any attention to me. He asked my sister: "Can I leave my bag with you? I'd like to go swimming." Then he went to swim.
>
> Suddenly, I started worrying about him. It had been 45 minutes. I said [to my sister]: "Sonya, something happened to him." She said, "Don't worry, he'll come back, his things are all here." Indeed, he soon came back, thanked my sister, took his things, and left. He didn't even look at me... I hadn't seen the young man for several days. My sister left, but I stayed to enjoy the sea a little more...
>
> One day I went to a bathhouse. I stood in the line, and suddenly, I saw him behind me... There was a long line, and we stood together for a while... Then we went together to wait for the tram. Then he said: "Let's take a walk." We walked together. I had a wonderful feeling ... Eventually, we took the tram, he wanted to pay for me, but I paid for myself. Then he walked me home, and asked me out to the theater. I agreed. I still don't know how I agreed so easily to go out with an unknown man.
>
> He came to pick me up at home. My mother met him, and she liked him. We went to the theater. In the theater, he only looked at me. That is how our romance started. But then I found out he was Russian ... And I didn't want to upset my family. So we broke up. I thought about him all the time. I thought about him during the war, when I was already married. But I wasn't brought up that way. I couldn't be with him. It still hurts when I think about him.

A.S.: So the only reason you didn't pursue him was that he wasn't a Jew. Is that right?

L.S.: I couldn't upset my mother.

A.S.: How did your mother argue that you had to marry a Jew?

L.S.: My mother didn't say that. She explained that all nationalities are equal. We didn't think that Jews were special. However, I remembered that my grandfather called every gentile a "goy." I didn't want him to call my husband that. I later married a Jew. He was a wonderful man. We have great children. And I always thought that I did the right thing. But I missed Shura [the Russian man].[11]

Lilya's story shows us some of the doubts and contradictions which could surround the choice of a spouse for young Jewish women in the late 1920s. Although she emphasized that the final decision was her own and that her mother did not interfere with it, it was clear that her family background and the values of her upbringing, asserted by her grandfather, played a more important role in the young woman's life than those she learned from her schooling. It is also quite possible that Lilya chose to tell only part of the truth, and that her parents protested more than she remembered (or chose to tell) in order to smooth out the conflicts and contradictions. Importantly, Lilya decided to present her decision to marry a Jew as a conscious choice and not as a matter of accident.

Some people remembered sharper arguments within their families that centered on intermarriage. The story of Esfir A. (born in Orsha, Belorussia, in 1908), a Jewish woman who married a Russian man, is illustrative:

I met my future husband accidentally. I finished university, came back home, then met with an old grade-school friend, Vasily. We had studied together until fifth grade. He introduced me to a friend of his, whose name was also Vasily. They were close friends, and they both fell in love with me. I liked the first Vasily, but he was drafted into the military in 1937 and was killed. The second Vasily came to tell me the news, and brought a picture of me that was found in Vasily (the soldier's) pocket. Then we started dating, and I eventually married him.

A.S.: He wasn't Jewish, was he?

E.A.: He was Russian. I am the only one of my four sisters who married a Russian man. The other three all married Jews, but my brothers married non-Jews. They both have Russian wives.

A.S.: What was your parents' attitude to the fact that you married a non-Jew?

E.A.: My mother died young, when I was sixteen. My father married again, and his wife was scum, even though she was Jewish. So he could not really argue with me. When I married a Russian man, my father didn't tell me anything. He just said: "I'm so glad your grandfather didn't live to see this." Do you know why I married a Russian man? When I graduated, I couldn't find work for myself. When I would come to the cadres department, they would look at my passport and say that the position had already been filled.... But after I got married, I had a Russian last name, even though my first name and patronymic [remained Jewish].[12]

Esfir suggests that her father could not protest effectively against her decision to marry a non-Jew because his second marriage to a Jewish woman was not successful. In her mind, these were important arguments, which could not have been countered by Jewish tradition. Practicality and humanistic values were more important than the desire to continue the trend of marrying within the ethnic group, as her ancestors had done. Also, Esfir's statement that marrying a Russian man would help her social mobility was perhaps stronger than the argument from her father, which suggested the need to have a Jewish family. It is not clear whether Esfir's internal passport reported her ethnicity as Jewish or as Russian as a result of this marriage. More than a Jewish-sounding name or patronymic, a passport record would have affected her social mobility, but the fact that Esfir did not discuss it in the interview suggests that her passport recorded her as a Russian, not as a Jew. Otherwise, that fact would have made it into the story. Moreover, "nationality," the infamous "fifth line" in the passport, the result of a 1932 ordinance that recorded ethnicity (natsional'nost') in Soviet internal passports (clearly identifying Jews as such), began to play an important role in denying Jews employment only in the late 1940s, not in the late 1930s, which Esfir describes. Thus it is likely that Esfir's story of advantages given to her by a Russian last name projects the situation of the 1940s, rather than the time when she made the decision to marry a non-Jew.

Esfir's father (who was obviously unhappy with her choice) lacked the persuasive arguments to prevent her from marrying a non-Jew. First, he might simply have felt guilty for marrying a second time. Second, reasons such as having Jewish children, creating a Jewish family, and observing Jewish religious laws were not relevant in rapidly modernizing Soviet Russia. A remarkable feature of this testimony is that while Esfir's father was strongly against her marriage, she presented it as an almost conflict-free situation. (When asked whether her father protested, Esfir's first reaction was "no.") One explanation is that the process of life review eliminated the memory of the sharpness of the conflict. After all, Esfir was interviewed almost seventy years after these events took place, and family contradictions and conflicts that took place in the 1930s may seem less sharp or painful now.

Esfir, like most participants in the study, stayed married to her non-Jewish husband for decades. It is possible that in describing her father's attitude toward the choice of spouse, she was projecting the later relationship, not the initial reaction. In addition, the lack of description of conflict in testimonies might be explained by the fact that articulated choices did not contradict their parents' wishes radically; perhaps most parents did not see intermarriage as a family tragedy. Indeed, many interviewees who were married in the 1930s, especially in larger towns or cities, asserted that their parents did not oppose intermarriage. On the contrary, they often thought that Soviet policies of national equality were beneficial to the Jewish community.

Between 1936 and 1938, the rate of intermarriage by Jews in large cities outside the Pale was much higher than in smaller towns within the Pale. More than 37 percent of men and 26.7 percent of women were intermarried in Leningrad and Kharkov, for example. In smaller towns within the former Pale, by contrast, the numbers were 13.5 percent for men and 12.4 percent for women.[13] In Moscow, nearly 50 percent of all Jews intermarried by 1939.[14] Residents of shtetlekh were more inclined to marry Jews than non-Jews even if they moved to bigger cities in their early twenties.[15]

Interviewees constitute a nonrepresentative sample, because only a small percentage of them (fewer than 5 percent) were married to a non-Jewish partner before the war. Even given the fact that most of them were born in shtetlekh rather than cities, the number of intermarriage is still lower than a statistically representative sample would have shown. This probably means that the majority of the people interviewed had a more pronounced Jewish consciousness compared to other Jews of their generation. However, even these people did not have clear reasons and motivations for marrying Jews. They insisted that choosing a Jewish partner was a matter of instinct rather than principle, and very few were able to present any intellectual justification of this choice. The desire "not to upset my parents" was the only explicit argument I was given.

Despite the fact that a similar number of men and women in this survey chose to marry non-Jews, women seemed more willing to emphasize their Jewish identity and the role it played in their personal choices. The closer ties that women maintained with their families, as well as the different patterns for raising boys and girls, could explain this. Sometimes, interviewees suggested it would be easier to build a family with someone of a similar background (thus choosing a Jewish mate). Some women stated that they did not think about marrying a non-Jew because their circle of friends consisted almost entirely of Jews. Still, an absolute majority asserted that they "coincidentally" chose a Jew, and that they did not think about the ethnicity of their partner.

## Wedding? What Wedding? Marriage Ceremonies of the 1930s

Before interviews, I would ask people to prepare photographs that they considered important to show me during the conversations. Almost no one prepared their own wedding picture. It seemed strange at first, as today's society puts such significance on weddings. Moreover, for centuries the wedding ceremony has been one of the most elaborate rituals among East European Jews. The full ceremony can last for several days, and preparations can take years.[16] Ever since the late nineteenth century, ethnographers have studied the meanings of elements of Jewish weddings in different areas of Eastern Europe.[17] Overall, while not a strictly religious ceremony, Jewish weddings had deep religious significance and definitely cultural impact on their participants.[18] In fact, as central events of small-town life, Jewish weddings often seemed one of the most popular Jewish religious and communal rituals.[19]

Surprisingly, despite decreasing levels of religious observances among upper- and middle-class Jews in the Russian Empire,[20] as well as numerous variations among religious Jewish groups, the wedding ceremony continued to be extremely popular throughout the nineteenth century.[21] Even more astonishing, however, is the rapid disappearance of the ceremony from the daily lives of Soviet Jews. Not a single one of my interviewees went through a Jewish wedding ceremony if they were married before 1946 (after 1946, the story is quite different). In the eyes of my narrators, religious weddings among Jews declined dramatically in the 1920s and almost disappeared in the 1930s.[22]

Most interviewees who were married in the 1930s did not have any wedding celebration, whether secular or religious. Especially for young, urban Jews, weddings consisted of the act of signing registration documents at a ZAGS. Even people who were meticulous in describing every single other detail of their lives did not give much thought or significance to their wedding story. For example, a retired scientist, Fira G. (born in Odessa, Ukraine, in 1921), spent a long time talking about her decisions on what hat to wear in 1937 for a special occasion, then whether or not to join the troops to fight the Finnish war of 1939–40 (she joined as part of the secretarial staff), but she was quite laconic when it came to the story of her wedding:

> Vitya and I studied together at the university. In 1941, we were both supposed to graduate. Right before final exams, he suggested that we go to the ZAGS and register. I replied, "All right, let's go." That was it. We went there and signed the papers. The office was located right in front of the Odessa Opera Theater. Then I took my final exams and moved into his empty apartment with him.[23]

Fira did not even recall telling her parents about the event, let alone a having a celebratory dinner.

Similarly, Ilya Sh. (born in Voznesensk, Ukraine, in 1908), a retired physician whom I interviewed in Moscow and who spent a few years writing short stories about his life, could not quite understand why I wanted to hear about how he met his first wife. I initially attributed his hesitation to the fact that his current (second) wife was present at the interview, but this turned out not to be an issue. The reason for hesitation was that, in Ilya's opinion, there was no real story. He recalls the wedding as something he took care of in between other errands on the same day in 1935:

> I was friends with this woman for a long time. We studied together at the university. We both majored in medicine. We spent all our time together: we studied for tests, and we saw each other every day. But then we decided that we were not destined to get married, even though we loved each other. Then, for a year, we stopped dating. Then I was at some party, and realized that she was the one for me. I walked into her apartment, and told her, "I think we should get married."

She said: "I am going to take a vacation in Koktebel [in Crimea] tomorrow, with my girlfriend. I'll come back in a month, and then we can talk about it." I said, "No, I need an answer now." She said, "No answer." I said, "Then it's 'no.'" So we said goodbye to each other.

I walked home. It was midnight. I came home, my parents were awake (at that time I still lived with my parents). My mother said, "A woman came and brought you this letter." I opened the letter, and it said, "I agree." I ran to the post office to call her (we didn't have a phone at home). I told her I got her letter. She said: "That's good. But tomorrow I'm still going to Crimea. If you can, join me."

Immediately, I went to the railway station and bought a ticket. Then I called her again, and said, "I'm all set to go to Crimea." She replied, "That's wonderful, but first we have to get married." We met the next day at 10 a.m., went to the ZAGS with our passports, and got married. Then I went home to pack my things. My train was leaving at 2 p.m. and hers at 6 p.m. We met in Crimea, and spent our honeymoon there.[24]

The process of the legal wedding registration is described as a technicality, not as a major event recording a rite of passage. Although Ilya's bride insisted on registering their relationship officially, she did not care about a wedding or even a celebration of the process.

I recorded only one story of a special celebration from someone who was married before the war and lived in a large city. The woman who shared it was Olga K. (born in Kamenka, Ukraine, in 1905). At the time of the interview, she was 96 years old. She was in bed, and she was not very enthusiastic about the interview. In fact, she agreed to meet with me thinking that I was a nurse who could help her get the palliative care she needed and help relieve her 70-year-old daughter. She showed me a lot of documents, including her marriage certificate, dated 1937. The certificate recorded both her Jewish-sounding maiden name and her German-sounding married name. She was quite proud of that name. When I asked her about the story behind her wedding, she said that she had done something extraordinary for her time—had a dinner to celebrate her marriage:

I got married to an Austrian man. We registered at a ZAGS. But in Austria, you see, they had weddings. Even though he was a communist, he wanted a wedding. So we had a little evening, mostly with his Austrian friends, ten or fifteen people. We were very poor, so there was not much to eat. But it was a dinner, and most of my friends who got married at the time had no celebration at all.[25]

Like Olga, most interviewees did not feel that they needed to justify the absence of a wedding ceremony. In fact, they needed to justify why they did it. A former engineer, who worked on the inaugural construction of the Moscow Metro system and later held a higher-up managerial position there, Venyamin Sh. (born in Sobolevka, Ukraine, in 1908), explained that when he got married in 1929, his family hosted a small dinner for him, his wife, and a couple of relatives only because "that was not an easy year, there was absolutely no food."[26]

It is hard to say whether Venyamin explained events of the past from his current perspective or as he understood it then. It is remarkable, however, that even though he grew up in a town densely populated by Jews, he did not think a wedding could serve as an expression of religious or ethnic identity. Rather, he saw it as a social event that reflected the wealth of the family.[27] Many people attribute the lack of observance of religious holidays and customs to poverty, not to the fact that Soviet ideology did not support religious ritual.

The decline of religious wedding celebrations, both Christian and Jewish, was a trend not only in urban centers but also in smaller villages and shtetlekh. Although elaborate church weddings became rarer during the 1930s, two-day dinner celebrations remained standard for anyone getting married in a village.[28] Similarly, the only interviewees who reported having attended or even having had a Jewish wedding came from smaller towns within the former Pale of Settlement, where some interviewees reported that they had gone to a wedding before the war (though usually not their own). A few even chose to speak about weddings as the most memorable aspect of shtetl life before the war. However, these were usually interviewees who spent their leisure researching shtetl culture, conducting genealogical research, and thinking about the shtetl past. Consider, for example Grigorii B. (born in Orynin, Ukraine, in 1918), who, following his parents' arrest in 1927, left his native shtetl at the age of nine and ended up in a Jewish orphanage in Leningrad. Yet he wrote a memoir in which he savored every little thing he could remember about his life in Orynin, including the weddings. He reiterated the memory during the interview: "There were chuppot, and lots of music at those weddings. When there was a wedding, I ate everything I wanted ... everyone was invited."[29] Indeed, as historian Jeffrey Veidlinger observed, weddings were one of the few opportunities that people had to eat well, especially if a wealthier community member hosted a celebration.[30]

Several people were able to recall some specific customs associated with Jewish weddings in the shtetl. For example, Mariya K. (born in Ekaterinopol, Ukraine, in 1920), a former actress of the Moscow State Yiddish Theater, was most impressed with the klezmer music performed at the Jewish weddings she attended:

> When I was a child, I attended Jewish weddings. I remember klezmer bands. Musicians who lived in our town sometimes teamed up to play at weddings. The usual klezmer bands consisted of four people. For weddings, there was always a fiddler, a drummer, a flutist, and a cello. My two cousins got married, and I danced at their weddings. I was eight. The guests used to pay the musicians, but I didn't pay. I just danced, and I danced really well, and guests asked me to dance more.[31]

The details of the account of the wedding, such the payments to the musicians and her own dancing, suggest that Mariya was probably quite accurate in her description. Indeed, Jewish wedding music made the biggest impression on those who attended such events in the 1930s.[32]

A rare exception from the trend of describing the weddings of other people as opposed to their own came from Fira F. (born in Volsk, Ukraine, in 1919), who asserted that she had a chuppah at her own wedding in 1939:

> F.F.: We had a very modest wedding. There was a chuppah, and everything else necessary. We were very poor, we didn't have money to pay for everything, so we had a very modest wedding, but all the customs were observed.
>
> A.S.: How did your wedding go?
>
> F.F.: I only remember the chuppah, but it was all according to the rules...
>
> A.S.: Were there musicians at your wedding?
>
> F.F.: Oh yes, we had klezmorim, they played *freylekhs* and all the other necessary music.... I've been at other real Jewish weddings. There were rich Jews, they had handmade things ... But our wedding was simple.[33]

Some people called their wedding Jewish simply because no non-Jews were invited. Iona K. (born in Parichi, Belorussia, in 1907), who also had a wedding before the war, described the ceremony of his wedding as modest, but "proper":

> *A.S.:* Did you have a wedding with your first wife [in 1928]?
>
> I.K.: Yes, we had a wedding in Bobruisk, in my wife's parents' house.
>
> *A.S.:* Was it a Jewish wedding?
>
> I.K.: Well, there were no Russians invited, only Jews.
>
> *A.S.:* Did you have a chuppah?
>
> I.K.: No, we didn't.
>
> *A.S.:* Who officiated at the ceremony?
>
> I.K.: We went to the ZAGS.
>
> *A.S.:* Were there musicians at the wedding?
>
> I.K.: There were no musicians; one person played accordion, but especially for us. It was a small ceremony, just for the family. I didn't want to organize anything in a club.[34]

Indeed, the only Jewish element of this wedding that was mentioned in Iona's story was that all the guests were Jewish. However, for Iona, the fact the wedding took place among Jewish friends and family was sufficient to feel that he had a "proper" Jewish celebration. He did not mention the possibility of getting married in a synagogue, but suggested a club as a viable alternative. Even though Iona was proud of retaining "Jewish values" in the organization of his marriage ceremony, he did not see religion as a necessary or integral part of a Jewish wedding. Some aspects of the celebration, perhaps unexpressed, created an association between the wedding and being Jewish; commemorating it in his wife's parents' house, most likely enjoying Jewish festive foods, speaking Yiddish with guests—all these things could be meant by the statement "all the guests were Jewish, so the wedding was Jewish."

Shtetl residents, who were more familiar with Jewish traditions, were more likely to organize a celebratory party or dinner for their wedding. They were also more inclined to add a specifically "Jewish" feature to their ceremony (such as inviting only Jewish guests, playing Jewish music, or serving Jewish food), even though they did not include elements of a traditional wedding. In other words, this study of interwar shtetl weddings illustrates how what was considered "Jewish" among Soviet Jews had been transformed. In the case of weddings, as exemplified in Iona's story, the notion of what was "Jewish" changed from one based on a religiously Jewish ceremony to simply a gathering of Jewish people. This transformation played an important role in shaping Jewish identity in the Soviet Union in subsequent years, when religious expressions of Jewish culture ceased to be public and "being with other Jews" became a primary expression of Jewish culture and identity.

That interviewees did not associate their prewar life, including courtships and weddings, with "being Jewish" can also explain their lack of emphasis on the Jewish nature of weddings as well as the decreased significance of the ethnicity of their spouses. As contradictory as it sounds, especially after reading the descriptions of dilemmas associated with choosing Jewish partners, the majority of narrators seemingly connected being Jewish with persecution and antisemitism. The stories of prewar marriages and weddings belong to a happy realm, and, in their minds, being happy and being Jewish stand in contradiction. The stories of courtship before the war are not associated with antisemitism. When this changes, and the stories of courtships begin to be influenced by government discriminatory policies in the 1940s, the narratives transform into detailed, emotional, and passionate stories of being Jewish.

# 5

## Lost, Found, and Guilty

### The War and the Family

World War II left women widowed, children orphaned, and the entire institution of marriage and family desirable and prestigious. The "Great Retreat" from radical communist values into a more conservative, traditional, almost prerevolutionary society, which had begun in the 1930s, went into full swing after the war.[1] Jewish families experienced a profound change as well. First, the war changed the gender balance among Soviet Jews. In 1939, for 100 Jewish men age 20 to 39, there were 111 Jewish women. By 1949, for 100 Jewish men of this age, there were 133 women (for non-Jews, the numbers were 106 and 141 respectively).[2] The gender balance among Jews was not as skewed as in the general population because Jewish women and children were killed at a higher rate than non-Jewish women and children. Additionally, Jewish draftees had a higher chance of survival than Jewish civilians who remained at home. Jewish men, therefore, had a theoretically larger pool of Jewish and non-Jewish women from whom to choose.

### Courtship and Choice of Partner

Most interviewed men served in the military during World War II; some even met their future spouses then. Yet unlike their older counterparts, men who married in the 1940s (especially war veterans) usually spoke about both their spouses and their casual extramarital relationships. These relationships were popularly referred to as "field marriages," and the women involved in these unions were mockingly called "field wives" (in Russian *pokhodno-polevye zheny*).[3]

Women were usually reluctant to talk about these relations. Not Anna M., however. I interviewed Anna in her Moscow apartment, where she lived, by herself, at the age of 89. She was born in 1912 in Vitebsk, graduated from Moscow State University in 1937 with a degree in communism studies, and served in SMERSH (counterintelligence unit) during the war.[4] Anna's apartment was furnished with bookshelves filled with volumes of classic Russian and Soviet novels, Western literature, many new paperbacks, and, unusually, thick celebratory editions of works by Marx and Lenin. Some books were in German (Anna had worked as a translator during the war, helping to interrogate captured German soldiers and officers), many had bookmarks in them, and many were stacked horizontally. It was clear that she was still a very active reader. When I asked her whether she made close friends during her service in the army, she replied:

> I had a relationship. I don't want to tell you the details, because you're taping this conversation. But it was beautiful. It wasn't a marriage, but men felt freer to start affairs with women there, because many considered themselves widowers. Many had families left in Kyiv, and they had heard about Babi Yar [the mass shooting of the Jews of Kyiv in 1941]. [Sigh.] But life is life. That is why they wanted to consider themselves free. I was also young, and many things happened. [Sigh.] [Silence.] After the war, I gave birth to our son. [Silence.] I am already a great-grandmother. Life goes on. But that was the real page of my life. I know what love is.[5]

Although Anna was not very open when speaking about her relationship, she could have chosen not to speak about it at all. Frequent pauses and sighs after sentences about Jewish men and her own youth stood out in Anna's story, who was otherwise verbose. Commonplace use of Soviet rhetoric like "Life continues" or "the real page of my life" and even "I know what love is" hide Anna's mixed emotions about what happened. She justified the men who had extramarital relationships because they could have lost their spouses during the Holocaust, and she attributed her own choices to love and youth, notions acceptable and respected in modern society. Anna did not see her extramarital relationships during the war as anything unusual (though the beauty of it was described as extraordinary). She repeatedly emphasized that "everyone," both men and women, lived like this and that "no one got married" during the war.

Other women expressed resentment of their wartime partners and claimed that these men took advantage of them. Mira G. (born in Uman, Ukraine, in 1923) approached me and asked to be interviewed when I visited a Philadelphia Jewish adult day-care center that catered to elderly Russian Jews. She had heard from her friends that someone was interested in talking about Soviet Jewish life, and she wanted to make sure that I wrote down that "not all Jews were equal," even during the war. Mira ended up in the Uman ghetto during the first days of war and then the concentration camp Umanskaya Yama.[6] In 1942, she met a man she called her "unlawful husband":

> I met Voresaev, who was a prisoner of war. He worked in the camp, he was a driver. I met him, and he was my husband, but we didn't register [our marriage]. I got pregnant, and seven months later gave birth to my baby boy. I tried to hide the pregnancy under my clothes, so that I wouldn't be killed. The clothes were all rags, so it wasn't very difficult. . . .
>
> Some women who were in the camp with me were doctors and nurses, so they helped deliver the baby. But I don't even know how it all happened, I think it [the baby] jumped out by itself.
>
> Now I have this son, who is fifty-eight years old. He suffers from depression. My son is not registered as a Jew, because his father wasn't a Jew. He was from Baku, he was Azeri. . . . We lived together, but we didn't register. . .
>
> I was tired and sick, and he began to search for younger, more beautiful women. I got sick and was admitted to the hospital. It turned out to be sepsis, and then it was tuberculosis of the bone. I spent twenty months in a hospital. But he was a man, he didn't marry again, but brought [lovers] home. . . I couldn't forgive him, and told him that the war was over, and I didn't need a husband. He didn't insist. But then they wanted to draft him again, he came back to me, took our son, and went with him to the draft office, so that they didn't draft him.
>
> I was deathly ill at the time, and couldn't stop him, and there were no orphanages then. . . So he said he was the primary caregiver, but he didn't do anything. My son saved him, because otherwise he would have had to serve in the *shtrafnaia* [penal company] detachment, because he had been a prisoner of war and that was considered as if he had voluntarily surrendered [*sdalsia*].[7]

The tone of Mira's story is very different from that of Anna M.'s. Anna did not want to mention any difficulties associated with being a single mother. In contrast, Mira stressed the vulnerabilities of her personal situation and blamed her wartime partner for taking advantage of her and their child. The immediate danger of being pregnant in a camp has been documented, but not in descriptions of Ukrainian camps.[8] Mira, however, did not blame the political situation or her imprisonment, but instead emphasized that her sufferings, such as giving birth in the concentration camp and a life-threatening illness, were in many ways the result of poor treatment by the father of her child. Perhaps the difference in approach stems from the fact that Anna M. met the father of her child in a SMERSH unit, while she was serving in the Red Army. While she might have felt betrayed on a personal level, her public expectations did not include his leaving his first family for her. Mira, on the other hand, was a prisoner in a concentration camp. The father of her child was a driver who worked there (probably a POW). It is possible that the relationship was imposed upon her with a threat or that she chose it in order to have some protection against potential rapists—the Uman concentration camp is known for the prevalence of rape, which routinely took place at night.[9] Mira's story serves not only as a rare glimpse into women's lives in the Uman camp and their survival strategies as inmates, but also how she chose to smooth out the contradictions of her past in the story, designing it for the future. For example, she refers to Voresaev as her husband rather than a man who took advantage of her. His abuse goes beyond mistreating her: he took advantage of their son, whom he allegedly used to avoid returning to the front. The message of the story is clear: Mira emphasized that she was abused in the camp, and so was her son, both during his incarceration and beyond.[10]

Throughout her story, Mira stressed that Voresaev was not Jewish, and she attributes some of his negative behavior to that fact. Significantly, her second partner was also a non-Jew, but because Mira was happy with him, she never said anything about his ethnicity and did not raise direct parallels between his ethnicity and personal characteristics.

Both Mira and Anna hint at the stigma that poisoned the lives of women war veterans in the early postwar years. Haunted by the stereotypes of surviving the war through sleeping with commanding officers, formerly enlisted women were perceived as immoral. In order to avoid stigmatization, some women sacrificed their veterans' benefits and threw away the documents showing that they had served in the war in order to have a chance to get married and live a peaceful life.[11] In this sense, the stories of female Jewish war veterans do not stand out when compared to non-Jews who had similar experiences. Indeed, Anna M. and Mira probably used the interview to a certain degree to "normalize" the stories of their wartime experiences, to make peace with the past and smooth out the contradictions (in the spirit of life review). This is similar to how women spoke about ethnicity with regard to their future spouses in the 1930s.

Many men interviewed confirmed the widespread nature of extramarital romance during the war and spoke about it unapologetically. Usually such conversations happened towards the middle of the interview and often after a drink. For example, when I came to interview David S. (born in Zhitomir, Ukraine, in 1921), a retired military professional and a 1940 graduate of the Moscow military academy, he set up a table laid out with numerous appetizers, vodka, and sweet wine. David insisted that I drink wine while he helped himself to some vodka and food. He spent about half an hour of his interview telling anecdotes about the "field wives" of his commanding officer. However, he asked me to turn off the tape recorder when he told me about the affairs in which he had been involved during the war. When I asked why he did not want to have this on the record, he said, "I don't want people to think that Jewish men behaved as I did."[12]

David S. resorted to "the Jewish factor" to explain his choices during the war. He saw our interview as a chance to transmit a message to future generations. Therefore, the only information he volunteered was what he thought would educate listeners about the "heroic" aspects of his story, especially because the interview was focused on the "Jewish" side of his life. For David, to be Jewish meant to be a good, moral person. His war adventures did not fit this image. Indeed, some men proudly asserted that, despite the temptation, they never allowed themselves to start an affair simply because "Jewish men should not do this."[13] A variation on this attitude was that some men did not mind having extramarital relationships with non-Jewish women, whereas they did not consider such relationships with Jews a possibility. In any case, all male interviewees agreed that having extramarital affairs was not considered typical Jewish behavior.

Significantly, most women disagreed. They believed that Jewish men were frequently involved in such relationships. The testimony of Anna M. provides one of the reasons for such behavior: the likelihood that Jewish men had lost their families in the Holocaust. Female veterans who married Jewish officers and soldiers stressed that they insisted their union be legally registered in order to distinguish themselves from field wives (which many Jewish soldiers had). A retired physician, Ava T. (born in Cherkassy, Ukraine, in 1921), who married an officer from her military unit, said that she refused to have any sexual relations with her fiancé until they registered at a ZAGS. Olga K. (born in Mytishchi, Russia, in 1921) similarly stated that even though she fell in love with her future husband, a Jew, when he was an officer in her unit, she did not want to live with him until they were discharged. She did not want people to consider her a field wife, and she also wanted to make sure that he was not already married to a woman back home.[14] Numerous responses indicate that, among Jewish women, the postwar view of Jewish men was far from favorable. Women, and men as well, often mentioned that distrust was prevalent. Evgeniia B. (born in Algopol, Ukraine, in 1928),[15] for example, says that she initially refused to marry her future husband because she thought he would be unfaithful, since that was the reputation of Jewish men at the time.[16]

Some women spoke from firsthand experience of men abandoning their prewar families. Bella G. (born in Bulovka, Ukraine, in 1928) recalls that her father did not come home until four years after his discharge:

We lived in a small shtetl. . . The war was over, it was 1945, then 1946, but we heard nothing. Finally, a letter arrived. There was a rumor in the army that all the Jews in Ukraine had perished. He [her father] sent a message to the village council to inquire about us.

He received a reply that indicated that we were alive. But he was already living with another woman. When he was about to be discharged, he said that he had no family left, so he was sent to Kyiv. But even when he found out we were still alive, he didn't hurry home.

My older sister was sixteen or seventeen then (she was born in 1924), and someone from the village council told her: "If you don't go there and bring him home, he'll never come back." At that time, very many [Jewish] men started going out with Russian women. He was then forty-five years old, a young handsome fellow. So we collected money for her to travel.

She found him. . . He was living with a Ukrainian woman from Kyiv, in her apartment. He had access to a lot of food at the warehouse where he worked, so he brought her food. She was happy. When my sister came, he said to her: "I can't get released, they won't let me go." She said: "I don't believe that." A neighbor told her to go to my father's boss and demand that he be released. She said: "Go to the office, and say: 'Let our father go. He has seven children and we are all naked and barefoot.'" She did so. He was called in and shamed. . . They released him, almost by force. And then he came home and bought us presents.[17]

Bella G. takes it for granted that it was common for Jewish men to build new families during the war. This observation is consistent with a number of other interviews suggesting that prewar views of Jewish men as better husbands and fathers did not hold up during the immediate postwar years. Men who did not have extramarital affairs or abandon their families for younger women were seen as the exception rather than the rule.

A retired teacher, Liusia G. (born in Kyiv, Ukraine, in 1925), was present when I interviewed her husband, the retired surgeon Semyon Sh. (born in Kuty, Ukraine, in 1918). When I asked him about his war experience, she interrupted to say, "Make sure that you write it down for the record when you write about him. He went through the entire war and did not have a single field wife. Few men, especially Jewish men, can boast of anything like that!"[18]

The evaluation of extramarital affairs that took place 50 to 60 years prior to the interviews can certainly tell us more about the interviewee's current views than those they held in the 1940s or 1950s. In fact, it is likely that the stories resurface as reactions to the choices of grandchildren, who increasingly marry non-Jews. However, it is still noteworthy that there is a significant difference between evaluations of relationships among those who married in the 1920s and 1930s and those who did so in the 1940s and 1950s. For example, those married after the war, both men and women, took marriage and courtship more seriously than their older counterparts. Perhaps the transition from wartime uncertainty led to an increased desire for stability and normalcy in all aspects of daily life. Many people saw the creation of a family as the basis for such a stable existence.

Despite their strong condemnation of Jewish men's behavior during the war, most women interviewed eventually married Jews. Mariya P. was born in Ianovo, Ukraine, in 1928 and was in high school when the war began. After the war, she returned to her village and worked on a kolkhoz (collective farm). She recounted, "I met my husband in my shtetl. Our family returned from the evacuation, so did his. There were very few young people there, so we met, and then decided to get married." When asked if it was important for her to marry a Jew, she answered, "No one even thought of marrying a Russian. I had a lot of [Russian] admirers, but I avoided them. I used to run away to the lake and sit there, so that they would leave me alone ... Like a typical Jewish girl, I was innocent, beautiful. They were handsome guys, good guys, but I was not interested in non-Jews. It was not the custom at that time to marry a non-Jew."[19]

Although Mariya insisted that she wanted to marry a Jew, she pointed out that she had had other choices. This was a tendency that appeared anew in the testimonies of brides of the 1940s. Liusia G., for example, proudly noted that, when she was a high school student, all of her boyfriends were non-Jews and she was an object of envy among her Jewish girlfriends.[20] Notably, while the assertion of her popularity among non-Jews suggested that she considered herself beautiful and associated her rejection of their advances with modesty, she related both beauty and modesty to her ethnic identity.

In the late 1940s, the political climate in the country made it hard for Jews to intermarry, and the wish to have a Jewish spouse declined dramatically for non-Jews. However, none of the interviewees spoke about this factor when they shared their stories of finding a spouse. Rather, people found other reasons to justify marrying a Jew. Men, for the most part, explained that Jewish women made "better wives." Often, this was the only ethnic sentiment they expressed.

The high death toll among men during the war created a situation in which it was much easier for men to find wives than for women to find husbands. For Jews, the situation was slightly different. More women than men were killed during the Holocaust (the survival rate for Soviet Jewish enlisted personnel was higher when compared to Jewish civilians in the parts of the Soviet Union occupied by Germany and its allies).[21] In turn, this meant that Jewish men had the potential to enjoy interest from both Jews and non-Jews. Yet no woman who participated in the survey spoke about any difficulty of finding a partner, Jewish or non-Jewish. On the contrary, almost every female narrator stressed that she was popular and that men were "fighting over her." It is revealing to analyze the qualities that these women chose to list as worthy.

An overwhelming majority of women emphasized that their main virtue (in addition to exceptional beauty, mentioned by about 80 percent) was decent conduct. Dozens of interviewees revealed numerous aspects of proper behavior, ranging from celibacy until marriage to the unwillingness to commit to a man of "doubtful background." Significantly, almost all the women directly or indirectly attributed this value to the fact that they were Jewish.

However, in each case, their Jewishness was depicted somewhat differently. Mariya D. (born in Mikhalevo, Ukraine, in 1928) was a student at the Jewish State Theater studio when she met her first husband in 1948. She related:

> I had never had a boyfriend. For some reason, boys thought they had to protect me. They thought of me as their comrade. They always took me everywhere, they walked me home, they loved me, and they loved my mother. They used to come to our place, my mother used to make a pot of potatoes, and if there was herring, that was even better. We would stay up all night and talk—my mother was with us. But I didn't have a boyfriend. . . .
>
> Once I was at some party, and I sat in the corner and cried. I asked [a friend]: "Vitya, please, help me get out of here!" It wasn't my crowd. They were all prostitutes. . . . How I met my [first] husband is an interesting story. . . . There was a concert. I have to say that my parents and I never spared any expense when it came to theater, concerts, or museums. . . . After the concert, the guys who invited me said: "Let's go to a restaurant this time!" That was my first visit to a restaurant. Iura Cherniavskii played [piano] there. . . . Our table was near the stage. I looked at him. . . he was tall and very handsome. He must have liked me a lot, because he came to our table and introduced himself. Later he walked me home. We ended up getting married. I didn't have any boyfriends before him; I had never even been kissed before. . . . I had a Jewish upbringing. That was how I was raised. [22]

Mariya provided information about her single life in order to emphasize her chaste behavior and, perhaps, to compensate for the fact that she met her husband at a restaurant, a place she might have considered inappropriate for a decent woman. She also spoke of her first husband as an intellectual, who worked in a restaurant to supplement his income. The details about her single life stressed the fact that, even though she had male friends, she did not have any affairs. She claimed that her "proper" behavior was the result of her Jewish upbringing, which taught that modesty was a female Jewish characteristic. For her, to be "Jewish" meant to be decent and proper; that is, it was more relevant to her gender identity than her ethnic one.

An illustration of this point is the way Mariya is passing on these values to her 16-year-old granddaughter Karina (for whom she serves as primary caregiver). Mariya explained that she has tried to raise Karina in an "internationalist spirit" rather than in a "narrow-minded worldview like that of traditional Judaism" (which, according to Mariya, includes observance of religious holidays, traditions, and synagogue attendance). She repeated the following advice: "A Jewish girl must know that if one plays with dogs, one can get fleas, and if one plays with men, one gets children."[23] When asked whether this knowledge is valuable only to a Jewish girl or to girls in general, Mariya replied, "Of course, I am not a nationalist. Everyone should know that, but a Jewish girl has to know it especially well, because she will have more difficulties in life than non-Jewish women will."[24]

Mariya D. was not alone in suggesting that Jewish women need certain survival skills. However, another woman, also an actress, Mariya K. (born in Ekaterinopol, Ukraine, in 1921) told the following story when I asked her about the challenges of being a single woman in her profession:

My friends and I performed a concert in Peredelkino [a writers' village near Moscow]. After that, we were invited to the dining hall. There were bottles of vodka on the tables... There were four of us: me, a singer who was my very good friend, and a couple, Iura and his wife... Suddenly, two colonels came to our table. They were both handsome and tall. They asked Iura: "Can we invite these two girls to our table?" We looked at each other: how could we say no, that wouldn't be polite because we were guests. . . .

So we went to their table. Soon bottles of cognac appeared... They poured us half a glass... First, they said: "[Let us drink] to our getting to know each other." We drank. Then, they said: "Now [we should drink for] to our homeland!" How could we not drink to our country? We drank a bit. Then they said: "To Stalin!" We were terrified. It was impossible not to drink to Stalin! We sat a bit more. Then they both said: "Now we have to drink to victory!" We said: "We can't drink anymore, we won't be able to get home!" They said: "How can you not drink to victory?" We drank.

What saved me was that I knew how to drink. I had that skill. I never "lost my head" even when I was drunk... After that, we found ourselves in a vehicle; it was a truck with an open roof. I knew I was drunk... It was wild: everyone was drunk because of vodka. My friend Chana was drunk, too. She shrieked and yelled.... One actor began to bother her, she screamed, and everyone laughed, but I didn't interfere.

I didn't even look at them. Eventually, I got out of the truck and tried to walk. A professor helped me get home. But, even though I was drunk, I understood what was going on and I didn't lose consciousness. That is one of the important qualities of a Jewish woman. She has to know how to drink yet not get drunk![25]

Mariya K. saw "the ability to drink yet not to get drunk" as an aspect of modesty appropriate specifically for a Jewish woman. Like Mariya D. and Mariya K., other women had somewhat different interpretations of what virtues characterize them, but all agreed that there were virtues that good Jewish women possessed.

Mariya K.'s story about the colonels who manipulated women into drinking by using notions of the "Motherland" and the name of Stalin provides a glimpse into the cultural atmosphere of the early 1950s. Many women mentioned that their courtship was directly influenced by Soviet political rhetoric of the time, and for many it was hard to separate the public aspects of their lives from the private and the personal from the communal.[26] People of various backgrounds and places of residence agreed that political rhetoric was an important part of their daily lives and even affected their selection of potential spouses. Mila Ch. (born in Mstislavl, Belorussia, in 1928), for example, remembered that she and her fiancé applied for a wedding license at a ZAGS the day Stalin died in March 1953. The ZAGS official shamed both of them for ignoring "the tragedy of the country" and did not issue them a license.[27]

The virtues that women spoke about, such as modest behavior, were quite popular in general Soviet society, not only among Jews. Nevertheless, the assertion that Jewish women were better than others was quite popular among female interviewees. This phenomenon was certainly not unique to wartime and the postwar Jewish community. Non-Jewish Polish refugees considered themselves to be better mothers and better wives than the surrounding population.[28] However, Polish women also spoke their national language, tried to maintain their observance of religious (Catholic) customs, and attempted to educate their children about their history and culture, whereas my interviewees did not consider those issues important. Moreover, unlike the Jews, the Polish women were not Soviet citizens, but rather refugees forced to leave their native cities and villages and live among strangers. Russian Jews grew up with Soviet values, many did not speak Yiddish on a daily basis, and an absolute majority did not practice or observe Jewish traditions and rituals.

Instead of defining themselves vis-à-vis others in terms of social and cultural background, many Jews used ethnicity as the basis for comparison. Many interviewees elaborated on what they considered important behaviors for Jewish women. Modesty—with regard to praise, material wealth, and desires—was expressed by both men and women as a Jewish woman's most important characteristic. In fact, many testimonies portrayed Jewish men as irresponsible, but Jewish women were described (by both men and women) as modest, trustworthy, and potentially better wives, both during and after the war.

Faithful behavior was the most valued trait for Jewish men as well. As shown, women were quite reluctant to marry demobilized Jewish officers and soldiers for a variety of reasons, some of which had a direct connection with ethnicity and some with the men's military background. Above all, however, was the fear that their potential partners would exhibit unfaithful behavior. The most vivid story of this comes from Mila Ch., who refused to go out with the man she loved because she did not want to be one of his many girlfriends:

> I studied at the Lvov architecture vocational school. When I finished my third year, he came to study in our school. This is how we met. Wolf was already twenty-five years old. It was in 1950. I was almost twenty. He began to court me, but I had boyfriends who were nineteen or twenty years old, we had different relations. But he had already been "around the block," he came from the army... I was afraid of him, and used to run away from him. But still, deep in my heart, I liked him. He was handsome, healthy, cheerful, and I was flattered that he had a lot of girls, but still liked me. In short, we began dating, but then started arguing. He was an adult, he wanted different relationships, but I did not want that. In short, I broke up with him.[29]

Mila's story had a twist. She married another man in 1953, and Wolf got married to someone else as well. Twenty years later, when Mila got divorced and Wolf lost his wife to a long-term illness, they met again. This time their courtship was more successful, and the couple got married. Moreover, the children from their first marriages (Mila's son and Wolf's daughter) got married to each other and had a son, who became the couple's common grandchild. During our conversation, Mila stressed that although she married another man, she continued to love Wolf all her life, but she was unable to become, as she puts it, "one of those sluts [*shalava*], who sleeps around instead of getting married." In other words, she felt that her integrity would be jeopardized if she gave in to her feelings and gave up the values with which she was raised.

The message of the story becomes even more apparent if one applies a genre reading. It is a narrative of restored justice and divine test; the couple is meant to be together, but obstacles stand in their way. These obstacles test the couple's virtues, especially that of the woman, who cannot compromise her integrity (in religious tales, it would be love for the divine) for the pleasure of earthly love. The reward comes later, when the couple survive their tribulations and have a virtual child together, through their own children who fulfill the desires of their parents. The obstacle here is not government antisemitism, not even the Holocaust (at least not directly), but the poor reputation of Jewish military men, so poor that even a Jewish woman in love cannot give in to her feelings for a Jewish man.

When I asked Mila whether her behavior was different from that of other women of her age and background, she replied:

My parents divorced soon after the war, because my father left my mother for an eighteen-year-old actress. We later became good friends. But my mother suffered a lot, and I didn't want to repeat her mistakes. She trusted my dad, who wasn't faithful to her. I wanted a man who would be loyal to me. And Jewish men who came back from the war, like Wolf, they weren't reliable, as they had relations before, and I did not want that. But now I understand it was a mistake.[30]

Numerous interviews suggest that the prewar stereotypes of Jewish men as better husbands and fathers did not hold up during the years immediately following the war. Evgeniya B. (born in Odessa, Ukraine, in 1928), for example, says that she initially refused to marry her future husband because she did not think he would be faithful to her—"Jewish men had that reputation at the time."[31] When men did not have "field wives" or did not abandon their families for younger women, it was seen as the exception rather than the rule.

Despite the overwhelmingly strong condemnation of Jewish men's behavior during the war, most of the female interviewees eventually married Jews. Like their counterparts who got married in the 1930s, they insisted that they did so for one of two reasons: not to upset their parents, or because they did not think that there were other possibilities. The majority of male interviewees who got married after the war took Jewish wives, but "ethnic" factors alone did not influence such decisions. For example, permission to live in Moscow and Leningrad was difficult to obtain during the postwar years. One legitimate way to receive permission was to marry a Muscovite or Leningrader or someone who had a legal right to live there. Many men hinted that a Jewish woman from Moscow or Leningrad would be more likely to marry an out-of-town Jew than a non-Jew, as many men used this circumstance to get into a desirable city. In effect, some women married such men to help to get them into Moscow or Leningrad. Few people openly spoke about this, but stories about obtaining the *propiska* (legal residence registration) through marriage were numerous. For example, Vladimir K. (born in Nikopol, Ukraine, in 1927) said that he liked two things about his wife: that she was a Muscovite and that she was a Jew. He said, "I don't know which was more important. But she was intelligent, and lived in Moscow, and happened to be Jewish, so it all came together. I don't think ethnicity was that important then. . ."[32]

The important factor in the decision to marry a Jew was increasing ethnic intolerance. When asked whether it was important for them to marry a Jew, many men replied that, although initially they did not give it much thought, later they changed their minds. The most frequent reason for this change of heart was hearing antisemitic remarks by a non-Jewish girlfriend or one's parents. One man, Lazar F. (born in Orel, Russia, in 1924) related his postwar experience in seeking a wife: "My first wife was my cousin. We got married in 1949, and it was not a good marriage. I think the biggest problem was my mother-in-law. . . . Finally, we got divorced. Then I married again, also to a Jewish woman." When asked if it was important for him to marry a Jewish woman, he explained:

Absolutely not. I can't say I was looking for a Jewish woman. The thing is that after the divorce, I didn't want to get married at all. I thought I had had enough. I already had a son, and this boy was growing up without a father ... but I dated women, I dated girls. I was infatuated with my [non-Jewish] colleague Liudmila Alexandrovna Matveeva. We had a wonderful relationship. We even were together, spent nights together. Then we went to apply for a marriage license at the ZAGS. Her father was an alcoholic. When my family found out, they said: "Do you need a son who is an alcoholic?" They protested, but I didn't listen. I had a condition for marriage: if we had a son, his name would be Aaron, after my deceased father.

But one day before we had to go register, Liudmila called me. She said: "What about my family?" Their last name was Matveev [a Russian name]. "Are you suggesting my parents have a grandson named Aaron? They wouldn't survive that!" So we broke up.

Then I dated a beautiful Armenian girl. When I proposed, she refused. Then I proposed to another girl, she was Russian and agreed to name a future son Aaron, but she didn't want to leave her three aunts (my second condition was that we would live separately, without in-laws). Then my neighbor, who was Jewish, introduced me to my future wife ... Eventually, I married her.

When our son was born, she called him Arik. But when the time came to register his name, she said: "That's such a Jewish name, everybody will make fun of him. Do you want to ruin your son's life?" I didn't want to ruin my son's life, but I insisted on registering him as Aaron. We didn't register him for two months. Then someone told my wife to register him as Arkadii. And we did that. Now he lives in Israel and has become religious. He goes by the name Aaron.[33]

Lazar later explained that he wanted to name his son Aaron because he felt guilty about how he had treated his own father. His father was arrested in 1937 and remained imprisoned until 1954. Lazar signed numerous documents in which he declared that he had agreed with the state's verdict and considered his father an "enemy of the people." He never visited his father in jail (though of course, it was not easy to visit anyone in a Soviet jail)[34] and broke off contact with his mother and sisters, who continued to stay in touch with Aaron after his arrest. Lazar's father was released in 1954 and died shortly thereafter. Lazar thought that naming his son Aaron would help him atone for his guilt.

Lazar replied "no" to a direct question about whether or not it was important for him to marry a Jew, but he indicated that the attitude he sought in a wife was one that only a Jewish woman would likely have. However, this specific concern (giving their son the Jewish name of his father) revealed that he was willing to marry a non-Jewish woman if she was prepared to accept some parts of his ethnic identity.

Lazar was not the only interviewee who was willing to marry a non-Jew as long as she was able to do something Jewish. For example, one man, who I interviewed on a street in Brighton Beach in New York and who refused to give me his name, said, "Ethnicity did not matter to me, as long as she knew how to make gefilte fish."[35] Another interviewee, Lev G. (born in Berdichev, Ukraine, in 1918) agreed: "I didn't care whether she was Jewish, I just wanted her to like my family and understand them. But my mother spoke only Yiddish at home, so I had to find a non-Jewish woman who spoke Yiddish."[36] Lisa G. (born in 1922, in Zhitomir, Ukraine) stressed, "I didn't care whether he was a Jew as long as my husband didn't object to my son being circumcised."[37]

The frequency of such comments, combined with the research on prewar Soviet Jewish culture, which asserted the importance of Jews doing things together as opposed to "correctly,"[38] suggests that they may illustrate a common trend in 1950s Jewish culture. Nearly all of the interviewees did not observe most Jewish traditions and, usually, did not speak Yiddish on a daily basis. Perhaps, by expecting at least a minimal acquiescence to some Jewish "requirements," these men wanted to ensure that their potential wife was not an antisemite and would not call them a "kike" in the heat of an argument.

In general, the genre of the stories of marriages and courtships conducted in the 1950s is the "test" as opposed to a "quest" or "love story." In a typical folk story, a test serves as an indicator of a hero's true commitment to the cause. From Abraham taking Isaac to slaughter on the request of the divine to a prince trying to win over the princess in the name of true love, the test genre usually addresses anxiety associated with surviving impossibly difficult circumstances. Similarly, the story of attempting to marry a non-Jew, whose structural details are so remarkably similar that it can be called a genre, describes a Lazar's anxious desire to devise a litmus test to verify their potential spouse's attitudes toward Jews and possibly identify their antisemitism before it was too late.

Consider, for example, how Ava T. (born in Cherkassy, Ukraine, in 1919), a chief medical officer in the army who married an Azeri officer from her unit, presented her account of her first meeting with her future husband:

> Once we were called in for a meeting. It turned out it was for a comrade's court appearance. One officer accused another one of cowardice, saying: "You're afraid because you're a Jew!" The Jewish officer beat up the one who said that. So the one who said that all Jews are cowards was put on trial. The chairman of the court began to speak. He had a beautiful voice, but I didn't like what he said. Then another officer spoke. He explained that it was wrong to accuse Jews of cowardice, because they fought harder than others. When he finished, I looked at him, and he looked back at me. I was beautiful then. It was love at first sight.[39]

The story displays the typical features of the "divine test" story: the protagonist is put in a situation where he can make a choice between a moral decision that might seem dangerous or illogical and an immoral option that may lead to an immediate reward. The protagonist passes the test successfully and is rewarded by a beautiful girl. In this instance, the test is whether or not he would defend a Jew in a fight with an antisemite. Like Ava, other interviewees who married non-Jews emphasized that their future spouses passed "a test for antisemitism" with flying colors. Some spoke of the fact that their spouse's family had helped hide Jews during the Holocaust or mentioned a non-Jewish spouse who went to a concentration camp in order not to be parted from his or her Jewish spouse or, on a banal level, prized a non-Jewish wife who "could cook gefilte fish better than most Jewish women."[40]

Some people emphasized that they married a non-Jew because they felt that such a marriage would help their children live a "normal life," one free from antisemitism. All the interviewees who married non-Jews in the 1940s and 1950s indicated that they had married for a specific reason, not because the ethnicity of their partner was irrelevant to them.

Still, the majority of interviewees, both men and women, married Jews. As mentioned, their chief motivation was to avoid the risk of marrying an antisemite. Samuil G. (born in Khmelnik, Ukraine, in 1924) expressed this idea most concisely:

"I did not even think that I could marry a Russian [woman]. Theoretically, there could be some circumstances, for example, he is in the military and she is a nurse and saves his life, then love. . . Love, you see, is stronger than anything. But when it cools a bit, she says one nasty thing or another and he looks back and says: 'What have I done?' "[41]

I initially suspected that one of the reasons for the stronger motivation to marry Jews during the postwar period was the impact of the Holocaust.[42] It could be that the knowledge of how local civilians helped kill their Jewish neighbors, as well as the loss of immediate relatives, would increase the desire to marry within the Jewish community. When asked directly, most often people did not understand the connection between these two issues. Certainly numerous testimonies speak of betrayal by non-Jewish spouses during the Holocaust, but the interviewees usually balanced these testimonies with stories of heroism and self-sacrifice by Ukrainian and Russian wives and husbands to save their beloved spouses. While many noted that they felt it was important to transmit the knowledge of the Holocaust to their children and grandchildren, no one suggested that it motivated them to marry a Jew in the 1940s or 1950s. Instead, the motivation to marry another Jew was predominantly to avoid antisemitism within the family, both for men and women. It seems that the context of the late 1940s, with the official restrictive policies toward Jews, played a more important role than the need to commemorate a devastating past.

## The Return of the Shadkhan: Matchmaking in the 1940s and 1950s

Traditional Jewish practices, including matchmaking, made a triumphant return in the late 1940s—most surprisingly, in large cities such as Moscow and Leningrad. Indeed, by 1948 the majority of Soviet Jews lived in bigger cities with dispersed Jewish communities. Traditional Jewish places of gathering, such as synagogues, were rare and unpopular. Secular institutions, such as Yiddish theaters, had been shut down by the end of the 1940s. Matchmaking, performed by older family members or even by "professional" matchmakers (called shadkhans), was often the only way to meet a future Jewish spouse. An astonishing fact is that three out of every ten men interviewed reported that they met their future spouse in the late 1940s or 1950s through matchmaking, and many more knew of its existence. (By comparison, only four men and two women out of 129 spoke of direct or indirect matchmaking in the 1930s.)

Most stories about matchmaking came from the war veterans, who asserted that during the immediate postwar period, they usually lived a "free life," which, in their language, meant living with women without registration or having multiple partners. When they decided to settle down, often pressured by their extended family, they were able to use the services of a matchmaker. For example, in 1946, the war veteran Vladimir Ya. (born in Purkhov, Belorussia, in 1921) returned to Leningrad. For several years, he lived with a woman, but he did not marry her "because she was older than me, and could not have children. Also, she was Georgian, and had a wild temper." Finally, Vladimir decided to find himself a "proper" wife:

> In order to find a wife, I talked to Roza. Auntie Roza; she was a matchmaker. She used to offer me brides.
>
> Everyone knew her in Leningrad. If you wanted to find a Jewish wife, she was the one to talk to. I can tell you a couple of stories. Once she took me to some family to introduce me. I was laughing: "Auntie Roza, we saw so many girls, and I didn't like any of them. Give me twenty-five rubles, and I will go with you!" Finally, we went to see the family. The girl came out, walked around a little bit, then she left the room. I whisper to Roza: "She's lame! She can't walk!" Then Roza replies: "Don't whisper, she can't hear either!" This girl also had small eyes. How can a Jewish woman have small eyes? So they tried to trick me.
>
> Finally, she introduced me to Lida. She was from a Jewish family. Her father was a butcher; her mother was a housewife and didn't work. Even though they were poor, I liked her, and I married her.[43]

Vladimir's story resonates with many Jewish jokes (and is possibly borrowed from them). But it also discusses the qualities of a potential bride that were important to him. Certainly, physical appearance played the most important role, but Vladimir also mentions family background as well as financial stability. It went without saying that the bride had to be Jewish. For Vladimir, matchmaking was the only way to find a suitable woman, even though he joked and complained about it.

Another man, Muscovite Yakov B. (born in Moscow in 1920), asserted that the only reason he married a non-Jewish woman was that "it was impossible to meet a Jewish girl without a matchmaker, and I was shy about talking to them, so I married a Russian woman."[44]

Matchmaking services were provided by both semi-professionals, like the "Auntie Roza" described by Vladimir, and by older members of the family. Ilya Sh. (born in Voznesensk, Ukraine, in 1908), who married his first wife in between errands in 1920s and notified his parents much later, explained that when he decided to get married for the second time, in 1951, it was his father who began to introduce him to potential brides. He recalled, "My father went to synagogue. He had a friend there, and that friend had a daughter. They introduced us, and we got married."[45]

Many men and women confessed that they were embarrassed to admit to their friends and colleagues that they had met through older relatives and especially professional matchmakers. Perhaps this explains why very few women admitted to being introduced to a man by a friend or a match-maker. Nevertheless, women readily stated that their female friends had met their husbands that way, or that they themselves often introduced their younger acquaintances to each other. Thus, there is strong evidence that matchmaking, which was disregarded and ridiculed in the 1930s, was significantly regenerated in the late 1940s and 1950s, when most Jews lived in larger urban communities. The sheer size of larger cities, combined with the absence of a formal or informal meeting place for young Jews interested in creating endogamous families, created a situation of demand for informal matchmaking services. Moreover, matchmaking was not the only "traditional" practice that was resurrected. The second major comeback was a renewed interest in wedding ceremonies, testified to and experienced by many of the interviewees.

## A Modest Wedding, but the Best One

Attitudes toward weddings in general, and Jewish weddings in particular, are visibly different among the people who married after the war. Most men and women who were married in the 1940s and early 1950s report having some sort of celebratory ceremony in addition to the ZAGS registration. While interviewees still complained about poverty, many recall having a celebratory dinner and even buying special clothes for the wedding, which was not mentioned by those who married in the 1930s.

Sima F. (born in Medzhibozh, Ukraine, in 1928) got married in 1946, right after her future husband was released from the army. During the interview, she showed me a picture of her wedding, in which she is wearing a beautiful gray dress. Her husband Ilya wears a military uniform. When I asked whether it was not customary to wear a white dress for the wedding, she replied, "The problem was that there were no dresses at all. My uncle, my mother's brother, served in Dresden, Germany, during the war, so he sent us some [fabric to make a dress]. So I had a new dress for the wedding, and Ilya's parents hosted a wedding celebration."[46]

A similar account comes from Semyon Y. (born in Mogilev Podolsky, Ukraine, in 1915), who returned from the front in 1945 and married Faina, the daughter of his parents' neighbor (born in Mogilev Podolsky, Ukraine in 1919). Because Faina and her family had survived three years in a ghetto, they had no money for a wedding celebration, but Semyon made sure that she had a "decent" dress:

> We didn't have a large wedding, we just liked each other and that was that. But she was from the camp, so she had absolutely no clothes. When I came back from Germany, I brought some military mattresses. They had upholstery with a square pattern on them. I gave her those mattresses, and she made herself a skirt. Then we got married, and she wore that skirt.[47]

Semyon made quite an effort to get the dress for his bride. This story shows quite a striking difference in attitudes compared to people who got married before the war, who thought that a celebratory dinner was something extraordinary. Those who married after the war thought that having neither a beautiful dress for the celebratory dinner nor a lot of guests at the wedding was a sign of poverty. Only two of the people who were married after the war reported not having any ceremony at all. The overwhelming majority told stories of at least some preparation and celebration.

Attention to fashion and women's clothes increased in the postwar years, partly for ideological reasons and partly out of the popular desire for a peaceful life.[48] After four years of service in the military, men wanted to see women dressed in "feminine" clothes. The choice of specifically styled hats, narrow trousers, and wide ties for men and bright, wide skirts for women was a political decision, a way for young people to "argue" with the Soviet system. By the early 1950s, the "action through fashion" turned into a popular *stiliagi* movement, which swept the urban Soviet Union.[49] Choosing dresses for weddings, however, and caring about them in the first place, was not part of this resistance. Instead, it was a sign of the increased perceived significance of wedding ceremonies and family. It seems that the government ideology of the late 1930s, which put a reemphasis on family values and allowed the production of champagne and other luxury consumption items, took off soon after the war. This emphasis on "enjoying life" translated into a desire for celebrations, including weddings.[50]

Such attitudes are not surprising, because, as a whole, the number of marriages increased during the postwar period in the Soviet Union. In the mid-1940s, celebrations of the legal registration of marriage marked the difference between the casual relations of men and women during the war and the onset of "normality" in the postwar lifestyle. Women who served in the army during the war and married their fellow soldiers and officers especially insisted on having a wedding ceremony, because they felt it would distinguish them from field wives. Ava T., a military doctor during the war, touched upon many factors that accompanied her decision to have a wedding ceremony in 1945. She provided some fascinating details of her engagement and wedding:

> At that time, we were serving in Germany, it was in October 1945. Once I was in some basement, or in a dugout. I was sitting in a chair there and working. He was working in the same room. Then suddenly he got on his knees, and said: "Please, I ask you, become my wife." I looked at him. I didn't expect that. I said, "How do you mean, your wife?" He said, "I mean it, please marry me!" I said, "There are no ZAGS here in Germany, and I won't marry you without a ZAGS." He thought a bit, then he said: "Don't worry, I'll take care of that."
>
> He then went to the commanding officer, and asked for permission to go to Kaunas in Lithuania. That was the nearest city with a ZAGS. We were two officers, so we couldn't travel alone. We had to be guarded. According to the instructions, each of us had to have two soldiers with guns to accompany us. But they only gave us two soldiers, because the war was just over.
>
> So we went to Kaunas. We got there, and he asked a lady in the street: "Where is the ZAGS?" She said, "My boy, I got married forty years ago, I don't remember where it is." He said, "I know where to ask." He went to the railway station and saw a young woman there. She said, "Go

that way, you'll see a destroyed house, and a staircase outside. Go to the fourth floor, that's where the ZAGS is."

We went there, and the soldiers waited downstairs. We went there without any witnesses or anything like that. The woman officer asked him his ethnicity, and he said "Azeri." Then she asked me, and I said, "Jewish." She looked at me surprised, as if it surprised her that Jews were still alive. . . Then she registered us, and we became husband and wife.

Then we wanted to take some pictures. I said, the wedding picture shouldn't be taken in a military uniform. Then we went to the flea market. We had enough money to buy me a dress, but not enough to buy shoes. So I changed, and wore that dress, a nice hat, but military boots. The photographer said, "I'll make the picture so that no one can see your boots." And that's why here in the picture you can't see my legs and feet. After that, we wanted to buy some schnapps to celebrate with our division. Everyone knew me, so we had to provide it for the party. He was known too, as he was a battalion commander.

Then we needed to sleep together. But it was hard to find a hotel. There was a hotel for soldiers. Our soldiers were allowed to stay there, but they wouldn't admit us officers, and the soldiers weren't permitted to leave us alone. So we went to the officers' hotel. They let us into one room, which had two beds. The soldiers slept on the floor, I slept on one bed, and my husband slept on the other. That was our wedding night. The next morning we went back to Germany and celebrated the wedding in our division.[51]

This couple went through considerable difficulties in order to make their wedding legal, and they both felt it was worth the effort and expense. Ava's interpretation of the comment of the ZAGS officer reveals some unexpected features of her identity. During the interview, Ava repeatedly emphasized that nationality did not matter to her and proudly reported that her extended family can count at least thirteen ethnic groups. Still, during the interview, she produced a "story" every time she mentioned the word "Jew."

Both Ava T. and her husband understood the necessity of the wedding celebration, and their first step after legal registration was to buy alcohol for the party. She also paid considerable attention to her attire. It was important for her, as for many other women who were married during that time, to look "wedding-like" in the picture and not like a military veteran. Such attitudes about the celebratory nature of the occasion were not manifested before the war; people saw official registration alone as sufficient to start married life. For Ava, registration at a ZAGS, "without witnesses," followed by a celebration in her division did not seem like a huge affair, but it was a more elaborate affair than those of her counterparts who got married before the war.

Other women mentioned frequently that registering legally was the condition of their agreement that officially consummated a relationship. Many women and men asserted that Jewish young women (as opposed to Russian and Ukrainians) were especially insistent on legal registration and, therefore, perceived as "more modest." This was true both for women who were veterans and for those who did not serve in the army. That is why the wedding celebration, which followed the official registration in ZAGS, signified an important change in a couple's life, not merely in the relationship's legal status.

The wedding ritual of the late 1940s was not usually very elaborate. It consisted of registration at a ZAGS with two witnesses and then a celebratory lunch and dinner. In other words, it was very similar to the ritual of the late 1930s. What is different is how people evaluate this celebration. Vera L. (born in Kyiv, Ukraine, in 1920) got married in 1947, and to describe her wedding she said, "We had a room in a dormitory. One morning we went to register at the ZAGS, and after that, we had a dinner for family and friends, for about thirty to forty people. That was it."[52]

Similarly, Elizaveta Z. (born in Nemirov, Ukraine, in 1923), who was married in 1948, emphasized that poverty did not allow her to have a "real celebration":

We didn't have a real wedding. We went to the ZAGS with some witnesses. I remember my brother went with us. Then we had a celebratory dinner for family and friends, and then a big lunch for other friends the next day. But when we came to Riga to live with his parents, they organized a bigger celebration there.[53]

Vera L. and Elizaveta Z. describe their weddings as "poor" because there were no sophisticated celebrations, whereas whose who got married in the 1930s (such as Olga K.) considered their weddings rich if they had a dinner at all. The women belong to the same generation in terms of age and went through similar career and other experiences, but they expressed different attitudes based on whether they got married before, during, or after the war. Such attitudes demonstrate the increasing value of marriage and associated rituals in the popular mentality that appeared in the late 1940s and continued through the entire postwar period.

People who were married between 1945 and 1953 were more likely to observe Jewish rituals while celebrating their wedding than couples married before the war, regardless of whether they lived in small towns or big cities. Their descriptions of the rituals present a fascinating picture of the incorporation of Jewish tradition into secular Soviet celebrations.

Liza K. (born in Poltava, Ukraine, in 1928) was married in Kyiv in 1952. She told the following story of her wedding:

> We had a real wedding with a chuppah. Everything was closed: the doors, the windows… Imagine if then, in 1952, when I was a student, someone had found out that we had a chuppah and all those other things. All the guests were warned not to say anything… His parents insisted that we have a Jewish wedding. They took four poles and put some fabric on top, and they broke a plate for happiness. I went around him. We did everything that was necessary. This was all inside. And after it was over, we had a huge dinner for fifty people, but only the closest family members saw the chuppah. We didn't have many relatives, because they had all died during the war, but we had a lot of friends. It was a merry wedding.[54]

Liza K. emphasized that her in-laws insisted on a Jewish wedding and that she merely respected their wishes. This solicitude for the requests of parents, and especially the obedience she described, stand in stark contrast to the attitudes of respondents who married during the 1930s. The latter emphasized that parents were excluded from organizing a wedding celebration (if it even took place). The women who married after the war expressed much more respect for and fear of their parents; organizing a Jewish wedding was seen as a token of respect for them. But none of the interviewees ever suggested that having a wedding was his or her own initiative.

Why would parents want such a celebration? One can only speculate on individual situations, but it appears that such an attitude was a direct result of Jews' changing position within Soviet society: the rise of state anti-semitism and the appearance of wide-ranging discrimination against Jews at workplaces and schools, as well as daily manifestations of racial intolerance or acts of active and "silent" resistance. While many wrote letters of complaint to government offices and central newspapers,[55] others expressed their protests in less pronounced ways. Organizing Jewish weddings which incorporated at least some religious rituals may have been one form of such protest.

Another reason for the increase in Jewish weddings during this period was that less-assimilated Jews from the newly annexed territories of eastern Poland (western Ukraine and western Belorussia), Romania, and the Baltic states now lived and socialized with Soviet Jews. Jewish weddings had been widespread in these areas before the war and continued to thrive during the Stalinist years as well. Even some formerly assimilated Soviet Jews who settled in Lithuania and Western Ukraine after the war reported having Jewish weddings. Bella G. (born in Mikhalevo, Ukraine, in 1928), who was married in 1947 in Chernovtsy (Bukovina turned western Ukraine), explained that her wedding, organized according to "all of the Jewish rules," was not a hidden affair:

> I decided to get married, and my father organized the wedding for me. They put a chuppah in our backyard. But the wedding itself was upstairs, at my husband's parents' apartment, because they had two rooms. His father's sister also had two rooms, so they opened all four rooms to create space, and put big tables there to accommodate all of the guests.
>
> A.S.: Did your neighbors know that you had a Jewish wedding?
> B.G.: At that time, my husband wasn't a communist yet, so we didn't hide anything. Even after he became a communist, we had a son, and immediately we went to circumcise him.[56]

Bella's old friend from Chernovtsy, Klara R. (born in Uman, Ukraine, in 1928), was present at our interview. When she heard my question about hiding the fact of having a Jewish wedding, she commented, "Everyone in Chernovtsy had a wedding; it was unheard of to get married without a celebration. And if you were Jewish, you had to have a chuppah, to break a plate, and to have a nice banquet."[57]

Klara R.'s comments stand in striking contrast to the testimonies of women who got married before the war, who had never even heard of a chuppah and considered the entire wedding ritual unnecessary. Such remarks suggest that, in some families, people born during the late 1910s and early 1920s who were married before the war did not consider the wedding itself, and its accompanying Jewish customs, necessary; their younger siblings often had more elaborate celebrations if they were married during the late 1940s.

While collecting testimonies of weddings ceremonies of the 1940s, I was especially interested in what traditional Jewish wedding customs became incorporated into these celebrations. Most people mentioned three common elements in their weddings: the chuppah, breaking a plate, and Jewish cuisine at the celebratory dinner. Some also remembered that Jewish music and dances like *freylekhs* and *sher*, as well as the "chair dance" for the bride and groom, were part of the ceremonies. None knew any of the explanations behind these customs, and most just followed the lead of the older generation in observing rituals. Lyubov B. (born in Berdichev, Ukraine, in 1925) was married in Berdichev in 1945, and proudly asserted that she had a "real" Jewish wedding:

We had everything done properly. The plate was broken. We became groom and bride. Then we got married.

A.S.: Did you have a wedding celebration?

L.B.: It was a party. It was a party for our closest friends.

A.S.: Did you have a chuppah?

L.B.: No, there was no chuppah. My husband was a member of the Communist Party, and his father was a member of the Communist Party. So there was no chuppah.

A.S.: Was a plate broken?

L.B.: There is a Jewish law of engagement, so before you get married a plate has to be broken. Otherwise, it isn't a Jewish wedding.[58]

Lyubov considered her wedding Jewish because a plate was broken, but did not think that a chuppah, or *ketubah* (marriage contract), or *kiddushin* (the first part of the marriage ceremony), all crucial components of a traditional Jewish wedding, were relevant. Her story is probably influenced by the fact that she lives in Germany, where she is often challenged by members of the local Jewish communities who do not find her sufficiently "Jewish" because of her lack of religious observance. Her story fights against this perception. She chooses to focus on the Jewish wedding as representing the ultimate performance of Jewishness in the Soviet Union, a celebration despite persecution. Her story of a wedding story is a tale of laughter in the face of danger, persistence despite oppression. Ultimately, it is a story of expressing pride *despite* being a Jew in the Soviet Union.

# 6

# How Not to Learn about Antisemitism at Home

## Soviet Jewish Family Values after the War

A large-scale interview project with Soviet refugees conducted in 1951 in the United States, known as the Harvard Project, revealed that patterns of family life, including its structure and inner relationships, went through significant changes during the Soviet period.[1] Women's increased involvement in the workforce, the creation of a new system of education for children, and the processes of industrialization, urbanization, and internal migration (along with Soviet family policies, which included abortion rights) each influenced a family's development.

Compared with imperial Russia, families became smaller as the number of children decreased during the Soviet period.[2] This was also true of Jewish families. Between 1926 and 1939, the fertility of Jewish women dropped as a result of the urbanization and modernization of the Jewish population.[3] Unlike in Western European countries, which experienced a considerable baby boom, the birth rate in the Soviet Union continued to fall. This decline affected the Jewish population as well.[4] In fact, by the 1970s, the birthrate of Jewish women was among the lowest in the country.[5] Most of the interviewees had no more than three children, but the majority had two or fewer, typical among Soviet Jews during the postwar period.

More than half of the Harvard Project respondents asserted that their families became more cohesive under the Soviet regime.[6] Growing closeness between family members was probably a reflection of the increasing role of the family as a refuge from the growing pressure of the state on the individual.[7] Because the state policies of the late 1940s and 1950s were especially oppressive toward Jews, these two tendencies might have been especially pronounced within Soviet Jewish families. Parents generally tried to do everything possible to ensure that their children would succeed despite obstacles put in place by the state. Unwritten restrictions on the enrollment of Jews in institutions of higher education stimulated parents to encourage their children to get higher grades in high school in order to "beat the system." But beating the system also meant being incorporated into the system and following the rules practiced there. In this sense, the Jewish family was perhaps the most "Soviet" in its spirit and intentions.[8]

On the other hand, disagreement with state policies toward Jews led to the conception of the family as an escape from Soviet rhetoric. The family became a refuge from official culture and a forum for expressing genuine views on current events.[9] Only family members and very close friends could completely trust each other to express critical opinions of government policies. After 1953, the Soviet family gradually emerged as a cohesive unit that confronted the state rather than served it. One of the goals of the interviews was to understand how these two contradictory trends were combined in individual families and whether these families developed strategies of coping with the regime, adjusting to it, and resisting it.

During the interviews, I often observed how people described the relationships in their family and how they saw the roles of husbands and wives. Significantly, just as in description of courtships, many narrators attributed certain qualities of a person (positive or negative) to their being Jewish. Although most interviewees did not directly talk about the specifically Jewish characteristics of their spouses (or ideal spouses), they often understood ethnicity as a character feature rather than as a description of background. It seems that in the absence of safe opportunities to express ethnic sentiments publicly, people developed a system of identifying appealing characteristics as Jewish. One such characteristic was modesty (*skromnost'*). Another, typically attributed to men, was the ability to stand up to a hostile society. Such attitudes were especially visible when informants spoke about mixed marriages, both their own and those of their acquaintances.

Dora Z. (born in Odessa in 1923), for example, asserted in her interview that her daughter's life had been unhappy because she married a non-Jewish man and, according to her, "all non-Jewish men are alcoholics."[10] When I asked why she thought it was better to marry a Jew, she replied, "I don't know. I just know that Jewish men are better. Maybe it's because Russians don't like us, Jews ... But it is better to marry a Jew."[11] Many others shared Dora Z.'s sentiments. Though Dora Z. stressed that nationality did not matter in choosing friends and partners, her attitude changed radically when she spoke about marriage. Some testimonies about marriage evoke the entire range of contradictions of Dora's story.

A monologue by Mariya D. (born in Mikhalevo, Ukraine, in 1928) discusses issues of Jewish identity, religion, and intermarriage:

After the war, when my mother died, my [first] husband died, a priest suggested that I get baptized. I then said: "Do you understand, Father Alexander, I can't do that for many reasons. Why do you think that God's son will save me, whereas God's father won't? Yes, Christ was sent by God in order to enlighten Jewish people. I know it for sure. I know Jews didn't do the right thing then."

This is the same as they do in Israel now. What do they do? If, God forbid, there is mixed blood there, this person is not kosher anymore. It angers me tremendously. Why can't they see a person first, and then see if this person is circumcised or not circumcised, does he have the right blood and so on. A human being must come first.

But in Jewish teaching, I do not understand a lot. Why do Hasidim, or, as I call them, *"peysatye"* [derogatory term for Jews with earlocks, called payess; ultra-Orthodox Jews] care so much about pure blood?

Yes, I tell my granddaughter: "It is better to marry a Jew. It is better. But if you fall in love with a non-Jew, and he loves you too, let it be so." I will never protest and yell: "No, only marry a Jew." I won't do that, because love is. . . Love is either there or it isn't. If it truly comes, it can't be replaced by any ethnicity. That's for sure.

Yes, I am married to a Jew, and I was married to a Jew, and I was never married to a Russian. My son, though, married a Russian woman. He married a woman with a child. There's not much good in it. I'm being honest. There's not much good. But did I tell him not to do that? No. Children have to decide their own fate. Parents can suggest, if children want to listen. . . But if they don't want to listen, you shouldn't tell them.[12]

Mariya rejects the traditional notion of Judaism and reveals that she understands the Christian doctrine better than the Jewish one. She repeatedly criticizes ultra-Orthodox Jews and protests against the notion of "pure blood," which, in her understanding, limits the definition of Jewishness. Had Mariya been born in the United States, she would have been considered entirely devoid of Jewish identity. But she was born in the Soviet Union, and she considers herself a Jew, even a "better Jew" than religious Jews, primarily because her definitions are not limited by the external manifestations of Judaism, but rather incorporate "inner characteristics" such as "a human being with a good personality." But if personality and general characteristics come first, why is it better to marry a Jew? For Mariya, this is not an easy matter. Though her ideas about religion, and human values such as love, come from her general secular background (partly derived from her Soviet-imposed ideology and education, which promoted both internationalism and the value of romantic love in marriage),[13] her attitude toward marrying a Jew is a result of her own life experience and the experience of her children.

When Mariya D. describes the unsuccessful marriage of her son, the first thing she mentions about her daughter in-law is that she is a non-Jew. She blames the failure of that marriage on ethnicity rather than on other factors, such as the child from a previous marriage. When asked to name reasons "Why it is better to marry a Jew?" Mariya is lost and cannot offer any valid explanation. In fact, everything she intellectually believes contradicts this assertion. She simply thinks that experiences of daily life prove that marrying a Jew is "better." This conviction is perhaps a combination of her parents' values with numerous encounters with popular antisemitism; it does not come from Jewish education or even any positive associations with Jewish identity.

Mariya D. was married three times, and each match was unsuccessful. Yet she did not attribute their failures to the fact that her husbands were Jewish. The contradictions in this testimony represent a common attitude among both men and women in their evaluation and description of mixed marriages. If a marriage was successful, it was attributed to general humanitarian characteristics, but if a union fails, it was most frequently explained by the non-Jewish ethnicity of one of the spouses. It seems that attribution bias, the mechanism understood in social psychology as a device that attributes successes to internal or personal factors and failures to external or situational factors, is at work here.[14] In other words, being Jewish was understood as a personal achievement in marriage that could claim responsibility for success, but could not be blamed for failure.

Most of the narrators believed that marrying a non-Jew could lead to problems within the family. The reason for this belief was most frequently explained by popular antisemitism within the country at the time. Many attributed specific characteristics to an ideal Jewish spouse. In most cases, interviewees were not able to explain why a Jew should have these features, but it was surprising that, in the absence of knowledge associated with a traditional Jewish way of life, they were quite consistent in their opinions of what makes a good Jewish wife or a husband. Both men and women agreed on these definitions. Almost none of the characteristics that they named had anything to do with a Jewish way of life, Judaism, or Jewish traditions. Men and women named reliability, a "good profession," and kindness as important for both sexes, being a "good cook" for a woman, and being a "good father" for a man. Interestingly, "being smart" or "being funny," universally attractive qualities for men, did not make it onto the list. This probably happened not because the interviewees did not value these characteristics, but because the conversation focused on being Jewish. They did not believe that the universally agreed-upon characteristics of a fruitful partnership belonged in this conversation. Instead, most likely they chose to speak about positive characteristics that they associated with being Jewish without explicitly actually naming them as "Jewish." Following that logic, it seems that the above-mentioned characteristics were attributed to being Jewish because possessing them could enable a Jew to live a successful and happy life in the Soviet Union.

The analysis of interviews reveals that it was impossible to practice Soviet Jewish identity in an atmosphere of acceptance and tolerance. Even in descriptions of mundane duties such as cooking, cleaning, and taking care of children, which most people thought of as the primary tasks of a woman,[15] being Jewish meant being able to survive in a hostile environment. Consider, for example, cooking. Most interviewees suggest that a good wife (not necessarily Jewish) had to know how to cook well (or she had to know how to cook at all).[16] Everyone agreed that a good Jewish wife was expected to impress visitors and be familiar with traditional Jewish cuisine. Some women spoke of the difficulties they had to go through in order to "fit the standards." A story by Fira F. (born in Pereyaslav, Ukraine, in 1920) describes the process of her husband's acceptance into a prestigious military academy in 1949:

> When my husband found out that he had been accepted into the Military
> Academy, he immediately sent a telegram to me through his local division

staff. It said, "I am enlisted into the Academy. Prepare pierogi with sour cherries." It was his favorite dish. Yes, it was perfect, that dish. It was always seen as a reward in our family. He knew that if he asked, I would make it, of course. But making it was another story. By the time the telegram had reached me, it had many signatures on it. They said, "I read it, and signed. Ivan. Stepan. See reverse." I turned the paper around, and saw that every single member of the Staff of the Division signed the telegram. It meant they were all coming over.

I realized, oy, oy, oy. I had to buy sour cherries and flour and to make enough pierogis for the entire division staff. I took old children's clothes and went to the mountains, to the Armenian Gypsies, they're called Kurds there. I went to the Kurds to exchange my clothes for cherries and flour. When my husband found out I did that, he almost shot me. He said, "You're crazy to go to the mountains, to Gypsies, by yourself." When he sent the telegram he didn't know the entire staff would read it. He thought I would buy a kilo of cherries and a kilo of flour, and make it for him. But now I needed a whole bucket of cherries and a whole bag of flour.

I carried it all home by myself, no one helped me. They gave me the most beautiful cherries. I came home, put the kids to sleep, and spent the entire night pitting the cherries, using a hairpin. I did the entire bucket, and made the filling. In the morning I made the dough. My neighbor took the kids, and I made the dumplings. Someone brought me a board, and I put them on the board. I boiled water in huge buckets, and boiled dumplings in them. Then I made the special syrup. I make it like my mother taught me.

It's a special way, not with sour cream, like Russians and Ukrainians eat. It has a special syrup. First, you roll all the cherries in flour, then in sugar, and that keeps each berry separate from the others. Then I put it on a strainer, let the liquid drip, and use the liquid to make the syrup.

After the dumplings are done, I put them on a dish, and cover with the syrup. The taste of this dish is divine. I only make it on very special occasions: for my son's birthday, for example.

But now I made it for the entire division staff. They all came and ate, one after another. And all praised my husband for getting into the Academy. But after we moved to Moscow, we went through hell. It was 1949, no one wanted to rent to Jews. We could find an apartment only in the Moscow region, not in Moscow itself. We lived under terrible conditions; it was hard to get fuel to warm up the house. All of that was my responsibility, because he left for work before dawn and came back late. Everything about our daily life was my work.

And, with my weak hands, I moved all the coal and wood, and fed, and bathed, and washed. We used a primus stove for cooking, because gas stoves were not yet available.[17]

Fira described the process of obtaining the ingredients for and the method of preparing pierogis in such great detail because these facts indicate what she saw as the sacrificial nature of her role in the family. In addition, she felt that her spousal duty included ensuring that her husband's colleagues and bosses appreciated the hospitality and stability of his family.

Although the choice of dish was her husband's, it was Fira's decision to make dumplings in a "proper" way, that is, the hardest way, despite the large quantity involved. One hears the pride, the sense of accomplishment, but also a hint of the lack of appreciation or acknowledgement by her husband. She says repeatedly that she put herself at physical risk in order to get the necessary ingredients. Though Fira never directly articulates it, the listener understands that keeping up the appearance of a successful housekeeper was more important to her than personal safety.

The story itself belongs to the genre of quest. Reaching the goal requires sacrifice, wit, resourcefulness, and physical endurance. The goal was to feed the entire division staff with the best possible celebratory food, a dish which was not necessarily recognized as Jewish by others, but which just happened to be cooked according to Jewish custom.

The story of the dumplings was the first time in the entire interview that Fira brought up the Jewish aspect of her behavior. Her pierogis were prepared according to a Jewish custom (she did not say this directly, but it was strongly implied). The Jewish method was then associated with the hardships of living in postwar Moscow, which was, in turn, immediately associated with antisemitism and with other adversities. The testimony is a statement of the close association of hardships with the difficulties of being a Jew, especially a Jewish woman. Even the memory of a celebratory dish, whose recipe had been transmitted from generation to generation, is associated with exhausting labor, deprivation, and an unfairly heavy share of chores.

Fira's testimony touches upon an issue important to many other interviewees: one of the reasons that a good Jewish wife had to know how to cook was that her talents were needed to impress colleagues (who were sometimes hostile toward Jews) and to help their husbands in career promotion. Fira emphasized that she could not even think of not making enough for the entire unit, because "then they would say that we were typical greedy Jews!" When the narrators spoke about discrimination, they often mentioned creating a positive image of a Jew for non-Jewish acquaintances at work in order not to be referred to as a "Yid." Cooking a beautiful meal was described as one of the strategies to win friendship and respect from colleagues, bosses, and neighbors. Liza R. (born in Romanov, Ukraine, in 1918) explains:

> My husband's colleague was non-Jewish. He and his wife loved coming to our house, because I cooked those very special *varnechkes* (dumplings). They loved it. His wife would come to the kitchen with me and say, "I love it when you cook this Jewish *osek fleysh* [sweet and sour meat], and my husband likes when you cook those *varnechkes*." But when I saw her at the office (we worked together), she would always tell me, "I am so tired of you Jews. When are you going to Israel?" And sometimes she would come to me and say: "Give me gold, I need new teeth." I would ask, "Why do you ask me?" And she would answer, "Because you Jews always have gold."

> A.S.: Why did you keep inviting her over to your place, then, if she made such remarks?
> L.F.: Because everyone thought like that. If we took such comments seriously, we'd never have any non-Jews over.[18]

Preparing Jewish food for antisemitic acquaintances would contradict the wishes of Liza or Fira to demonstrate that Jews were making an effort to be integrated and accepted, that they were just "like everyone else." But perhaps there are no contradictions in such behavior. Cooking Jewish food was meant to demonstrate, perhaps subconsciously, that there was no mystery in how Soviet Jews lived and how they cooked. Although interviewees were not consciously aware of reasons for their behavior, many emphasized that their guests often commented that they had no idea Jewish food could be so delicious. Sometimes women proudly noticed that their cooking changed former antisemites into "friends of the Jewish people."

Women who recalled their culinary extravaganzas (and often demonstrated them for me) spoke specifically about Jewish dishes. I was able to record dozens of family recipes, many of which were said to be "Jewish."

Women described several ways to make traditional Sabbath and festive meals, such as gefilte fish, sweet and sour meat, tsimmes, dumplings, borscht, blintzes, cholent, and many other Ashkenazic dishes. Most did not mention the rules associated with kashruth. In fact, many mentioned that in making these dishes, they combined dairy and meat products (forbidden by Jewish law) in order to improve the taste of a dish, such as sautéing beef in butter instead of oil, or, like Klara, adding a little pork to a meat dish to improve the taste.

Yet most of the women insisted that, for special occasions, they would cook Jewish dishes, the recipes for which they learned from their mothers and other Jewish relatives, and not traditional dishes of Russian or Ukrainian cuisine, with which many were familiar. Why? One obvious explanation would be that these were the dishes that women had learned as youngsters and therefore continued to cook as adults. Although this generation did not practice most of the family customs associated with a Jewish way of life, traditional cuisine was not attacked by official anti-religious propaganda, and it survived the radical assimilation and modernization of the Jewish community. However, it would seem that preparing Jewish food for non-Jewish or even antisemitic acquaintances contradicts the desire to demonstrate that Jews were making an effort to be integrated and accepted. Cooking different food would emphasize the differences rather than encourage friendships.

Paradoxically, the existence of popular antisemitism helped some families keep traces of Jewish tradition. In this sense, Jewish women's cooking was one way for Jewish spouses to support each other in a hostile society. A woman's ability to cook a fancy Jewish meal was as desirable as men's ability to protect their women from derogatory remarks, which was described by women as an important quality for a husband. They praised husbands who were able to respond to hostile comments by strangers and neighbors. Mila Ch.'s testimony is representative:

I never encountered personal antisemitism in my life. But once, my first husband and I took a tram together. It was very crowded. And one man, a bastard, told me "Sarochka [little Sarah], go ahead, go!" I asked him: "Are you leaving the tram now?" He said: "Go, go!" I went ahead and left the tram. My husband left too, he followed me. This man left as well. Then my husband took the man and hit him against the tram. That other man didn't do anything, he just said: "What are you doing?" And my husband said: "This is for Sarochka!" He protected me.[19]

Mila did not imply that a husband had to be Jewish in order to protect his wife from antisemitic remarks. In fact, many women who were married to non-Jews emphasized that their husbands were more "useful" as protectors against antisemitism than were their friends' Jewish spouses. In other words, many seem to have internalized the antisemitic perception that diminished Jewish physical strength and masculinity.

Elizaveta K. (born in Chernigov, Ukraine, in 1910) explained, "No matter what they say now, Jewish men are not brave. And if he can't protect his own dignity, how will he protect the dignity of his wife? And in the Soviet Union, we really needed to be protected."[20] Evgeniya R. (born in Kharkov, Ukraine, in 1909), agreed:

My husband wasn't Jewish. He was Russian, but he was in Buchenwald, together with many Jews. When he heard an antisemitic remark, he would get more upset than I would. He knew that Jews suffered so much during the war. Even our Jewish friends often said antisemitic things, but he would always say to them, "Jews are heroic people, and you have to be proud that you are a Jew."[21]

Evgeniya R. told me this story when I asked her whether her deceased husband was Jewish. She emphasized that, even though he was not Jewish, he had one characteristic that "almost" made him a Jew—a negative attitude toward expressions of antisemitism. Thus, resentment of antisemitism and antisemites makes a spouse almost ethnically Jewish.

Interviewees provided contradictory characteristics for typical Jewish wives. Some asserted that Jewish wives were not afraid of hard household work (unlike non-Jews),[22] others insisted that Jewish women ran extremely messy households. Some women suggested that they did not get married because they did not want to do household chores for their husbands and also did not want to be considered imperfect wives.[23] Others said that they were not that good with housework and always tried to avoid it.[24] Some asserted that good Jewish wives were good with children[25] and were more likely to want children than non-Jews.[26] Some even suggested that they brought up extremely spoiled children.[27] There was no agreement among interviewees about which qualities they considered specifically Jewish and which were just universally accepted positive characteristics. Such attitudes express one of the specific features of Soviet Jewish identity: the conflation of universally appealing characteristics with being Jewish, as a defensive reaction to popular and state antisemitism.

Like Jewish wives, ideal Jewish husbands were described by both men and women as fitting within Soviet society's general expectations of being honest, kind, and supportive (these qualities were called "Jewish"). Interestingly, unlike descriptions of Jewish wives, the testimonies about Jewish husbands were quite consistent. Narrators said that Jewish husbands did not drink (unlike their non-Jewish counterparts), did not waste money, and were extremely loyal to their families and their wives. The last was especially popular among women, who were insistent that, unlike other men, Jewish husbands "do not cheat." One woman even confessed that her biggest shock of immigration to the United States in 1990 was finding out that there were cases when "American Jewish men cheat, even though they have children." Mila Ch. (born in Mstislavl, Belorussia, in 1928), further explained, "It was such a blow to me. Every person has weaknesses, but not this. . . I always thought that Jewish husbands are the most loyal ones, and I just could not believe that they cheat here in America. . ."[28]

Women attributed many other positive characteristics to Jewish husbands. For example, they often said that Jewish husbands were more likely to encourage their wives to develop professionally and to have careers of their own. Vera L. (born in Kyiv, Ukraine, in 1920), a singer and actress, explained, "Only a Jewish husband would allow me to travel around the country and to do what I did. Maybe he was jealous, but he never said anything to me. He always supported me. Many other singers were not married, because what husband, except for a Jewish one, would allow his wife to travel so much!"[29] In other words, just as with Jewish wives, all the characteristics which people thought were positive were attributed to the fact that the husbands were Jewish. When narrators' experiences contradicted positive stereotypes, they made a point of emphasizing it. Even if the person's empirical experience suggested otherwise, stereotypes were often stronger than reality. Klara G., for example, spent about half an hour of the interview telling me that her Jewish father cheated on her mother and that he was an alcoholic. When I asked her, at some other point during the interview, why it was important for Klara to marry a Jew, she answered:

> First, I couldn't break my parents' heart by marrying a Russian. It just wasn't done in those days. Second, Russian husbands cheat on their wives and drink. My husband didn't earn much money, but I knew that he brought all the money he earned home, he never had anything to drink, and he never looked at any other woman. Jewish husbands are different from non-Jews.[30]

As mentioned, Klara does not connect her empirical experience with an abstract stereotype. But the stereotypes and beliefs went far beyond harmless conversations. They often served as arguments in important decisions regarding the choice of a spouse. Elizaveta K., for example, says that she did not marry the man of her choice simply because of these beliefs:

> I had a boyfriend, he wasn't Jewish. But my mother used to say to me, "Liza, remember, they [non-Jews] are not our friends." I remember that. She would tell me, "Liza, how can you marry a Russian? He'll hit you!" There was more fear than truth in that. But I couldn't find a Jew, and as a result, I never got married.[31]

There were most likely other reasons why Elizaveta did not get married, but the reason she chose to present involved stereotypes based on ethnicity, like, for example, "Russian men beat their wives." Apparently, this was not the first time she had told this story, and she expected her listeners (who usually came from the same background as she did) and interviewer to sympathize with and understand her dilemmas, which would be seen as sufficient grounds for her choices.

During the interviews, I also asked whether people thought that relationships between spouses in Jewish families were different from those of non-Jews. The majority were not able to provide answers to this direct question and said it had no validity (the typical answer was that "it depends on the person"). Still, indirectly, they often asserted that Jewish families were different from others, and, once again, this was usually described as a positive characteristic. For example, when I asked whether a person had a happy marriage, they replied "We had a Jewish family, what else do I need to say?"[32] When asked to elaborate, the familiar positive descriptions of Jewish spouses surfaced.

Many people emphasized that they were especially close to their spouse because they often shared knowledge about each other's background and the past that was secret not only from acquaintances, colleagues, and friends, but even from their own children. The closeness within Jewish families was often based on the fact that spouses knew things about each other that, if they became public, could slow down their career and seriously harm their quality of life and that of their children. While such a situation was perhaps true for many Soviet families (their secrets could include arrested relatives, for example),[33] in the Jewish case, these secrets often revolved around specifically Jewish issues, one of which was the story of survival during the Holocaust.

People who survived ghettos and concentration camps frequently mentioned that they did not publicize what had happened to them during the war in order not to risk possible discrimination in the workplace and at school. For example, Mariya S. (born in Zlatopol, Ukraine, in 1927) said that only her husband knew that she had survived three years in a ghetto, and they vowed not to tell their children so that this information would not hurt them.[34] Information about the Holocaust in the Soviet Union during the immediate postwar years was scarce and sporadic, and state ideology emphasized that Jews suffered no more than other Soviet peoples.[35] Mentioning Soviet collaborators was taboo. Many Holocaust survivors preferred not to speak about their experiences publicly, and once again, their own family became a refuge where they were able to speak about this perhaps most significant part of their lives. Thus, the kinds of relationships within their families that the interviewees referred to as specifically Jewish were direct consequences of state policies that targeted Jews in the Soviet Union, rather than a continuation of traditions of the prerevolutionary Jewish family.

State policies that were aimed toward Jews, in combination with popular antisemitism, played the most important role in forming specific expressions of ethnic identity among the first generation of Soviet Jews. The process is not dissimilar to the peasant resistance of the 1930s, the suppression of which led to the actual strengthening of grass-roots peasant culture, though in a different form. [36] When the Soviet state began to attack Jews, they had to come up with a culture that would allow them to survive. Some pre-Soviet or early Soviet Jewish customs, such as the use of a matchmaker and organizing Jewish celebrations, became helpful in this mission and appeared in places where they were not seen before—Moscow, Leningrad, and other large urban centers. These were areas where, during the 1930s, Jews escaped specifically from these traditions. Somehow, the Soviet policies that took Judaism out of Soviet Jewish culture brought them back, in a shifted but still recognizable form.

## Passing on Soviet Jewish Values

A common feature of all narrators, with the exception of some of those from Moscow, is that their children decided to leave Russia in the 1990s.[37] The reasons for emigration that they cited included: the desire for a better future for their children and grandchildren, hope for stability, a war-free environment, and, of course, increasing opportunities for social and economic mobility. In other words, narrators' children developed a deep dissatisfaction with the status quo and who decided not to take their chances on Soviet perestroika in the late 1980s.

The analysis of *what* the people actually said about their children answers the ever probing question: what kind of "Jewish" values would a non-religious person who has somewhat internalized the antisemitic sentiments of their society pass on to their children? The interviewees provided a surprisingly universal answer to this question, which did not differ much across countries or across backgrounds. They all universally believed in the power of higher education, "transferrable" skills, and hard work.[38] All of them encouraged their children to stay ahead of the curve. All of them used all of the connections that they had, paid all the bribes that they could, and generally made sure they would succeed in classrooms and get in to the first, or at least second, institute of higher education of their choice.

Interestingly, when asked about antisemitism directly, the interviewees who had survived the Holocaust and postwar Stalinism universally started by describing discrimination that their children faced when they first went to school, a time when they were denied admission to a prestigious institute, difficulties in trying obtain a raise at work, a refused promotion, or some other experience of unfair treatment. Sometimes, people blamed their overwhelmingly non-Jewish sons- and daughters-in-law for their children's misfortunes. At other times, they emphasized the good natured qualities of their sons- and daughters-in-law *despite* their not being Jewish. The description of Jewishness when it comes to children's partners appeared without prompting, but I do not know whether the subject of the interview made them think in this direction. Still, the prevalence of the "Jewish" factor in describing the marital choices of children and grandchildren suggests that interviewees continue to pay attention to the ethnic makeup of their families, even when this make it does not have much influence on the situation.

The interviewees now live in countries that are, for the most part, free from state antisemitic policies. Consequently, they do not consider creating a Jewish family a priority for their grandchildren. However, they see values of social mobility, such as excelling in science, math, music, and other easily quantifiable skills, as still relevant, because their grandchildren now have to succeed as children of immigrants rather than children of a persecuted minority.

## The Soviet Jewish Family: Not What It Seems

When American Jews of the baby-boomer generation decided to marry other Jews, they were largely driven by the desire to have Jewish children and provide a Jewish upbringing for them.[39] Other factors, such as "feeling comfortable" with a person of the same ethnic group and intending to celebrate Jewish holidays, were quite meaningful as well.

Since the late 1940s, Soviet Jews had the opposite reasons for marrying Jews. They wanted Jewish partners in order to postpone the time when their children would find out that they were born Jewish. They wanted to prolong the experience of a happy childhood free of antisemitism. Observing Jewish traditions and holidays, providing a Jewish upbringing for their children, and "preserving the family tree" were largely irrelevant to them. Before the war, when state-run antisemitic policies were waning, many interviewees did not consider ethnicity to be an important factor in their marital choice. Those who married within the group did so because their circle of friends consisted largely of Jews. After the war, due to a change in their image, Jewish men were viewed as less- desirable husbands. Yet Jewish women married Jewish men, because they had limited choices among non-Jewish partners. The justification for this was their own desire to decrease the personal impact of antisemitism. While many interviewees stated that said they did not mind having a non-Jewish spouse, they indicated that it was important to them for a potential spouse to have some Jewish attributes or affinity. Subconsciously, these narrators were probably hoping to find a spouse who would not be antisemitic. Despite the decline in the reputation of Jewish men after the war, most of the interviewed women married Jewish men. It seems that the prospect of marrying an antisemite was considered more daunting than that of being married to an unfaithful Jewish husband.

Although interviewees often cited positive Jewish characteristics when justifying their choice of a Jewish spouse, unlike their non-observant American counterparts, none spoke nostalgically about celebrating Jewish holidays. Rather, they often emphasized their "internationalist" background and respect for Russian culture. The majority wanted their children to be registered as Russians, not as Jews, so that they would not suffer from discrimination in their education or career. But the majority of participants of the project who created Jewish families spoke of it unapologetically because they believed that they had created the an environment which that would delay the onset of the inevitable trauma that they felt their children would experience when they were to found out that they had been born Jewish. In other words, they wanted to create Jewish families in order to avoid teaching their children, for as long as possible, that they were Jews. Thus, the interviews suggest that the antisemitism of Soviet society was largely responsible for the relatively high level of endogamous marriage among Soviet Jews during the 1940s and 1950s.

The return of the necessity of Jewish marriages to other Jews in the 1940s led to the re-establishment of traditional Jewish institutions associated with the family: the institution of formal and informal matchmaking, and even some Jewish rituals at weddings. Even assimilated urban interviewees from Moscow and Leningrad spoke of such events and encounters, to say nothing about of those who came from smaller Ukrainian or Belorussian towns. Yet the return of the Jewish wedding ritual did not signal the resurrection of the Jewish religious way of life. Instead, the meaning of the Jewish family changed to signify the a unit that protects its members, especially children, from antisemitism (by providing internal support, reinforcing a positive self-image, and other strategies). Finally, a Jewish family would teach a child how to succeed in a hostile society by developing the survival skills and moral strength. When taken out of context, those family values do not seem all that different from middle-class childrearing strategies in many urban societies, but the Jews of the first Soviet generation understood them as their response to antisemitism and as an attempt to create a positive association with being Jewish in a country where such an association seemed irrational.

# Part III

From Enthusiasm to More
Enthusiasm: Jews in the
Soviet Workplace

# 7

## What My Country Needs and Where My Aunt Lives

### Choosing a Profession in Stalin's Soviet Union

By the time Victor Kh. reached his sixteenth birthday in 1932, he had witnessed many tragedies. He was born in the small shtetl of Piliava in the Kamenetsk-Podolsk region of Ukraine. When he was three years old, one of his brothers was killed in a pogrom. Shortly after his brother's murder, his father suffered a fatal heart attack. His mother fell into a severe depression, which left her unable to function for twelve years. Victor and his two older brothers became the providers for the family; they worked on a collective farm on the weekends (but not on Saturdays) and during summers to support themselves and their mother after Victor turned twelve, but they never had enough to eat. When Victor turned sixteen, he went to Khmelnik, a town in the Vinnitsa region of Ukraine, to try to find a place to study:

> Once in Khmelnik, I went to the *rabfak* [educational courses for workers] affiliated with the medical school. My brother lived well there, so I stayed with him. I studied there for one and a half years, and then I got really sick. You see, those were years of famine. My brother couldn't take care of me, so I left the institute. I went to my cousin in Gaisin.[1] My cousin worked as a chief accountant in the state timber enterprise [*lespromkhoz*]. I stayed with him, but then he was sent, like some other Jews, to build new settlements in Kherson. I couldn't stay with him any longer, so I had to find a place to study in Gaisin. So I went to the cavalry school.[2]

Seemingly eclectic in subject matter, ranging from a medical prep course to a cavalry school, Victor's scholastic trajectory is not unusual. Like many people of his age and background, he was limited not by what he *wanted* to study but by where he could live while studying. The availability of a corner, or a couch in a room, or—much rarer—a family member's apartment determined many people's professional choices in the 1920s and 1930s. With the relaxed admission requirements in many institutes of higher education,[3] as well as limited dormitory opportunities, a place to sleep while studying seems to have been the most important factor in choosing a profession.[4] Altogether, this explains the fact that most interviewees did not want to spend much time elaborating on why and how they chose their occupation.

### Studying Where My Aunt Lives: The 1930s

Young Jews probably chose to study some professions because of the traditional appreciation for this occupation that was cultivated within their families.[5] Even people who went through medical instruction, arguably the hardest training that exists, talked about their choice casually, as an "accident." For example, a retired doctor, Ilya Sh. (born in 1904 in Voznesensk, Ukraine), moved to Moscow in 1919 and found a job as a plumber's apprentice. A few years later, he entered the *rabfak* associated with the engineering institute. Upon completion of the course, he began to doubt whether he wanted to continue his studies at that institute:

> I didn't like the idea at all. So my friends and I made a plan to walk around the city and to attend "Open Door Day" at all the institutes, not just ours. Five or six people got together and walked around to see what and where things were. We saw one institute and didn't like it. Then someone said, "Let's walk to the Medical Institute. It's interesting there. They have corpses. They cut them open. They study anatomy." We were interested in that. None of us, including me, of course, had thought about the medical profession, but it was an open door day, so we decided to go and take a look. We all went. We all were *otlichniki* [straight-A students], except for one girl. Their entrance committee wasn't in session that day. We went to the secretarial desk and asked the secretary, "Can we walk around? We want to go see the morgue, to see things." As we were talking, one man came out of the door. With his hat on, he looked tall and interesting.
>
> "Who are these people?" he asked.

The secretary said, "These are *abiturienty* [prospective students]. They are looking around institutes."

"Ah, I see. Do you want to go to the Medical Institute?"

"Yes, of course."

"How many are you?"

"There are six of us."

"What grades do you have?"

"We're all *otlichniki,* except for her."

"Is that so? All right, please enroll all of them in the institute, they don't need exams, all six of them."

That is how we all became students of Moscow Second Medical Institute. I graduated in 1933 and became a doctor.[6]

It is possible that the simplicity of enrolling in medical school was exaggerated; later in the interview, Ilya did mention the completion of forms, searching for the dorm, finding out details, and getting the correct documents. However, like Ilya, many people with similar experiences emphasized the accidental choice of their profession, as opposed to a thoroughly thought-out decision, planned together with parents and discussed with teachers. Unprompted, Ilya did not even begin to talk about *what* he actually studied. His emphasis was on *where* he studied. Other people who studied in the 1930s talked about similar logistical factors. Olga K. (born in 1918 in Kamenka, Ukraine) recalls her first schooling:

I finished school. Someone said, "Go to the town of Ziun, near Kharkov, they have a professional school there at the factory. Maybe you'll learn a profession." I had an aunt there, so I went. That's how I became a mechanic toolmaker. As I studied, I realized I really liked making things from metal. And I worked as a toolmaker for over fifty years, beginning in 1933.[7]

Once again, Olga cites logistics, such as the presence of an aunt in town, as the most important factor in her choice of profession. Although she does admit that her profession became her calling later in life, her own pursuits had no role in her career choice.

In fact, quite often personal interests and preferences in career choices were completely disregarded in favor of logistics and convenience. Faina

D. was born in 1922 in Ekaterinoslav (later Dnepropetrovsk), a large industrial city in southeast Ukraine. In 1926, her father took his family to work at
a Jewish agricultural colony in the Kherson region of Ukraine. When Faina
turned twelve, she went back to Dnepropetrovsk to study:

> My family was beyond poor. We didn't have anything, not even an apart-
> ment. But my aunt lived in Dnepropetrovsk, and I went to her. I worked at
> a tailoring factory and studied at a pedagogical *technikum*. I was studying
> to be a teacher of Russian. But I spoke Russian poorly; I made forty-nine
> mistakes in the spelling test [*diktant*]. I studied there because it was close,
> and I could study in the evening. Later, I became a good student, and
> eventually a teacher of Russian.[8]

Economic considerations (for instance, whether she had enough money or
would be able to support themselves as students) played an important role
in Faina's decisions about where she studied, but the choice of a particular
subject or institute is presented as a matter of happenstance.

It is possible that, just as in the discussion of marriage and intermarriage,
people downplay the internal soul searching and other factors that mattered to them in the 1930s. Interviewees eventually made peace with their
choices, and many were happy with their careers. After all, they made these
decisions as teenagers, most between the ages of fourteen and sixteen, long
before their personalities, preferences, and interests were fully formed. In
addition, the life review process helped them smooth over the contradictions and regrets of their past.

Although their own choices were presented as accidental, most people
seemed, in general, to consider work very important. First, the narrators
often spoke about the importance of "having a good profession" in regard
to their children and grandchildren. By "good," they meant a profession
that provided a stable income in various economic and cultural environments (they considered engineering and medicine more appealing choices
for their grandchildren than, say, banking).[9]

Second, interviewees emphasized that they could not imagine their lives
without studying. They did not seem to care *what* they studied, as long as
they were learning. This observation is generally in line with Yuri Slezkine's
assertion of the unprecedented, fast-paced process of social mobility among
the young generation of Soviet Jews in the 1930s.[10] Perhaps the desire to

get out of the shtetl and away from their parents' way of life explains the seeming indifference to the method of doing so. In other words, the choice of profession mattered only insofar as it could help interviewees relocate to larger cities.

Narrators' chosen paths of study were not guided or influenced by their parents. Stories to this effect came from all professions, ranging from scientists, doctors, engineers, teachers, and accountants to metalworkers and other trades. The only (very small) group of interviewees who told stories of their parents taking an interest in what they studied in the 1930s were those who became musicians. For example, one woman recalled that her entire family moved from Odessa to Moscow so that she could study in the best possible music school.[11] However, these stories were exceptions to the rule.

Many people implied that despite their indifference to the topic of study or the importance of logistics for their decision, they ultimately succeeded. Olga K. stressed that she grew to like metalwork, and Faina D. eventually became a competent Russian language teacher. In other words, the stories of choosing a profession can be seen as stories of success when faced with difficult circumstances. Similarly, the stories can be read as narratives of ultimate success resulting from intellectual superiority, good ability, and hard work in overcoming humble beginnings—not dissimilar in character to the story of the American Dream. The stories present a complex amalgam of Soviet values (working selflessly without expectation of reward and for the sake of the greater good or, at least, because of the absence of choice)[12] with elements of the American success story (rising from humble beginnings though hard work and talent resulting in success).[13] In fact, almost all stories of "making the best of a bad situation," including those of having to study or work in a field that was available rather than on that was desirable, come from United States–based participants.

## Whatever the Country Needs (and Wherever My Aunt Was Evacuated): Choosing a Profession, 1941–1947

From 1941 to 1945, 233 interviewees fought in the Red Army and partisan units, 64 lived in Transnistrian ghettos under Romanian rule, and 187 worked in the Soviet home front in Central Asia, the Urals, or Siberia. Some did two of those things; others did all three. As part of their army service, some people, in addition to performing actual military duties, were assigned and trained for a profession (a nurse, radio operator, or driver, to name a few). Others served as military doctors. The majority of narrators who did not enroll in post-secondary education by 1941, even many of those who became students, did not have the opportunity or luxury to think about their interests, callings, or professional ambitions. Based on their location and age, they either studied in schools that were in close proximity or, more often, worked at assigned positions at factories or in the agricultural fields. Nevertheless, a remarkable number of interviewees—52 of them—began their studies during the war in "evacuation," usually in Central Asia, but also in the Urals and Siberia.[14]

Beginning in 1941, all boys aged 15 to 17 and girls aged 16 to 18 were required to report to local authorities for full-time work assignments, and children over 10 years old were required to work during school breaks.[15] Work ensured survival, because payment consisted of a "bread card," which provided sustenance and was otherwise unavailable.[16] Many interviewees spoke of the joy, pride, and responsibility that came along with earning a bread card. Many did not remember much about the actual work that they did, however, and definitely not the specifics. But they commented that work challenged them, helped them grow up faster, and made them proud for contributing to the Soviet war effort.

The tone and genre of stories about choosing a profession, or an institute or *technikum* (vocational school) to attend from 1941 to 1945, are similar to the ones told about career choices in the 1930s—that is, people emphasized opportunities and logistics as opposed to their own interests. One significant variation is the fact that the process took place during the chaos, deprivation, and uncertainties of the war. Yet some interviewees discussed the educational *opportunities* that were created for them because of the war. A retired parasitologist, Fira G. (born in 1925 in Efingar, in the Nikolaev region of Ukraine) recalls how she ended up as a student in the Perm (then called Molotov) Medical Institute in 1943:

> I went to study in Perm. One neighbor harnessed horses and took me there in a sled. I didn't have a coat, it had been stolen from me, so I borrowed a jacket, covered my feet with cotton balls, wrapped them with ropes, and took a forest dirt road to Perm. When I got to Perm, I first went to the Department of Literature at the university. I really wanted to study literature, because, I wanted to be a writer. I arrived and the director of the university came out and said, "If you pass the exams, we

will settle you in the dormitory." I said, "Give me a roof over my head."
Then he said, "We have already finished with the Old Slavonic language,
and you don't know it." I said, "True, I don't know it." He said, "Then
study it, pass the tests, and come back." I understood that it wasn't going
to work out. Then the old man who drove me said, "What shall we do,
girl? I brought you here alive through the forest for 120 kilometers. What
are you going to do?" I said to him, "Take me to the Medical Institute, I'll
definitely get in, my mother is a paramedic." And so he took me to the
medical school, and they accepted me. They took everyone after the eighth
grade, without exams.[17]

It is remarkable how easy it was for Fira G. to change her career path and
even more remarkable how easy it was to be accepted into the medical
school at the age of fifteen, given that she started her education in 1943. In
addition to being a story of miracles, this is also a story of opportunities,
because Fira went to have a long career as a successful and important medical scientist with hundreds of publications on the subject of epidemiology.
It was her life's calling after all, but she did not know that in 1943. Choosing
a profession as a physician was an accident, a way to avoid starvation and
cold during the war.

A similar story comes from Roza K. (born in 1922), a refugee from
Zhitomir, Ukraine, who escaped on foot with her mother, running for over
200 kilometers until she reached a train that took her to Alma-Ata, the
capital of Kazakhstan, in December 1941. After her mother had ("miraculously") found a menial job at the local hospital as a cleaner, the family
received a bread card. Finding the job seemed especially lucky because
Roza and her mother had lost their suitcase, which carried documents
that certified their occupations as well as Roza's high school diploma.
After her mother settled in at work, Roza began to think about her own
education:

I found out from a newspaper that the Moscow Geological Exploration
Institute had moved to Semipalatinsk, a town a hundred kilometers from
us.[18] But before the war I had dreamed about [attending] the Mendeleev
Institute [of Chemical Engineering]. So we can't think about our dreams. . .
We have to think that we have nothing. We are the poorest of the poor, we
are beggars, we are homeless. . .

Yet we got the nerve to dream that I would go to Semipalatinsk. They organized preparatory courses there for the geological exploration institute. We didn't have anything—no clothes, no shoes. But I was going. Yes! I wrote to the director of the institute that the documents had been in the suitcase, that we lost them during the war. And that I had lost everything, my clothes, my shoes, the means to exist, all of it, except for my desire to study. Imagine my cheekiness! And we received an invitation from the director, complete with the money to buy the ticket. You can't imagine how happy everyone was in the hospital [where the mother worked—A.S]. The director wrote in his letter that I needed a note, signed by two witnesses, that I had indeed finished ten classes. Can you imagine finding witnesses in Kazakhstan that I finished school with a gold medal? But get this, people are people. Miraculous, kind, nice people... They all ran to me and said, "I would sign, I would sign" . . . They wrote the note together. Then I received an invitation (at that time you could not buy a ticket without an invitation). They also wrote that they would give me a dorm room. I set off. I arrived a month after classes had started. But nevertheless, I got admitted to the hydrogeological department. I could study. But I realized that I didn't have anything to wear in that cold climate, I had nothing to eat, nothing to use as a blanket at night. I wrote a letter to my mother saying, "get me out of here."

My mother arranged for the hospital chief to send a telegram, which said, "get here urgently, your mother is sick." I took the telegram to the director of the institute. I asked him for permission to go there and return. That convinced him that I would indeed come back, and he gave me permission to leave, and money for the ticket. I went back to that hospital to be with my mother. I never returned.

In 1945, I went to Moscow, where my father's relatives lived. My mother and I had nothing—no home, no shelter, no clothes, no shoes, nothing. I came to Moscow so I could study and work. But no one would hire me without a *propiska* [registration], or admit me to an institute. Then someone advised me to try the Institute of Economics. I didn't want to go there. It was my least favorite option. My father used to say: don't go there. But I went there because I decided that I would study there for a year, get a Moscow registration, then find work, then finally get into my favorite Mendeleev Institute.

A year passed. I realized I had no right to waste time, I had already lost three or four years because of the war. I needed to work and to find a room for myself and my mother. And I graduated from the Institute of Economics. But the hardest thing began after the graduation. I got an "unrestricted placement," and nobody would hire me.[19]

In addition to the beautifully articulated individual details, the story is filled with trajectories and mechanisms of survival in the Soviet rear during the war. Roza depends on the informal discretion of individuals: the hospital chief who hired her mother and later sent the deceptive telegram, the director of the institute of higher education who admitted her based on the handwritten "trust letter" signed by strangers, people willing to sign the letter confirming a high school diploma, and others.

Roza does not discuss the government policies that enabled the relaxed rules of hiring to hospitals and admission to institutes of higher education during the war. Instead, she stresses that she made all her decisions independently and succeeded despite circumstances that seemed to push her down, such as poverty. She does not associate her family's lack of social or economic status with the Soviet regime or Soviet policies toward Jews. In fact, quite the opposite occurs. In her story, all the positive characters ("mentors") are empowered by the Soviet regime, even when the action required ignoring the rules (for example, signing the letter without knowing whether or not the information provided was true). Although she talked about working toward her goal of education, the story does not belong to the genre of a quest, but instead resembles a wonder-story, filled with miracles and miracle-makers. The obstacles are presented as out of the storyteller's control, and the happy endings are all the results of miracles, which in turn, are all associated with the Soviet regime.

Being Jewish does not appear in the story until the very last sentence, when Roza implies that the "real" quest began after the war, when she could not find work, presumably because of her Jewishness. Wartime is not associated with antisemitism, the difficulties were shared by all, and therefore, even though the details suggest a life full of hardship, Roza presents that period in her life as happy and miraculous. In her mind, it seems, the happiness is explained by the fact that no one harassed her for being Jewish.

Interviewees' discussion of professional ambition during the war is in stark contrast with the testimonies of non-Jewish Polish women who ended up in Kazakhstan during the same time as Roza. These women tended to see the wartime Soviet Union (in Siberia and Central Asia) as nothing short of hell on earth, with limited possibilities for survival, let alone personal or professional growth.[20] Even though my interviewees often described their living conditions in Central Asia and especially in Siberia as harsh (very cold or very hot, for example),[21] physically difficult, and often hopeless, they still overwhelmingly found positive aspects. They often spoke of unexpected opportunities, the miraculous kindness of strangers, bold risks that they took, and, most importantly, the happy endings that they lived to see. In other words, if one must choose a genre to describe the adventures of evacuation, a fairy tale, or even a magical tale, best suits the majority of the testimonies like Roza's. The Polish women's stories, on the other hand, belong to the realm of tragic tales. Also, just as for Roza, the tragic parts of the tales of Soviet Jewish interviewees came when they described "the hardest parts of their lives," which happened to them *after* the war.

How was this harder than wartime conditions—when they had no clothes, no shoes, no shelter, and no blanket? How was it worse than living thousands of kilometers away from family, from hearing bad news daily, compared to a miserable yet stable existence in Moscow? It seems that for Soviet Jews, just as for Polish and European Jews, the "hardest part" should indeed be the story of the war. Yet for Roza, the search for work in 1948 revealed that for the first time, when compared to her non-Jewish classmates, she was not on an equal footing in the Soviet state. The hardships of war, experienced by everyone, are not presented as the worst time of her life because she perceives it as a time of equal suffering, whereas 1948 began the period of singling Jews out. The "hardest" here does not mean the most challenging, but instead the hardest to explain, justify, and therefore talk about. The "hardest" is also associated with being Jewish, and being Jewish is associated with limits in career choices.

## In Between Storms: 1945–47

Shortly after the war, the number of Jewish students in institutions of higher education (which most interviewees attended) fell to 65,000 (compared to almost 100,000 in 1939).[22] By 1947, Belorussia had lost more than half of its Jewish student population; Ukraine lost almost half.[23] The people who started their post-secondary education as soon as the war ended described a lack of accommodations and means, but emphasized that their circumstances were no different from anyone else's. Moreover, because war veterans (*frontoviki*) were not required to take an entrance test to enroll in institutes of higher education, they enjoyed somewhat privileged choices compared to the prewar period, when their family background (*lishentsy*, arrested parents, and generally nonproletarian lineage) could limit their selection of future career paths.[24] Mikhail B. (born in 1923 in Zolotonosha, Poltava Region, Ukraine), who chose to become a radio engineer in 1945, explains:

> In 1945, when I entered the institute, the war had just ended, and no one cared whether you were a Jew or not. As long as you were alive. . . It crept out after graduation or toward the end of the studies. That's when I really felt that I was a Jew. Before that, I was a person like everyone else, I no longer felt any of that.[25]

The discussion of the watershed between feeling "like a person" and feeling like an "it" is found in virtually every testimony that details the years 1945–48. The period immediately after the war, which was full of poverty and unprecedented equal opportunity, is presented in stories as the quiet before the storm. "It," the thing that poisoned Mikhail's life, which we understand as government-sponsored antisemitism, is not named. He refers to the poisoning of their lives using a neutral pronoun, an all-encompassing shadow of evil that cannot be faced without fear, cannot be fully comprehended, and thus cannot be defined using words by someone who lived through it. Referring to the traumatic combination of events as "it" has been documented in scholarship that examines narratives of wars, famines, and natural disasters. Many stories of trauma include "ruptures" which divide the narrative into "before" (a period of good) and "after" (when all hell broke loose), with the actual rupture remaining unnamed and usually referred to as "it."[26] In testimonies of Soviet Jewish experiences, government-sponsored antisemitism is understood and presented as the too-traumatic-to-name "it" which ruptured the interviewees' lives into before and after, especially when people discuss their professional lives. When talking about 1945–47, the period right before the "it" overwhelmed the narrative, many people still spoke of following their hearts and interests in choosing their professions, often despite practical considerations. Importantly, they did not think that they needed to explain "it," because they trusted that anyone with any background in Soviet Jewish history would understand what "it" meant. The stories of choosing a profession between 1941 and 1947 do not include any elements that would define "the Jewish experience," whether in a positive or a negative fashion. As Roza K. said, the hardest part was about to begin in 1948.

## The "Black Years": 1948–53

Though my interviewees were unfamiliar with Yehoshua Gilboa's term "black years" to describe 1948–53, that is how they referred to this period. They *always* included episodes of discrimination and limitation, and heroic efforts in overcoming them. Choosing one's profession seemed to have left one of the most lasting impressions. Statisticians and demographers confirm that by 1948–49, the proportion of Jewish students in institutions of higher education had gone down compared to the prewar period, constituting 7 percent of all students (compared to 9 percent in the United States).[27] Moreover, it seems that Jews were the only non-Russian students who faced discrimination with regard to admission.[28] Analysis of admission and graduation records of Soviet institutes of higher education (which all recorded the ethnicity of their students) reveals that between 1948 and 1952 Jewish students were strongly discouraged from studying in certain areas, such as law (where the number of Jewish students declined from 9 percent to 1 percent in 1948), medical institutes (which reduced admission to Jewish students by half), and institutes of culture and art in Moscow and other central regions (which also reduced their Jewish enrollment by half). However, engineering schools, schools of economics, and trade schools (with the exception of international trade) continued to admit Jewish students, and their enrolment numbers went up.[29] By 1956, more than 55 percent of all Jewish students were studying engineering and technological disciplines.[30]

The statistics seem to present a clear picture: Jewish youth had fewer choices in selecting their education path as compared to the 1930s. However, when the members of this generation speak about choosing a profession during the "black years," they tend to focus on dilemmas, discussions, and the process of agonizing decision-making with regard to their futures. In fact, these are the only ones among the interviewees who remembered precisely the process of selecting a profession. In their stories, parental influence was significant, and, surprisingly, their own interests became important as well, despite the fact that the possibility of fulfilling those interests became more limited. In addition, many interviewees' parents lost their jobs (they think it was because they were Jewish). The loss of income and social status, in addition to admission policies, further decreased options in choosing suitable professions. Mila Ch. (born in Mstislavl, Belorussia, in 1931) recalls:

In 1948, when I was sixteen, I moved to Lvov to live with my mother, who was an actor in the Yiddish theater. The theater was closed, she lost her job, so we lost our registration. That same day, her landlady threw her out on the street. And every day we spent the night with different neighbors. We hid in the closet during the "check time," in the evening. That was a very scary time. We were hungry; we had absolutely nothing. Meanwhile, the Ukrainian Ensemble of Song and Dance went on a tour to Lvov, and its director, Shpritsman, hired mama. Mama left with him, and I stayed behind. I didn't know where to go, because I was only in the ninth grade. I decided to leave that school so that I could study somewhere where I could receive a stipend. I researched and found a *technikum* of architecture and construction. I did not know how to draw, how to do anything, really, but I learned later. After I finished the *technikum*, I went to study at the Polytechnical Institute. This was at the time of the Doctors' Plot, and I was kicked out. I was extremely upset. Though I wasn't at the Medical Institute, everyone was kicked out nevertheless. So I went to Moscow to fight for my rights, and there I met my first husband.[31]

On the surface, Mila's story has some similarities to the narrative by Faina D. There, Faina recalled that she had not been qualified to study in a teacher's college because she had made 49 mistakes in her Russian dictation test. But she succeeded because she wanted to study and was able to do so because of her intellectual abilities and the fact that she had a couch to sleep on. In Faina's story, both society and government policies motivated her and supported her studies.

In contrast, Mila presents her story of having to study architecture, a subject she disliked, as a consequence of society's antisemitism. It is not clear from her story why her mother had to leave Mila alone in the city, or why she was not able to support her. But the villain in the story is not her mother; it is the government's antisemitism, which caused her mother to lose a job, marry another man, and abandon Mila. Institutionalized state antisemitism also caused Mila to enroll in a vocational school, leading her toward a profession that she did not like.

It is possible that Mila decided not to join her mother—some details later in the story indicate that this could have been the case, as she speaks of disliking her mother's new husband—or perhaps there were other contributing circumstances. However, these factors do not belong in the story recounting Mila's experiences of discrimination and antisemitism in 1948. For her, describing the period of 1948–53 seems impossible and inappropriate without making antisemitism the main part of the story and everything else secondary.

Being Jewish and the specific difficulties associated with it dominate Mila's story. For example, she chose a profession she did not like. Regarding the 1930s, the story would have been told as a commonplace, but the in the 1940s, it becomes a narrative of persecution. The fallback to a polytechnic institute is not unexpected; many interviewees received their postwar degrees from polytechnic institutes. Engineers were in great demand in the war-ravaged Soviet economy, so the institutions that trained them do not seem to have received orders to limit the intake of Jewish students. The story of expulsion from a polytechnic or another engineer-training school, however, is neither clear nor typical. It is important that Mila emphasizes that "everyone"—meaning all Jews—was expelled during the Doctors' Plot of 1953 (a short but fierce campaign during which some high-positioned Jewish and non-Jewish doctors were arrested on accusation of trying to poison Joseph Stalin).

The choice of professional occupation during this period is almost always a story associated with antisemitism. Antisemitism prevented people from following their passion, determined where they could study, and affected the nature and process of their education. Unaware, of course, of official restrictions that might have regulated the admission policies of institutions of higher learning, the people relied on rumors and indirect information in choosing their institution.

These stories of antisemitism are not solely tales of victimhood. Instead, some are heroic quests. Many people spoke of ways to manipulate the system and strategies of achieving professional successes despite imposed limitations. Such stories are likely to come from interviewees who became very successful in the Soviet Union and somehow managed to carry over this success after immigration. For example, Nissan K. (born in Gaisin, Ukraine, in 1932) who moved to the United States in 1987, became a paralegal in 1991 and worked in a busy law firm located in Brighton Beach, New York, that specialized in immigration law. Here is how Nissan recalls the process of enrolling in a law school in the Soviet Union:

> I left Gaisin [a small town in the Vinnitsa region of Ukraine] in 1947, when I was in the ninth grade. I had a very wise mother. She saw ahead. She understood. This was 1947; I was going to finish high school within a year. She needed to think about my further studies. In Ukraine, it was very hard for a Jew to enter an institute, so we decided to go back to Tashkent. We did so in 1947, and I finished the tenth grade there. I was always a very good student. So I entered law school. It was very fashionable then, because there was a special directive of the Central Party Committee about legal education in the country. I graduated from the Institute, became a lawyer, then entered academia and had a wonderful career, also in the Party.[32]

The "relaxed" situation in Central Asia, the Urals, and the North Caucasus was widely known: a network of educational and industrial institutions had developed during the war, and had been, according to rumor, deserted by the majority of specialists and the workforce as soon as the war turned the corner.[33] Indeed, during the black years, when the number of Jewish students was reduced everywhere within the Soviet Union, it went up in Uzbekistan, from 5.9 percent Jewish students in 1939 to 7.1 percent in 1948–49, and the percentage there remained consistently higher than in many other Soviet republics.[34] Rumors spread that Jews were not restricted in entering institutes there. Moreover, Jews who lived in the multiethnic surroundings of the Trans-Caucasian and Central Asian Soviet republics had to deal with fewer public expressions of popular antisemitism compared to the European part of the Soviet Union. While none of the interviewees stated that their families moved away from Ukraine because of antisemitism, almost all those who moved (at least 10 percent of Ukrainian-born narrators) cited the opportunity to study at a place where they were not discriminated against, as long as their relatives could offer them a bed.

A curious trend emerged from stories of choosing a profession between 1948 and 1953. If a person's own evaluation and explanation of their situation is removed from the story and the obstacles faced in choosing post-secondary education are analyzed as they are listed, no major difference is apparent among the four periods. In all, during the 1930s, 1941–45, 1945–47, and 1948–53, the major difficulties associated with choices of education were lack of availability of family support (funds) and accommodation. However, in stories from 1930 to 1947, these difficulties are not seen as being associated with Jewishness. Instead, the problems described are noted as common, and stories emphasized how their personal characteristics, even luck, or miracles helped them to overcome them. In stories of 1948–53, the tone is very different. Despite the fact that many of the difficulties were the same, the interpretation almost always suggests the impact of Jewishness. Moreover, the stories are told as illustrations of the prevalence of state-sponsored antisemitism in the Soviet Union. Without the use of oral history, and without the literary analysis of testimonies, we would not be able to trace the dramatic change in perceptions of Soviet regime among Jews. However, oral histories of choosing a profession during the black years do not seem to provide facts of actual discrimination, just evidence of the perception of discrimination. Fully verifiable discrimination associated with the choice of profession developed later, in the 1970s and '80s, when the interviewees' children began looking for a place to study. The narrators themselves, however, began to face difficulties associated with their careers *after* they graduated, not during their studies. The search for jobs after the war became a powerful test of their ability to survive in Soviet society.

# 8

# The Right Specialists with the Wrong Passports

## The Search for Employment

In the Soviet Union, graduates of institutions of higher education were not free to choose their place of employment, but instead were subjected to a mandatory three-year centrally administered placement.[1] After this period, the new specialists could either remain employed at the same place or search for work elsewhere.[2] Promoted by the Soviet government as a guaranteed job security program, the practice of placement (*raspredelenie*) was both corrupt and controversial. In theory, students with better grades received better placement options, but in practice, bribery, personal connections, and other subjective factors determined the placement process to a larger extent than one's grades. The most desirable cities for employment were Moscow and Leningrad, places for which one could not even receive a residence permit without a job or a marriage certificate that connected a person to a resident. Rural locations were considered the least prestigious placements, and came with less professional and logistical support.

Almost all interviewees who finished their studies in the late 1940s and early 1950s spoke about the process of *raspredelenie* as the first time that they had been reminded of their Jewish last name, patronymic, or the line in the passport that recorded their nationality. Good grades, good connections, family in town—all seem have been irrelevant to the decisions of the all-powerful *raspredelenie* committees. People of different occupations spoke of specifics relevant to their professions, yet pointed out the similar process of their gradual exclusion from the prestigious locations. A few common perceptions of tendencies within each emerged.

Newly minted engineers of the late 1940s, usually graduates of polytechnic institutes, recall being placed in strategically important plants or institutions located far away from the desirable cities of Moscow or Leningrad.
Mikhail B. (born in Zolotonosha, Poltava region of Ukraine, in 1923),
who studied in Moscow and wanted to stay there, shares the story of his
*raspredelenie*:

> I graduated from the Moscow Institute of Energy in 1951. As a true Jew,
> I was then deported to a plant in Novosibirsk. All the Jews from our
> Institute were sent there. It was a military plant in Novosibirsk. I worked
> there as a skilled worker until the day of Stalin's death and maybe just a
> little after that. I met Madame B. there. She worked there, and by then had
> been promoted to be the head of the workshop, a big deal. She was trans-
> ferred to Moscow, and eventually I was able to join her in 1953.[3]

The choice of the word "deported" (*ugnali*) is not a slip; it was a rhetorical
device commonly used by many people to describe their placements after
completing their degrees. The Russian word "*ugnali*" is normally used in
talking about deportations, exiles, and forced resettlements rather than job
placements. Its use here is indicative of Mikhail's perception, which might
not be obvious from the simple facts involved in his testimony. After all,
Novosibirsk was an important scientific center of the Soviet Union, and
placement there could be interpreted as an honor rather than an exile.
However, in Mikhail's eyes, such a placement was an expression of discrimination. Interestingly, he is less concerned with being appointed as a worker
(as opposed to an engineer), but instead complains about the location. He
finds little consolation that "all Jews" were sent to Novosibirsk. Instead, he
interprets it as a punishment.

The word "Jew" appears twice in the segment, which comes a full hour
into the interview; Mikhail had not used it previously. Moreover, he refers
to himself as a "true Jew" and alludes to the collective tragic fate of the
Jewish people. For the first time, Mikhail presents himself as part of a Jewish
collective. In the early parts of the interview, he had spoken of himself as
a typical Soviet student, a son, a brother, and an aspiring engineer. But he
constructs the story of *raspredelenie* in 1951 as a narrative of the suffering
of all Jewish people, an oppressed and discriminated group, described in
almost Biblical terms.

## War Veterans

As war veterans began to return to peaceful civilian life in 1945, they had to find work. It seemed that they had almost unlimited opportunities. Empowered by their recognized heroism and euphoric from the sheer drive to live and survive, male veterans constituted the "heart"—the elite, core, and hope—of Soviet society.[4] Interviewed veterans, especially those who lived in the United States at the time of their interview, told stories of placement without connotations of Jewish victimhood, but instead stressed their seemingly unlimited opportunities in 1945–48. Even their Jewishness seemed like an asset. Consider a story by already-mentioned Victor Kh. (born in Pilyava, Ukraine, in 1916), who by 1946 was a senior engineer:

> At the end of 1946, I arrived in Moscow and saw a crowd of people. I went into the office of a colonel. He looked at my file and asked me to wait in the hallway. The hallway doesn't have chairs, but rather, lots of people. I stand by the door. People go in and out of his door. Some time later, the colonel calls me, gives me my file, and tells me to go to another room. I enter; they give me a pen and ask me to fill out a form. I spent four hours working on that form. My answers were: a Jew, not a Party member. There were also questions about my mother and father, where they were buried, and their grave slot numbers. I had no idea what they were. They asked me to bring twelve photographs. Then they asked me to come back in two weeks. When I came back, they gave me a special pass, and asked me to go to.[5] A person, they said, will meet you there, and he'll take you where you need to go. I didn't understand much. I took a train, got off at Bolshevo, saw the sergeant. We went and arrived at a house, the Scientific Research Institute of the 4th Academy of Artillery Science. Apparently, they were forming a new unit. I entered the barrack. I see one Jew go, a second Jew goes, one is a major, another is a captain, another one is a colonel, all Jews. I realized that we were being prepared for Israel. That's what I thought.
>
> When the moment came, I saw a man by a table. He was a captain; his last name was Voloch, a Jew, with a pronounced Jewish face. I say to him, "Listen, captain, are we being sent to Israel?" He said, "What are you talking about? This is a top secret unit, soon we'll be dispatched to our destination." So [as it turned out], I did not understand.
>
> In July 1947, I learned that I was appointed as the head of the group that had to go to Kapustin Yar, This was the beginning of Baikonur. Very

many people came. There was nothing there; we had to live out of tents. The next day, the chief of staff came. He was a Jew, Matvei Zelikovich Slepakov. He lived in a train. Later it turned out that only Jews were sent there. Sergei Korolev arrived later. He was the head of construction. But everyone sent there was a Jew. There was a rumor that he specifically asked for Jews. That's why there were so many Jews there.[6]

Bolshevo, a small town some forty kilometers northeast of Moscow, was home to NII-4, which was established in 1946 as a secret research center for military space programs; it indeed recruited personnel for Kapustin Yar. That year, the construction of the rocket launch facility began in Kapustin Yar (later renamed Znamensk). It utilized technology, material, and scientific support from defeated Germany. Numerous test rocket launches for the Soviet military were carried out at the site. The first workers lived in tents; the military commanders lived out of a train. Matvei Slepakov's daughter, currently living in Israel, verified that her father was working in Kapustin Yar in 1947–49. [7] In other words, these details suggest a significant degree of historical accuracy in the testimony and demonstrate Victor's enviable memory.

How do we then deal with his story about his belief that he was sent to defend Israel? Most importantly, why is the Jewish community presented here almost as a privileged group rather than a persecuted one?

The key difference is that the story takes place *before* 1948. While some discrimination and smaller-scale limitations on Jewish occupations began to surface as early as 1943, they did not reach the scope that they did in 1948. Moreover, events in Palestine inspired many Soviet Jews. Many wrote letters to the Soviet government to ask to volunteer and help build a new Jewish state in Palestine.[8] In other words, Victor presents Jewish collectivity as a positive phenomenon. In fact, it does not even occur to him to think about antisemitism or being Jewish when he describes his appointment.

Recorded in Yiddish, the interview uncovered the life of a Jewish young man who grew up in a small shtetl, had intimate knowledge of Jewish traditional holidays and other customs,[9] and was acquainted with youth Zionist groups in the 1920s. In other words, Victor's background can be credited for allowing him to retain positive associations with being Jewish, thus providing space for Jewish pride and the mistaken belief that Soviet Jewish engineers would be sent to help Israel.

Victor Kh. was interviewed in New York, whereas Mikhail B. was interviewed in Berlin, and this factor affected both narratives. Mikhail B. strives to portray himself as devoid of any Jewishness, but punished for it during Soviet times and rewarded for it during his life in Germany. For Victor Kh., the content of his current Jewish life is more substantial. He speaks Yiddish, reads Yiddish newspapers, knows the words of Jewish prayers, and does not feel lost in synagogues or Jewish community centers in New York. But he started all these activities after his immigration to the United States in the 1970s (although, of course, he knew Yiddish before). It is possible that had Victor lived in Germany, he would not have revived his knowledge of Yiddish, as Yiddish publications are nonexistent in Germany, and Yiddish culture is generally not perceived as an integral part of being Jewish in the Russian-speaking Jewish community. In Germany, Victor would have probably remembered the prayers and his mother's religious lifestyle to a larger extent, and maybe would have evaluated his life through the lens of being an engineer, internationalist, and war hero rather than as a proud Jew. But he lives in the United States, where he constructs his story in American terms. The recollection of Jewish aspects of his life plays an important role in the process of his adaptation to life in the United States and finds its way into the story in a positive way.

Despite the different evaluations of what happened to them, both Mikhail B. and Victor Kh. spoke of working in far-away regions in 1946–51, and both attribute this move to being Jewish. Mikhail B.'s perspective, that Siberia was a punishment for being Jewish, is widespread. However, some people, especially those educated in the humanities (such as historians, teachers of scientific communism, philologists, and journalists) spoke of the benefits of being sent to *work* at a Siberian institute, as opposed to being deported to a Siberian Gulag. Such is the perspective of Froim B. (born in 1922 in Kyiv, Ukraine), who entered the history department of Kyiv University in 1941, went to the front in 1942, was wounded, came back in 1943, completed his degree in 1946, then entered graduate school and finished with a *kandidat* degree in 1950. Everything was going well until 1950, when things began to change:

I finished graduate school in 1950, defended my *kandidat* dissertation, and then was expelled [*vygnali*] to Siberia. Officially, I was placed there because they supposedly couldn't find me a placement in Kyiv. I lived in Kemerovo in Siberia for six years. I worked there.

A.S.: What do you mean by expelled?

F.B.: It means they didn't give me a placement in Kyiv.

A.S.: But does it mean you were sent away, like to a prison?

F.B. No, they didn't put me in prison, but almost. They gave me a paper.
If you want to work, go to Siberia, that is your place. All my classmates
stayed in Kyiv.[10]

Froim B. uses the verb *vygnali* (expelled) to describe his ordeal—diction reminiscent of Mikhail B.'s use of *ugnali* (deported). Both men imply involuntary, unwelcome placement, against their will and beyond their control. In Froim B.'s testimony, he does not discuss the issue of *all* Jews being exiled or deported, yet he mentions that he was sent away because he was the only Jew among his peers. Essentially, he is talking about the same collective identity of Jews as victims. The young scientist in this story does not belong among the cohort of his peers because he is a Jew. Therefore, he is "expelled" to Siberia. It is possible that other people were sent to places where they did not want to work. After all, obtaining a desirable job placement required connections that not everyone had. Yet Froim was confident that he suffered from an unfair placement largely because he was Jewish. And because people like Froim hear similar stories from their peers now—and heard them twenty or thirty or even fifty years earlier in the Soviet Union, perhaps in a less elaborate form—they have learned to use these stories to confirm their inferior status.

Scientists and engineers often spoke about cities in Siberia, the Soviet Far East, and Kazakhstan as unattractive placements. Teachers and doctors were more likely to speak about being sent to rural locations despite their good grades. A retired teacher of Russian language, Mariya (born in 1925 in Enakievo, Donetsk Region, Ukraine) recalls:

I graduated from the pedagogical institute in 1951, with good grades, thank God. And then I was sent to work, the devil knows where, to the Karakalpakskaya region [in Uzbekistan]. They did not care about my sick mother, about anything.[11]

Mariya does not explicitly say that she was sent to a remote village in Central Asia because she was Jewish, but she implies the unfairness by mentioning her good grades and her sick mother (family circumstances could informally influence a placement and helped to avoid faraway regions). Also significant is the choice of words used to describe the placement. A trained pedagogue, she spoke a refined Russian during the interview, except when she talked about the placement of 1951. Then she used the semi-vulgar expression "the devil knows where," which indicates her strong emotional investment in the unfairness of the situation.[12] Moreover, she told the story at the very beginning of the interview, minutes after I explained my goal of recording Jewish fates in the Soviet Union. Mariya did not see the need to spell out *why* she was sent to a remote village despite her good grades. It was important for her to emphasize that she, like other Jews whom she knew had received her share of injustice in the Soviet Union.

Compare this testimony to the statement by Nissan, who was proud that his mother moved him to Uzbekistan, where he could enroll into law school and live in a relatively friendly environment, free of antisemitism. The facts stated in these two responses are similar, and both Mariya and Nissan emphasize that the main reason for the move to Central Asia was to avoid the impact of antisemitism, yet their interpretations are radically different. Nissan speaks from a comfortable position in the United States, where his benefits and pensions are safely secured. Mariya, however, lives in Toronto as a "sponsored" parent, one of a special group of immigrants who are allowed to live in Canada on a humanitarian basis, provided that children or grandchildren agree to support them indefinitely, without the right to a pension, benefits, or any recognition for her suffering in the Soviet Union or for being Jewish.[13] Her story of Soviet placement in 1951 is a commentary on her poor current social status, and her emotionally charged language addresses both her past and her present.

## Loss of Networks

A job placement was not a jail sentence. There was no law that required the graduates to take the job offered to them through their institution. If they refused to accept the offered employment, they could be offered an unrestricted placement (*svobodnyi diplom*), which allowed them to do an independent job search. Though that was theoretically attractive because of the severe shortage of specialists in all areas of Soviet industry, the reality was that unrestricted placement essentially meant unemployment and therefore a sublegal, dangerous, and poor existence. Most often, Jews experienced these difficulties in Moscow, Leningrad, and Kyiv, which also happened to be among the most desirable places to live in the postwar Soviet Union, as well as the cities with the highest concentrations of Jewish population. For example, Roza K. (born in 1922 in Zhitomir, Ukraine), who barely survived the war and lost much of her family, remembers her search for work in Moscow as the hardest period of her life:

> I graduated from the institute. Then the fun part began. I got a *svobodnyi diplom*, and no one wanted to hire me. For nine months, I walked from one bank to another. I would call them and ask, "Do you hire graduates of MGRI [Moscow Geological Institute]? They would say, "Yes. Our institute ranks very well." They would tell me to come in. I'd go in. They'd open my passport, and say, "You know, we've already hired someone." I talked to the dean. He sent me to another institute. They couldn't say no to me. But they also didn't give me a job. They didn't say yes or no for six months. Finally, they rejected me. I spent another nine months looking. Then I realized that it was all about my last name, Bonchik at the time, a Jewish-sounding name. I found work many months later.[14]

A testimony by an engineer, Mikhail B. (born in Zolotonosha, Ukraine) tells a similar tale:

> All Jews who graduated from my institute received placements far away. Only those who were married to Moscow women were allowed to stay with a *svobodnyi diplom*. They suffered for so long with these "unrestricted placements." I came to Moscow in 1953 with an unrestricted placement. I spent a year, probably, without a job. I would come, or call and ask, "Do you need radio engineers?" "Yes." I'd arrive, he'd look at my passport: "You know, our worker Ivanov was planning to leave, but he hasn't left yet, come back in a month." And so on. I could not find work for a year. Thank god, my wife worked and fed me. Here I faced antisemitism. Even after Stalin's death, it was hard to find employment. Only two or three years later did it relax a little. . .[15]

The trajectory that both narrators described was typical of many stories of newly minted specialists. They would call ahead, or ask a friend for a reference to do so, only to find out, after showing their passport, that the position was taken. The story is an illustration of what sociologist Moshe Lewin described as the "microworlds" of Soviet urban life.[16] "Microworlds" were routes to success that were both defined by, and cut across, ethnicity, profession, and class. Loss of power within microworlds meant, for example, that very often, any *znakomstva* (acquaintances in a position of power) became useless, informal networks simply stopped working. Interviews suggest that the inability to use those presented a bigger obstacle to a successful career than official laws, directives, and instructions, which never explicitly stated limits on hiring Jews. Interviewees cited similar reasons for the inability to be hired used soon after they identified their passports: the job had just been taken, or someone had not yet left the position.

People who held positions of power and who were able to make hiring decisions often discussed their own inability to help Jews get work. This is how, for example, Esfir A. (born in Orsha, Belorussia, in 1908) recalled trying to help a Jewish friend get a job in 1951:

> In 1951, I was the head of the group of engineers in a construction bureau. My friend couldn't find work after the war. I decided to talk to the director and ask him to hire her. I generally was quite respected there. So I came to him and said, "Evgenii Alexandrovich, if you hire her, I promise to deliver 1.5 of the normal plan." He said, "It won't be necessary, one norm is fine. I'll help you." Indeed, he issued an order to hire her. She was scheduled to go to work next day. Suddenly, the secretary of the Party organization returned from his vacation, and the order was canceled. There was nothing anyone could do, she wasn't hired until after 1953.[17]

Typically, many people who did not get jobs during the late 1940s and the early 1950s recalled being asked to come back some time later. Probably both parties hoped that the unspoken resolution about not hiring Jews would be lifted because of the severe shortage of specialists. Yet respite was not apparent. Many people remember desperation, exhaustion, and a feeling of hopelessness. Not having a legitimate place to work meant no legal right to live anywhere and being ineligible for a state apartment. Associations with tsarist Russia, with its severe discrimination against Jews, began to resurface. David B. (born in Moscow in 1925) explains:

> I never hid that I was a Jew. Why hide it? It's not a source of pride, but still. I, so to say, have suffered quite a bit because I was a Jew. You couldn't get

a job if you were a Jew. For me it was harder than it was for my father. My father witnessed limitations before the Revolution. He would say, "You passed by a store, and there was a sign in the window: 'Jews are not welcome here.'" It was easier then. In our times, you come, you see "Wanted," and they don't hire you. And sometimes they even tell you the reason they don't hire you[18]

The stories of how people tried to hide their ethnicity (called nationality in the Soviet Union) are common. Passports with their nationality line seemed to be the most important obstacle in attempts to gain employment. Although changing nationality was officially prohibited during the 1930s, one could find ways to alter the document. Some claimed to have lost their passports during or after the war, and they registered under different names, and most importantly, with different nationalities.

Some people spoke of discrimination in employment practices as a challenge, something that needed to be overcome by proving the Jews' opponents wrong. Zhenya (born in Odessa, Ukraine, in 1924) explains:

I graduated from my institute in Odessa. Then I saw an ad that read, "Economists wanted, graduates of the financial-economic institute in Feodosia" [Crimea].[19] I went there, applied, and brought my documents, I had no experience at all. I was accepted [for the position]. Then I arrived for the first day of work, and they said, "You know, we decided that you don't have any experience. A woman applied who has twenty years of experience. If you want to work, you can go to a village nearby and work as an accountant there, they're building a plant." I had no choice, so I went to the village, because no one else wanted to go there. But it was good, because I learned all stages of financial planning there, as I was the only one. I learned the entire mechanism by myself... The irony is that later I was sent to Feodosia to consult for the same office that did not [originally] hire me. Eventually, they fired that woman who had experience, because she didn't do a good job, and they hired me.[20]

The story contains all of the typical elements of stories of discrimination in employment practices: an attractive location (Feodosia is located on the Black Sea) is off limits, unrestricted placement in possession, which essentially means blacklist, the advertised need for a specialist, an applicant possessing all the qualifications, and then refusal after an examination of the documents. Zhenya, however, focused on her success in overcoming prejudices and making herself indispensable, and thus hirable despite her background.

Zhenya's attitude is typical among interviewees who initially immigrated to Israel and lived there for more than just a few years. Zhenya was interviewed in Toronto, but prior to her move to Canada she had lived in Israel for more than ten years. In Israel, interviewees seemed to have acquired the ideology of Jewish strength, heroism, and resistance. They translate this into how they convey their life experience. The story of discrimination, therefore, becomes a story of fighting, of not giving up dreams, of not giving in to self-pity.

All the people who finished their education in 1948 insisted that their Jewish nationality played an important role in how they were assigned a job. All considered being sent to Siberia or a remote village anywhere as punishment. Some, especially those without families and friends, took the assignment in stride. Others put up a fight, sometimes successfully, while a subset saw it as a challenge and tried to overcome the obstacles with expected competence or work ethics. All in all, the interviewees believed that during this time, Jews of their background shared a collective fate by being placed at less prestigious locations and given less professional opportunities. Unlike the stories about their war experiences, where almost everyone emphasized that Jews fought as hard as everyone else and suffered as much as others, their stories about postwar placements and employment carried a message of collective punishment.

Collective punishment can explain many things: first, like victims of racism, the interviewees might use the collective analogy in order to justify their own failures with shared reasoning (all Jews were fired, so was I; all Jews were mistreated, so was I), thus eliminating individual factors such as grades, connections, and social origins.[21] Importantly, one's successes are never connected to collective identity, but are associated only with skills or lucky circumstances. The second explanation is that during this period, Jews were popularly perceived as members of a separate entity, as opposed to simply Soviet citizens. The testimonies document the beginning of the process of the transformation of the perception of the term "Jewish" from being synonymous with "Soviet" to being the opposite.

# 9

## "You Don't Seem Like a Jew at All"

### The Atmosphere at Work

"Whoever forgot that he was a Jew, or didn't know, learned about it in 1948!" Repeated by so many people that I lost count, the sentiment seemed to inform the stories of almost every interviewee. People of different backgrounds, different professions, different attitudes, people who disagreed with each other on almost everything, seemed to believe that the period between 1948 and 1953, the last five years of Stalin's reign, taught them "everything" about being Jewish and showed, in the words of so many, "the true colors of our friends and colleagues." Memories of the "black years" almost always included stories of the onset of negative remarks and smirks at their workplaces; some interviewees had their salaries lowered, and others lost their jobs altogether. The most difficult years were the end of 1952, soon after the former leaders of the Jewish Anti-Fascist Committee were secretly shot, and 1953, when Jewish doctors were arrested. People of all occupations were affected, and each of them made significant efforts to be able to survive in a society filled with discrimination against Jews on both the personal and the state levels. But teachers, academics, engineers, salesmen, medical professionals developed different mechanisms for coping during this tumultuous period because they faced different challenges.

### Teachers

About 3 percent of all employed Jews worked as teachers in Soviet schools during the 1940s,[1] but teachers constituted about 10 percent of my interviewees. Perhaps these numbers speak to the fact that teachers saw a clear connection between their lives and the historical processes that took place in the Soviet Union during the 1940s, and thus were more willing to volunteer for an interview. Or maybe the percentage of teachers among Jews of this generation still living was higher than among Jews employed in the 1940s. In any case, I did not complain.

Teachers were my favorite narrators. They were the most articulate, usually recalled events of the past with remarkable detail, were amazing storytellers, spoke loudly and clearly, and made sure the interviewer understood their point. On the flip side, they also quickly recognized the interviewer's agenda and sometimes exaggerated. Well-read and interested in the past, they often made up stories that borrowed characters and plots from recent publications about the historical period they discussed in the interviews. Still, these stories were fascinating: some belonged to the tragic genre, others were comedies, most were quests for justice, yet some were also miraculous, almost supernatural, tales.

Unlike people in other professions, teachers spoke less of worrying about being fired, but more about concerns about effectively performing their work. They worried about possible harassment from their principals. If they were principals, they worried about instructions from district authorities about "restricting" or otherwise harassing their Jewish colleagues. Most of all, they worried about not having enough authority over their students, and thus being unable to maintain discipline in the classroom, and consequently becoming ineffective professionals. Yet their stories usually had happy endings, and they attributed their ability to survive to their remarkable ability to maintain the respect of their colleagues. Usually teachers listed their professionalism, superior knowledge of the topic they taught, and integrity as the three most important reasons that they had not became victims of antisemitism.

Among the 49 teachers interviewed, 14 were instructors of Russian language and literature in Ukrainian and Belorussian schools. Proud carriers of "the Pushkin faith,"[2] almost all of them mentioned, in different contexts, that it was especially important for them to prove that they were able to do the job *despite* their ethnicity, which they all understood as a form of disability. They spoke of conscientious efforts to fight a "wrong perception" as well as additional pressure. Evgeniya K. (born in 1921 in Romanov [Dzerzhinsk, 1933–2003], Ukraine) recalled:

> One year I had a graduating class with only one Jewish student in it, her name was Lena. She was going to get a *gold medal*. It was a strain on my health. My blood pressure rose that day.
>
> The director marked the compositions [as part of the final exam], and she did not award Lena a 5 [A], but gave her a 4 [B]. She didn't give her the highest mark for the composition. That was the end of it. She got a silver medal eventually, but it cost me long years of my life. That girl was an orphan. Her mother died from cancer. Her father remarried and had another child, and she lived with the grandfather, the father didn't help, and can you imagine such a thing? She had to take this exam so that she could get into the institute without exams and get into a dorm. All the teachers helped her, and all gave her the highest marks. She was a very talented girl. . . But that director did everything to spoil her life.[3]

The testimony combines two stories. One is a tragic narrative featuring a helpless orphan, and the other is a story of triumph, with a brave and skillful heroine, Evgeniya herself, who is not broken by her malicious surroundings. Both stories ultimately have to do with the position of Jews in a Soviet school, both as teachers and students. The story of the student, complete with the unfortunate circumstances of her life (in addition to being Jewish), is the story of discrimination. According to Evgeniya, all the teachers wanted to help the orphan, and all of them did so despite the fact that the student was a Jew. The "evil" director, however, did not want to help; she probably had received informal instructions by phone not to allow any Jewish gold medalists. Receiving a silver medal had career implications—a silver medal meant that one had to take one entrance test to enter any institute, whereas a gold medal only required an interview[4]—but it was better than not getting a medal at all. In fact, many Jewish students were prevented from getting any medal, even a silver one, and as a result, the doors to prestigious institutes of higher education were essentially closed to them.[5]

One way to interpret the story is to see that the principal found a compromise by preventing the teacher from being fired and by not allowing a talented Jewish student to go without a medal. Or it can be seen as a story of support of individuals by a supervising commission (the ones who gave

her good recommendations instead of negative ones, probably again informally requested), and eventually a successful career as a Russian-language
schoolteacher. But such stories would not belong to the narrative of persecution in a Soviet school because they speak of the period of known antisemitism and come from a person who suffers from lack of respect in the
present.

A typical detail is Evgeniya's line of defense against possible accusations: the emphasis on her highest possible degree of professionalism. She
is qualified to such an extent that even a negatively inclined commission is
unable to find a flaw in her work. She does not credit the commission for
not exercising its right to write a negative (very subjective) report, but speaks
of herself only as a person able to defeat the odds. Many teachers, especially
Russian language teachers, and especially those interviewed in the United
States, spoke about their impeccable knowledge of the Russian language,
and therefore unbeatable qualifications for the job.

In fact, all interviewees expressed pride in their mastery of the Russian
language independent of their professional occupations (even if the interview was conducted in Yiddish). One reason for stressing knowledge of the
Russian language might be narrators' perception of Russian language and
literature as superior both to the local language of their Soviet past and
possibly the one of their post-Soviet present. Also, many did not want to be
seen as "shtetl Jews" (*mestechkovye evrei*), a title that they considered pejo-
rative despite the fact that most came from a shtetl. They often presented
mastery of the Russian language and literature as their not-so-secret weapon
against antisemitism. Liusia G. (born in Kyiv, Ukraine, in 1925), another
Russian language and literature teacher, structures her entire story around
this phenomenon:

> We lived in Tulchin. My husband was the head of the Ear and Nose
> Department of the local hospital, and I went to RONO[6] to ask for a job.
> My daughter was six months old then. When I was in the office of the head
> of RONO, a director of their methodology department entered the room.
> He asked me, "Are you a Russian language teacher?" I said, "Yes." He said,
> "Can you give a lecture about Radishchev?" (it was his 100th anniver-
> sary).[7] He was the first Russian revolutionary. I was uncomfortable saying
> no, and I replied "Yes." I prepared the lecture. Meanwhile, they appointed
> me to become the head teacher of the tenth grade, the graduating class.

Why then? They had a teacher, Dora Naumovna, who had graduated from the Teacher's Institute and wasn't allowed to teach the older grades.

So, right before the academic year began, I went to a teachers' conference. Teachers from eight districts gathered, the head of the Kyiv region was there, the secretary of the district Party committee, the presidium. The head of methodology came to me, he was white as a wall. He didn't know me. He thought I would be speaking at a small panel of Russian language teachers. But he just got an urgent telegram, I was the first speaker at the plenary session. He did not know me well, and he was shocked. He asked to see my text. He had no choice. If I failed, they would all fail. So I went first, before the Secretary of the Regional Party Committee. I was a young girl, I was wearing a short skirt. I said the first sentence, I will remember it all my life, "The first monument of the Great October Socialist Revolution was the monument of Alexander Nikolaevich Radishchev." That was my first sentence. When I finished, I got an explosion of applause. Everyone began to shake my hand. But no one knew me yet at the school. And here the principal, the famous Raisa Borisovna, went through the entire hall to tell me "Congratulations! This is our baptism by fire." Two days later she was fired, because her mother received a package from America.

Antisemitism began when the Doctors' Plot began. When Stalin died, I was afraid to go to work. My husband was a doctor, and I was afraid they would say that doctors killed Stalin. I was afraid to leave the house. When I finally arrived at school, I found the principal crying. Next day she screamed, "Long live our teacher and leader, Malenkov!" You know how much I suffered during the Doctors' Plot. . .

I was always a teacher of Russian language and literature. I loved my profession, and my pupils loved me. You came to interview my husband, because his story is more Jewish and more interesting to you. I am only telling you my biography because you asked. It is not as important to you, but you asked and I told you.[8]

Throughout the interview, Liusia mentions the names of quite a few individuals: her colleagues, bosses, friends, and acquaintances. All of the names were Jewish. If she spoke about non-Jews, she did not name them. All of the Jews in the story suffer for being Jewish. The former school principal is fired for a connection with the United States, a schoolteacher is not allowed to see her class through to graduation because of a bureaucratic formality, and Liusia herself is scared to go to work because her husband is a Jewish doctor. She presents all Jews as supportive of each other (the principal supports a young teacher), whereas non-Jews are shown as lacking integrity at best, and without intellectual skills at worst. For example, the non-Jewish principal cries over Stalin and then immediately changes to glorifying the newly elected Malenkov.

Liusia's apologies at the end of her story are also significant. Her husband, Semyon Sh. (born in 1908), whom I indeed came to interview, gave an entire interview in Yiddish. He spoke about being involved in the Zionist movement as a child, had gone to a cheder, and was quite aware of his Jewish roots. He also suffered quite significantly from the state-run campaigns during the Doctor's Plot. Compared to his background, Liusia considered herself not Jewish enough, not because of her lack of Jewish identity, but largely because she did not consider that she had experienced a sufficient level of antisemitism at the workplace to call herself a "real Jew."

Former teachers often spoke about episodes when they were forced to act against their convictions. Always, without exception, they reconciled their dislike for a lack of integrity (in themselves and others) by blaming antisemitism for it. For example, Mariya M. (born in Enakievo, in the Donetsk region of Ukraine, in 1925) recalls her work as a teacher-inspector in Ukraine in 1952:

At that time I worked as an inspector of children's institutions (schools, kindergartens). My direct boss, a Belorussian, was a true idiot. I had never heard that such idiots could work at such positions. He would come to the human resources department, where I worked, and talk about someone, saying, "That person is a bad kike." He knew I was a Jew, but he'd still say it. Once they had a situation. There was an issue in the kindergarten class that needed to be fixed. He said to someone, "Go call that female kike from human resources." Someone went to fetch me. She came and told me what he said. But I was stupid. Instead of confronting him, and saying, "The kike has arrived. What do you need, idiot?" I just came and said, "What's wrong? What do you need?" as if I didn't know anything. But I was afraid to betray the woman who told me. He knew I was a Jew, yet he always made remarks about Jews in front of me. That was the only antisemitism I encountered at work. Otherwise, I was very much loved and respected.[9]

For Mariya, a lack of integrity means not standing up to the supervisor's verbal abuse. She justifies it by not being willing to betray her colleague, but perhaps she was also afraid of losing her job. The antisemitic bosses, colleagues, and friends form the pieces of a puzzle where Mariya acts in discordance with her standards. In other words, she associates being Jewish with being forced to behave below universal moral standards.

Interviews with teachers tell a complex story centered on the balance between self-presentation as victims of antisemitism who were able to overcome prejudice and the portrayal of other Jews, who had to face unfair compromises because they had to adjust to antisemitism. Stories of respect illustrate this dichotomy. Beyond the measure of professional success (especially for teachers), the discussion of respect provides space to stress that despite oppressing circumstances that forced interviewees to lie, hide, and do unethical things, they managed to do positive deeds, which ultimately outweighed all the negatives, and resulted in the respect of others, usually non-Jews. In other words, for my narrators, to be a Jew also means to do an extra amount of "good things," that would compensate for the negativity. This notion that a Jew had to study harder than a non-Jew to get the same job and the same pay became a widespread and acknowledged Soviet Jewish value, which survived well beyond the collapse of the Soviet Union.[10] Testimonies of interviewees of the generation born in the 1920s help us ascertain how this social perception was born.

## Scientists and Academics

That Jews were highly involved in all areas of Soviet science is an undisputed (though some might add overdiscussed) fact.[11] One large-scale Moscow-based project designed to honor all Russian Jews who made contributions to Soviet culture (vaguely defined) ended up including more than 8,000 names involved in Soviet art, literature, science, and culture, with scientists taking up thousands of entries.[12] In the view of many Russian Jews, the work of these people arguably represents the most important Soviet Jewish contribution to civilization. At the same time, the most significant stories of discrimination against Soviet Jews in professional fields also come from scientists.[13] Complaints about working for less-than-deserved salaries, being awarded worse-than-deserved degrees, or being forced to write doctoral dissertations for scientific bosses or party officials dominate stories told by rank-and-file Jewish scientists.

The host of Jews that were drawn to science in the prewar Soviet Union is impressive. By 1939, 29 percent of all scientists in Ukraine, 33 percent in Belorussia, and about 18 percent in Leningrad were Jews, with a total of about 16,000 Jewish scientists working in the Soviet Union.[14] As many of them were evacuated during the war, their proportion went up in the late 1940s, with more than 26,000 Jews working in various areas of science by 1947.[15] However, during 1948–53, the number of Jewish scientists went down to 24,600, and proportionally began to constitute less than 11 percent of Soviet scientists.[16]

In the late 1940s, interpersonal relationships in academic circles were poisoned by a general atmosphere of suspiciousness and arrests that targeted scholars.[17] The wartime past also strongly informed the dynamics of the academic workplace. Professors and students developed closely knit networks, often in the form of research groups, based on where they had spent the war.[18] Belonging to such a network was essential if one sought to thrive in the profession. In fact, the biggest blow, aside from the arrests of colleagues, rumors of orders not to advance Jews' careers, and the general hardships of postwar times, was the feeling that despite being a fellow *frontovik*, or a fellow evacuee, a Jew no longer could fully belong to any internal network, professionally or personally. Moreover, being a Jewish academic was often a *disadvantage* for a family member who chose the same profession. Many interviewees spoke of how the system strongly discouraged Jews from forming professional dynasties, especially in engineering science. It was common for someone to hear "two Fishmans are way too many for one institute" as a justification for rejecting one's job application.

The networks built among Jewish workers were quickly destroyed when colleagues were abruptly transferred to remote locations. Yurii K. (born in Kyiv in 1923) recalls, "You come to work, and you see that your best colleagues are gone. In my institute, one day all the best professors were gone. And they were all Jews. They were sent to Perm or something."[19] It is not clear whether the realization that "they were all Jews" dawned on Yurii in 1951, when the event took place, or if it was a later reflection, or even the fruit of his imagination. But a sense of collective punishment informs his narrative, too, and also culminates in other stories depicting 1948–53.

Consider, for example, the narrative of Anna M. (born in Odessa in 1920). After two years working as a translator and interrogator for the special department of the Soviet army during the war, Anna was released because of an "accidental" pregnancy, the result of a short but passionate affair with an unnamed officer. As a Jewish single mother in postwar Moscow, Anna found herself in a difficult position. In the late 1940s, she was fired from a prestigious job at the French department of the Soviet Radio Committee[20] (the committee was reorganized in 1949,[21] but according to Anna, the only people who lost their jobs had distinctly Jewish-sounding names). Luckily, by the time of the "reorganization," Anna already had a degree in political economy. So she began searching for a less prestigious, lower-paying (compared to work at the Radio Committee) academic job:

My dissertation was titled "Economic Ways of Development of Russia in Works by Karl Marx and Friedrich Engels." It was based on the correspondence between Russian *narodniki* and those two great Germans. This was a solid work, my independent research. And theoretically, I could find a position as a university teacher in Moscow—especially since, at that time, *kandidat*s in science were still rare;[22] they became common much later. Everywhere I went, I was rejected. I had a long list of *VUZy* [institutes of higher education] and went to look for a vacancy in each of them. I made a list so that I wouldn't call twice. So I called and asked, "Do you need an instructor?" They would say: "Yes, yes." I would come, they would look at me, and say, "The position was withdrawn." I began to both feel and present myself as a beggar. I was the model victim of antisemitism. I once went into a dentistry institute, I knew they needed a political economist. I was sitting in the office of the chief, and he asked me, openly, "What is your nationality?"

A.S.: What did you say?

A.M.: I said, "I'm a Jew. Thank you, goodbye." He didn't answer, he just waited for me to leave. Then a friend of mine, who had spent the war in evacuation, she taught Western literature, wrote to me to say that Saratov University was looking for an instructor of political economy. My mama tells me, "Leave Andryusha [your son] with me, go there for two years. In two years, things will calm down." So I went. For two years, my son was without me, and I was without my son. I sent mama the money, and kept waiting. In 1952, it got a little easier and I came back to Moscow. This was the fate of Jewish mothers.

But even in the 1960s it was hard. I was feeling better, but I wanted to work at the Civil Engineering Institute. Then I called the MK, the Moscow Party Committee. I called them and said, "What's going on? I am a sole provider; I have to provide for my family. Tell me, could I have been more honest, could I have had a more honest life in order to serve the fatherland?" I reached a smart, kind woman official. She sent an official from the Party committee with me to the institute. He talked with the provost, and said something to him, I don't know what, and I got a job. I think they made an exception for me. So even in the Party they understood how wildly unfair it all was. Because there were many Jewish scholars, scientists and graduate students, they all complained and demanded work. They wanted to work anywhere, even for the lowest salary. But everyone was afraid to hire them.

In 1964 or '65, I was among a group that was sent to Sverdlovsk to audit the level of teaching of political economy in their institutes of higher education, among them the Sverdlovsk Polytechnic Institute. We took a train there, and were all sitting in one compartment. One man, who was the head of the History of the Communist Party department at the Civil Engineering Institute, sat across from me. He said a standard slur that, of course, Jews had been in Tashkent [during the war; i.e., safely evacuated to the rear rather than in danger at the front]. I don't know what I said back. Probably, in the heat of the moment, nothing that smart. Later, after we arrived and all settled in hotels, they organized a party. One young teacher invited me to join them, but I said, "No, I won't come." He tried to convince me, but I refused. Then another one came to invite me, but I said no. That was the only form of protest available to me. I said to one of them, "He probably lectures well about the friendship of peoples." I never spoke to him after that, and made sure that we never had any professional contact.[23]

The story contains almost all of the typical details of testimonies from academics recalling the tribulations of the late 1940s. It is unusual because it comes from an ambitious and educated single mother and war veteran, but it still names common obstacles remembered from the late 1940s and early 1950s. Anna speaks of difficulties during her job search, stories of overheard antisemitic remarks, and even a story of suppressed rage and quiet protest against individuals who openly expressed antisemitic views. Even the figures of "helpers" and "mentors" generally fit the pattern: one helper was a prewar colleague—a friend who does not abandon her despite circumstances—and the other one, the most important one, comes from a Communist Party executive office. Again typically, Anna explains the actions of people who helped her succeed or stood in her way as the result of personal choices rather than regulations, laws, and instructions.

Anna's job was to teach the foundations of Soviet ideology. Essentially, she could be seen as an integral part of the oppressive Soviet system, a person who validated the beliefs and ideologies that ultimately betrayed her personally and betrayed other Jews in her situation. Anna fully understands this contradiction, and reconciles it through a few concessions. First, she emphasizes that she took this job only because a more interesting and suitable one was not available to her. Second, she stresses how she refused to be part of the system by not befriending an important colleague (the chief of the department) because she believed it would betray her integrity.

For Anna, the articulation of the story allows her to believe that she *deserves* to be seen as a Jew in post-Soviet Russia. As a beneficiary of numerous charitable programs, all run by Jewish organizations in Moscow in the early 2000s, perhaps she feels the need to exaggerate and emphasize both her sufferings as a Jew during Soviet times and her role as a proud and strong member of the Jewish community.

All testimonies from former specialists in the humanities share a similar focus on episodes that demonstrate that being Jewish was a difficult ordeal for them; unlike their contemporaries in medicine, they did not talk about *overcoming* Jewishness, thus avoiding antisemitism. This may be because many in the immediate post-Soviet era looked down at the "perpetuators" of the Soviet system, Jews among them. Thus in some ways their emphasis on suffering from being Jewish balances out the presumed cooperation and enabling of the regime.

## Engineers

The single largest group of the interviewees were "engineers," which in Soviet terms also meant "technical intelligentsia": graduates of technical institutes of higher education. These included specialists trained for numerous industries, such as chemists, mechanical engineers, construction engineers, forest industry engineers, paper industry specialists, steel industry engineers, and many, many others. Engineering, broadly defined, was one of the most popular professions among Soviet Jews. The number of Jewish engineers grew tenfold between 1926 and 1939, reaching 43,000. By 1959, the number had grown even more, reaching 80,000.[24] During the late Soviet period, one out of every six employed Jews worked as an engineer.

During the late 1940s, freshly educated engineers could obtain three types of placements. The most desirable was in research institutes, organizations specifically designed to advance technical science through collaboration between theorists and engineers. A second path was to continue their studies through graduate school (*aspirantura*), often supervised and housed in one of the those research institutes. A third path, the most common and the least prestigious, was a direct placement in a manufacturing industry. There, after working at a junior position for some time, a young engineer could either be promoted to a managerial position or become the head of laboratory and research initiatives.

Of the 66 engineers interviewed for this project, 38 worked at research institutes, 17 worked or obtained a graduate degree in engineering and thus also worked at research institutes, and 11 worked in industry. In other words, a majority of interviewees represent arguably the "luckiest" segment of Soviet engineers—the ones who held the best jobs in the field and who enjoyed a higher level of salary compared to other Soviet engineers.

Analyzed together, the stories of engineers have a few unifying characteristics. First, none of them lost a job or was reduced in rank during the "black years," though everyone worried about the possibility. Second, they did not have trouble entering institutions granting engineering degrees. If anything, some chose to become engineers because of rumors that those institutions were the only ones without prohibitive restrictions for incoming Jewish students. Third, this group had the largest proportion of Yiddish speakers among all interviewees with advanced degrees. Similarly, of all interviewees with a higher education, this group had the largest proportion of people who lost their parents in the Great Terror, probably because of the leniency in admitting qualified students from troubled backgrounds into strategically important institutions of higher education. Finally, this group has the highest proportionate number of people who held positions of significant power (heads of labs, managers of scientific research teams, head engineers, and so forth). To be in such a position in Soviet society meant also holding a high rank within the Communist Party (although interviewees almost never wanted to discuss this aspect of their lives). As a whole, engineers represented both the most successful segments of Jews in Soviet society overall and the least troubled among all narrators.

Overall, engineers told stories of success, in spite of their Jewishness. Like teachers, engineers point to their personal traits, such as professional competence (for example, that they were impossible to replace), to account for their success during this difficult time. Two major themes emerged from their narratives. The first concerns the effect of rumors about the deportation of Jews to Birobidzhan. The second discussed the role that being Jewish played in their decision-making throughout their career, especially during the black years.

## Between Deportation and Promotion

Izrail N. (born in 1913 in Velizh, Vitebsk region, Russian Empire) started his career as a junior technician in Leningrad and moved up to become head of a construction bureau in Moscow by 1948.[25] His road to success was not smooth, however. His father, a former small business owner, became a *lishenets* - he was deprived of the right to vote or to be hired, and therefore was unable to provide for his family after 1925. Moreover, having *lishenets* on his record made it almost impossible for Izrail to enter the institute of higher education of his choice in 1929. He went to work in a factory, in the hope of being able to qualify later as a worker-student.[26]

Living in poverty and not succeeding at his studies or factory work, Izrail ended up living on the streets. Eventually, the OZET (Society for Settling Toiling Jews on the Land) helped him get a bed in a factory dorm. After injuring his finger in a work accident, he could not return to manual labor. His uncle, who worked in a chemical industry, found a way for him to enter the Leningrad Institute of Labor in 1930. The institute specialized in accelerated training of homeless and troubled youth, with the goal of their eventual employment in the metal industry. After completing a yearlong course, Izrail was sent to work at an airplane construction factory, where U-2s, an early variety of Soviet airplanes (made out of wood and fabric), were produced.[27] At the same time, he entered the *rabfak*, a workers' training facility, in order to study for the entrance exams for the Leningrad Institute of Labor. Eventually, he teamed up with three of his friends and hired a private teacher to help them pass the exams.

By 1935, Izrail and his friends were all admitted as students to the Leningrad Polytechnic Institute. Izrail finished his studies right before the war, in 1939, and then was hired as a junior engineer at a research institute in Leningrad. During the war, he was evacuated with other members of the institute to Uzbekistan, where he worked on developing Soviet warplanes. In 1945, he was sent back to Moscow and was appointed head of the construction bureau of a secret institute, again in charge of developing military aviation. With 50 people working under him by 1948, it seemed that Izrail had finally managed to overcome the disadvantages associated with being born into a family of *lishentsy*. But new troubles lay ahead. When asked about the atmosphere at work during the late 1940s, Izrail replied:

> To fill your tape, I'll tell you a story. A popular rumor circulated during this time. Ustinov, the Minister of Defense, personally oversaw our institute.[28] His deputy, Gerasimov, was the head of the *glavk* [*glavnyi komitet*, central directorate]—the department that supervised our institute.[29] I don't know whether the story is true or made up, but here it goes. When Ustinov and Gerasimov needed to visit our institute—it was located only two blocks away from the Ministry of Defense—Ustinov would tell Gerasimov, "Get ready, we're going to the synagogue today." Why did they call it a synagogue? Our director was Foshner, the chief constructor was Rabinovich, the chief technologist was Abram Ilich Khaikin. His deputy was Gurevich. The chief of the experimental lab was Torochansky, and the head of the construction lab was Izrail Evseevich Neishtadt. This was a small elite circle. There was also the head of the workshop, Sofrov, and another head of a large workshop, also a Jew, Klyuchevski. All of the key positions were held by Jews, so they called it a synagogue.

> A.S.: Do you think there existed tensions between Jews and non-Jews (at this workplace) during this time?
>
> I.N.: No. The relationships were very good. But there were some incidents. One day, Rodion Alekseevich Kuzmin [R.A.K.], the head of the personnel department called me and said, "The head of the personnel department of the ministry needs to send you to Yoshkar Ola, to head their construction bureau." I said, "Will there be an apartment there?" R.A.K. said, "They'll sort it out." I said, "What about the work? What

will I do there?" The next day, I called my boss, and told him, "Do what you want with me, I won't go."

A coincidence helped me. Marxism says there are no coincidences. Everything happens for a reason. But here, it was a coincidence. That was the time when [Lavrentii] Beria's son, S. L. Beria, decided to take over our territory, our lab. One evening, we got an order for our entire organization, with the exception of one part, to leave and move to Kuntsevo [a Moscow suburb in 1950s]. Complete chaos ensued, and they forgot about my appointment to Yoshkar Ola. Moreover, all of the Russians stayed in the old location, and all the Jews, well, almost all the Jews who worked with me, were sent to Kuntsevo in 1950. But as far as interpersonal relationships. . . I heard rumors that one of the higher-ups once said [about me], "Neishtadt can't be fired, he's a unique specialist."

In 1949 a strict law was instituted that said you couldn't disobey orders at work or give notice without the administration's permission. It was a very strict law. And I was in a management position. One day, I got a note. The note said that due to the dire need to strengthen Birobidzhan, we should allow Jews who wanted to leave to go to Birobidzhan voluntarily. I read between the lines. I knew that this directive could only mean that Jews would be sent to Birobidzhan. I also knew that it would be impossible for a Jew to find another job. I easily put two and two together. But then somehow that got dissolved too, and no one went to Birobidzhan.[30]

Izrail is talking about the Scientific Research Electromechanical Institute, which developed radiolocation technologies to track airplanes during World War II, and was then known as Top Secret Institute Number 20 (NII-20), which reported directly to the Soviet defense ministry. He continued working there until his retirement in the 1980s. He moved to Germany in 1998 to join his family.

The research institute that Izrail described was one of the most prestigious in the country, and he held a position of significant power there. In a way, Izrail is telling us the ultimate Soviet success story (from nothing to everything, from a shtetl to an advanced city, from a nontechnological world to state-of-the-art science, from nuisance to the salt of the earth). The testimony reads like a complicated wonder-story with unexpected twists, hidden forces in place, unexpected resolutions, and, ultimately, a happy ending. The Soviet government is presented ambivalently: on the one hand, it takes all of the power away from Izrail's father, but on the other hand, it provides Izrail himself with almost unlimited career opportunities, which eventually enabled him to restore his father's high position in society and, at times, surpass it. The message that "everything is not as it seems" is also quite typical of stories from interviewees now living in Germany; they are vehicles to address their own well-documented ambivalence about their current place of residence.[31] Testimonies often present the Soviet past as full of unexpected twists and outcomes, full of gray areas, and with no clear division between right and wrong. In this context, unexpected twists that seem to constitute the backbone of the story (such as the possible relocation of the hero into an undesirable remote city and rumors of deportation to Birobidzhan) should be understood as rhetorical tools rather than portrayals of moments that were actually important in the Izrail's life—especially when fact-checking reveals that the causes of these episodes differed from the stories told, and some did not happen at all.

Izrail emphasizes that he is telling me the story about Jews working in his institute in order to "fill the tape"; in other words, he speaks of it as something that is not necessarily important to him. Similarly, the story of antisemitism and rumors of deportation also appear after prompts. But he presents the story of OZET—an organization responsible for providing help to poor Jews, usually by involving them in agricultural work but also by training them in trades, which plays a crucial role in jumpstarting his work path and getting him off the streets—without any coaching. In that story, he speaks of being Jewish as an advantage, almost a privilege, something that helps rather than hurts the narrator. The tone of the story resonates with Victor Kh.'s statement about his false belief that Jewish engineers were specifically selected to work on the most important projects. Izrail's discussion of the war years, which he spent in Central Asia, does not include any Jewish characters or stories of antisemitism. Again, this is typical for Germany-based interviewees, who tend to downplay German or German-caused antisemitism, probably because they receive their benefits and access to social programs through the local Jewish community in Germany. At the time of the interview, they associated being Jewish with luck and prestige, and, if left to their own devices, their life story would portray such an outlook without mentioning persecution or harassment.[32] Finally, when asked about Jews, Izrail chose to tell his tale of overcoming potential difficulties associated with being Jewish. In other words, it is possible that, without prompts, his story would have been a tale of success and luck associated with being Jewish.

The question remains, however, why the response to a question about being Jewish does not include positive statements, but instead takes Izrail into the late 1940s. Despite being prompted (but, one hopes, not coached), the quoted part of the interview is significant, because Izrail uses it as an opportunity to contribute to what he thinks is an in-depth look into the history of Jews in the Soviet Union. And here he, like all other members of the technical intelligentsia, no matter where interviewed, chose to speak about 1948–53, and within this period about either antisemitism, the fear of antisemitism, or managing to overcome antisemitism in the workplace. In fact, Izrail associated the series of stories told in regard to the question about the relationships between Jews and non-Jews as his contribution to Soviet Jewish history.

The story about his institute referred to as a synagogue suggests that Izrail took a not-so-secret pride in the fact that all the key scientists at the institute were Jews. This joke is likely the culmination of a good-old-days story, when Jews enjoyed success in the Soviet Union. Then came the rupture point of the late 1940s, after which things took a turn for the worse. From that moment on, the story develops as a complex maneuvering quest to avoid persecution. Dangers come one after another. First, Izrail and all the Jews who work with him are threatened with deportation-like relocation to Yoshkar Ola, located 760 km east of Moscow. Then Jews are almost deported to Birobidzhan. Each time, they are saved by a miracle or a coincidence. With a sense of irony, Izrail remarks that "Marxism says there are no coincidences," making fun both of his familiarity with Marxist ideology and his own ability to avoid trouble. Overall, he describes the period between 1948 and 1952 vividly and is unapologetically influenced by pro- or anti-Jewish rhetoric, first with Jews as an asset and point of pride for the institute, and then as a liability.

The events in question did take place, and indeed, in 1951 the institute was split into two organizations. The first one became the research institute (NII 20) and the second one was experimental factory number 465, which was to implement the theoretical developments from NII 20. A little fact-checking, however, reveals that "the Jewish question" did not play a role in the restructuring of the institute. Instead, the split was motivated by the urgent need to develop a nuclear-bomb-carrying plane that could provide a system of defense against the potential threat of American offensive planes. A group led by engineers Sergei Beria and P. N. Kuksenko developed a system of defense against these types of weapons, and NII 20 was chosen to implement their theoretical findings. All available resources were mobilized to help them.[33] However, as M. V. Davydov, the author of the institutional history of NII-20, suggests, the secretive nature of the project, as well as the urgent nature of the restructuring, led to uncertainties, gossip, and rumors, all of which were partially reflected in Izrail's testimony. Indeed, according to Davydov, the scientists and the workers were given ten days to relocate their equipment to the village of Kuntsevo, where the new workspace seemed inadequate.

Many rumors circulated among workers at the time of the move. One was that the best specialists would stay in Moscow and the rest would be sent to Kuntsevo. The move reminded many of wartime evacuations: chaotic, fast, fearful, and full of uncertainty. The first months of work in Kuntsevo resembled the war years as well; for example, according to Davydov, the group headed by Izrail resided in a small room with no walls separating offices from workshops (a big change from the luxurious accommodations of Moscow).[34]

During the interview, Izrail did not mention these rumors, but instead spoke in detail about the "Jewish" aspect of the story. He alleged that "all Jews were exiled to Kuntsevo," whereas non-Jews remained in Moscow. He also conflated that episode with the one in which he was about to be sent to Yoshkar Ola and Birobidzhan in 1950.

Davydov's very detailed study of the institute lists names of many of its employees, including all engineers and scientific workers. There is no evidence that Jewish workers were all sent to Kuntsevo. A simple count of those with "Jewish-sounding names" at the institute did not reveal a higher percentage of Jews working in Kuntsevo as compared to Moscow. Moreover, NII 20, located in Kuntsevo, was a highly desirable place to work, with excellent salaries, the possibility of career growth, and interesting projects. In fact, a few testimonies of Jews who wanted to work at NII 20 included stories of being rejected in 1949–53. Many narrators thought this was because they were Jewish. Yet some interviewees were hired by the Institute in the 1950s, and they too, of course, were Jewish.

The story of Yoshkar Ola betrays Izrail's confusion: the institute's projects in Yoshkar Ola took place in the 1960s rather than the 1940s, and again, there is no reason to believe that Jews were sent there disproportionately. As far as the claim about Birobidzhan goes, there are no historical sources that prove either the existence or lack of such directives. Also, there were no plans to relocate Jews to Birobidzhan in the 1950s.[35]

The rumor that Jews were to be exiled or punished seems to be persistent in many testimonies, and many specific variations of it circulated (Izrail mentions a directive, others spoke about oral instructions, or a secret confidential meeting, or a phone call). It is not evident that the rumors came from the 1940s; rather, they were likely the product of the interviewees' post-Soviet familiarity with popular historical writings that argue that Stalin planned to deport the Jews.

Can we (and should we?) then conclude that Izrail made the story up in order to satisfy the interviewer's question about antisemitism? Definitely not. It is possible that much of the reply is inspired by the contemporary circumstance of Izrail's being actively involved in Jewish communal life. In addition, the question about ethnic relations might have triggered the memory of government-sanctioned antisemitism of the late 1940s, and the stories of two traumas (restructuring and antisemitism) merged into one narrative. But it is also possible that he and his Jewish colleagues indeed shared a different perspective on the restructuring of the institute and truly believed that Jews would be harassed. One fact that supports this hypothesis is that of all the historical events of Izrail's life (his father's arrest in the 1920s, the evacuation during the war, the immediate postwar period, the 1960s–1980s, and finally the collapse of the Soviet Union), he chose to speak about 1948–53 in the context of his workplace as the worst time for Jews and the worst period of Soviet antisemitism.

The testimony enriches our understanding of how Izrail (and probably other interviewees of his background) construct their life stories and their relationships with their Jewish nationality, how they pick and choose the periods when they saw their Jewishness as an asset and when they saw it as a great disadvantage. For the engineers and technical intelligentsia of this generation who were not arrested in 1937, the period 1948–53 represents the worst, the hardest, and the most challenging time in their lives.

## A Jew in Charge of Germans: Working with German POWs

Of the 66 engineers interviewed, 14 held managerial positions in the late 1940s. This was the only group of interviewees promoted at such a young age. At least half of them spoke about being in charge of German POWs; of these, five lived in Germany at the time of the interview, and the other two in the United States.

Millions of German prisoners of war worked in the Soviet Union as forced laborers between 1943 and 1956. They were forced to help rebuild factories, houses, buildings, infrastructure, and virtually every aspect of Soviet indus-try.[36] In their stories of managing German POWs, interviewees frequently discussed issues related to things Jewish, even when they were not explicitly asked about it. Grigorii B. (born in 1907 in Zakharivka, Crimea, Russian Empire), a specialist in woodwork and wood construction, was appointed in 1945 to supervise building projects in postwar Kyiv. Frustrated with local Soviet workers, who, in his words, were interested only in skipping work and stealing, he requested German POWs' involvement in his projects. After numerous consultations, his superiors approved the request. He could not have been happier:

> The POWs were great. I signed an agreement. I agreed [that they would receive] a change of their bedding every week, I promised that the sheets would be washed and starched. I didn't have to promise that, but I knew it was important for them, because they were cultured. I gave them extra food if they worked well. None of them stole anything; they worked amaz-ingly well. As a result, we finished construction well before the deadline. And they respected me, the POWs. I never wanted to take revenge on them because of what they did. But they knew I was a Jew, and it didn't matter.[37]

Probably many, if not all details of this testimony are strongly influenced by the fact that Grigorii B. lives in Germany today. As a recipient of a pen-sion awarded by the German government (not the Soviet one), he perhaps feels an obligation to speak to his fair treatment of German POWs. He also emphasizes their being "cultured" and their need for clean bedding, as opposed to Soviet workers, who did not request similar amenities. He praises the professional qualities of his workers and their work ethic, such as not stealing. Most interestingly, he brags about the respect he enjoyed from the POWs *despite* being a Jew. He does not speak about his own feelings of revenge, disgust, or hate, which could have accompanied his collabora-tion with former soldiers of the German army, something that came up in testimonies of non-German based interviewees. In essence, Grigorii has internalized his current position as an immigrant in Germany and projected this attitude onto his story of how he used to be fair to Germans, who are now fair to him.

Esfir A. (born in 1908 in Orsha, Belorussia), a construction engineer with a specialization in plumbing, was also put in charge of POWs in 1948. Unlike Grigorii, however, she did not speak about German workers in favorable terms:

> Right after the war, my husband and I lived in Gorky [now Nizhni Novgorod]. He taught at the military school. I didn't have a job. One day, he came home and said, "I saw a boat, they were recruiting brickworkers to work on construction in Leningrad. Go find out." I went there and said, "You know, I am a construction engineer, with a specialty in plumbing, but please hire me as a brickworker if you like. I can assure you that when you actually arrive in Leningrad, you'll find lots of masons there. But do you know what Leningrad means? There's water everywhere. You'll need to build the sewage system, furnaces, how will you do that? There are no specialists there, and you won't be able to use your masons until that is figured out." I convinced him, and they hired me. Very soon after, I was put in charge of German POWs, who were all employed to help with the rebuilding of Leningrad.
>
> German POWs lived in eighteen dormitory buildings which belonged to the "House of Officers" on Liteiny Prospect. It was an improvised camp. I had a translator. His name was Kolman, a former Volga German. I too spoke some German, but I didn't know much. Nevertheless, I was told to listen in to POWs' conversations and observe their behavior. You know, I found lots of SS members among them, you can't even imagine how many...
>
> For example, I would form a brigade. And I would notice that they were all scared of one person. I got it instantly. He was a nobody, not a brigade leader, nothing. He does nothing all day, but he gives orders, even to the brigade leader. "Oh," I think, "this is an SS member," I knew they were all scared of them. They thought the war wasn't over, and that they would return... I went to my superiors and said, "You know what, take him away from me. I don't need him." After that, they did a little investigation and they discovered he was indeed an SS member and took him away. I don't know what happened to him.

I remember another case. Once I caught an SS member in the follow-ing way. I said to him, "Why does it take you so long to mount this pipe? Give me the pipe! I'm a woman, and I'll do it. You need to put in the cement foundation and bolts. You know what to do. It's very simple. It's a small pump. And it is taking you six days to do it." I understood that he was sabotaging us. I approached his brigade leader, and said, "What is this? I'm a woman, and I can finish it in a day." And that man said to Kolman, "Tell her we killed many Communists and Jews, but it's a shame we didn't get all of them." I said to Kolman, "Kolman, what is he saying?" He said, "It will be done by tomorrow." I asked, "Is that really what he told you? We shall see." I went immediately to my superiors and told them to remove both the translator and the brigade leader.

Some Germans were nice. I remember one especially vividly. He was a coppersmith. Once a huge boiler broke. It hadn't been drained prop-erly, and it was impossible to replace it, the entire system needed to be redone. But if we didn't fix it, it would be impossible to heat the dorms for the thousands and thousands of students who would arrive in the fall. So I found that guy, who I realized was a specialist. I asked him whether the boiler could be repaired with some patches on the top and bottom. Normally, that isn't done because the pressure is too strong, but I had done some calculations and asked if it could be done. He said he could do it.

I went to the chief and requested that that person work for me. I explained the importance of the boiler, that without it the building would not be functional. The chief said to me, "Fine, take that German, but don't bring him here. I hate those Germans; they killed my son." I said to him, "I understand, but this German condemns Hitler and his policies." Later, I went to the chief and asked him to allow the five best German workers to send letters home. They were so desperate to know what had happened to their families, and I understood that it would stimulate them to work better. My coppersmith was allowed to send a letter home. I called him and said, "Here is your permission, write your letter home, but don't write anything. . ."

"I understand, I understand," he said. I told him that otherwise he wouldn't receive an answer.

A month or two passed. One day he ran to me, in tears. He kneeled and kissed my legs. He had found his wife, his kids. Everything was normal.

"Only my house," he said, "was destroyed." I saw him again a year or two later, I was walking on the street, and a truck was carrying POWs. They yelled, "Frau Ingenieur, Frau Ingenieur!" That's what they called me. I think he was sent home later.[38]

From the way Esfir A. structured her story, it is not immediately apparent that it took place at the peak of the antisemitic campaigns during the late 1940s and early 1950s. For example, there is nothing in it about being insecure about her career. If anything, she speaks of being treated with a greater degree of respect than others: she is hired for a position for which there was no opening, and she is entrusted to listen in on POWs (and she hints that this responsibility is given to her *because* she was a Jew, not despite of it). She does not speak about her personal motivation to take revenge on German POWs, even though earlier in the interview she spoke about losing her father, her siblings, and many, many cousins and uncles in the Holocaust. In her story, she is a person who expresses compassion for German POWs, advises them how to get around Soviet censorship and other restrictions, and sees them as human. In other words, she spoke about treating POWs as members of her own community—a community of people oppressed by the Soviet regime. In fact, Esfir's boss, a Soviet bureaucrat, a non-Jew, whose son was killed during the war, could not do the same. She proudly reported being able to rise above revenge to ensure the effective rebuilding of Soviet infrastructure.

The fact that Esfir was a Jew escaped neither the prisoners nor her colleagues. Yet the only time she mentioned antisemitism was when she described her interaction with the German soldier who was sabotaging the project. She described the openly antisemitic remark toward her, an anti-Soviet comment, as well as an attempt of the Volga German translator to cover it up. The translator was almost as much a villain in the story as the SS member himself.

The account is heavily influenced by contemporary perspective. Interviewed in Germany, where the tensions between Russian Jews and Russian Germans are pronounced, Esfir translates the severity into her account of the past. Moreover, like Grigorii B., Esfir proudly recalls the respect that she enjoyed from the German POWs. Once again, she projects craving for respect in her new adopted country onto the story of her past.

Similarly, her overall sympathy to German POWs is possibly exaggerated because of her encounters with contemporary Germans. Unexpectedly, she internalizes the anti-Soviet rhetoric and applies it to her story, thus creating a narrative of friendship between a Jew in charge and her German worker.

Esfir presents Jewishness as an asset in her work (her ability to speak Yiddish and her potential intolerance to Nazis and Germans in general), an aid in her career advancement, and a means through which to earn respect from both her Soviet bosses and German prisoners. Again, we can easily trace this message to contemporary circumstances: Esfir was able to immigrate to Germany because of being Jewish, despite her husband's Russian ethnicity and her children's and grandchildren's non-Jewish spouses. Moreover, she presented herself as always taking the initiative; she was the one who moved her family from remote Gorky, a city where many former political prisoners lived, to the more prestigious Leningrad. It is similar to how she took her family from the impoverished post-Soviet Russia of the 1990s to prosperous Germany. She also sees the benefits that her family receives from the Jewish community as a prize for her being Jewish. As a result, she did not speak much about antisemitism, and in general about being a victim, but instead emphasized the positive aspect of her Jewish ethnicity, despite the knowledge of widespread discrimination against Jews.

Esfir did not say that the worst period of her life was during the period of postwar antisemitism. Having lived through the death of her two children, the loss of her husband, and her painful immigration, she recalls the immediate postwar years with pleasure, pride, and an assertion of confidence. She did not see being Jewish as an obstacle.

Such optimism is rare among interviewees in general, but it is more common among engineers in positions of power in the early 1950s. In fact, many engineers in their thirties and early forties by 1951 spoke of the Great Terror of 1937–38 as their "black years." Grigorii B.; Venyamin S., who participated in construction of the Moscow subway; and many others were arrested in 1937 and released in 1941. They considered themselves lucky to avoid arrests between 1948 and 1953, and as a result did not stress either governmental or popular antisemitism at their workplaces. They knew that freedom, no matter how limited by Soviet shortages, deficiencies, and discrimination, was better than arrest.

## Accountants, Salespeople, and Blue-Collar Workers

A significant percentage of the interviewees (215 out of 433) never obtained the equivalent of a college degree. Many of them studied at professional or vocational schools, which trained teachers, accountants, Yiddish cultural workers, and sales personnel. My interviewees represented the last generation of Soviet Jews with a significant proportion employed in those occupations. Between 1926 and 1939, the number of Jewish trade professionals went down from 41 percent to 19 percent in Ukraine, and from 53 percent to 36 percent in Belorussia. By 1959, their absolute number decreased by a factor of two.[39]

My project collected a number of characteristics of such people, which sheds light on how they ended up in these occupations. The largest proportion among these interviewees (117 out of 215) witnessed their parents' arrests in 1937–38. Parents were arrested for various reasons: alleged economic crimes, religious "propaganda," and, most often, for no apparent reason (according to the interviewees). These parents usually worked for the Soviet system, either in the Communist Party or in other Soviet institutions. After their arrests, narrators were taken in by extended family members or by orphanages. In addition to being deprived of family support at a young age, people in this group had to deal with navigating poverty, chaos, and the uncertainties of Soviet society in the 1930s. Many had to begin supporting themselves soon after their parents' arrests, so they did not even have a chance to consider higher education, let alone completing their studies. A typical story is that of Evgeniya R. (born in 1922), who after her mother's arrest in 1938 gave up all of her dreams of becoming a teacher and worked as a janitor in a school. After the war, finding a work as a janitor in Moscow (where her husband lived) was hard, but she managed to secure one at the "school for difficult children" (special-needs education) where she worked until her retirement in 1977.[40]

A typical feature of people from this group is that most of them were educated in Yiddish primary schools. It has been documented that Yiddish school graduates experienced more difficulties continuing their education than those educated in Russian or Ukrainian-language schools, as only five Yiddish-language vocational schools operated in Ukraine in the 1930s. Russian-language institutes and vocational schools were more difficult for such students to enter. Though many interviewees were able to overcome their lack of knowledge of the Russian language and successfully completed their studies, others, all belonging to this group, spoke of their lack of mastery of the language as too high a barrier. For example, Mikhail K. (born in Korichi, Vitebsk region, Belorussia, in 1921) said that he could barely follow the math in his vocational school because he was not familiar with the Russian terminology. As a result, he could not even dream of higher education.[41]

Another common characteristic among this group is that many of them survived the war in Transnistrian ghettos, as opposed to the Soviet rear or the army. They usually described being in the ghetto as an experience that they needed to keep secret in order to be able to move on with their lives and careers. Soviet authorities treated people who survived the war in ghettos with suspicion. Everyone who declared this experience was subjected to interrogation, which in turn could lead to imprisonment. Often, only their spouses knew about their whereabouts during the war; their children typically discovered these parental "secrets" long after the collapse of the Soviet Union. In a practical sense, it was hard for interviewees to verify their whereabouts on application forms to universities and institutes, so they tended to choose positions for which no long, formal applications were required.

Just as among engineers, the major traumas of these narrators took place *before* 1948–53. As a result, they never begin conversations about that period without prompting. They do not recall it as a time of increased discrimination or of personal transformation, or as a period when they recognized for the first time that they were Jewish. Instead, they remember it as a difficult postwar era, with limited accommodations, poverty, and the communal sorrow of losing family members (Jews and non-Jews alike). Soviet antisemitism is not usually the central focus of their story.

A large proportion of the people from this group were interviewed in Russia and Germany; they either never left the former Soviet Union or left very late. Most interviewees from this group had experienced extreme poverty at some point in their lives, and many said they wanted to ensure that their children would not know it. Discussing finances seems to be more common among this group, too. Unlike others, they considered being poor a failure and the inability to earn money as a sign of discrimination against Jews.

Finally, university-educated interviewees usually saw their education, professional competence, respect at the workplace, and distance from their

Jewish origins in the Soviet Union (the further, the better) as social capital. But people from the group stressed, often unapologetically, their pride in being Jewish. Conversely, people who finished Soviet institutes of higher education took pride in how much they resembled non-Jews, whereas those without higher degrees took pride in how little in common they had with non-Jews.

## "I Was Lucky to be a Jew": Optimistic Perceptions of the "Black Years"

Olga K. (born in Kamenka, in the Kharkov region of Ukraine, in 1918) was born into a poor family that could not afford to send her to school. In 1937, she married an Austrian communist, a refugee who had fled to the Soviet Union a few years earlier. In 1939, he was arrested and presumably shot. She told their daughter that her father had been killed in an accident. Later, she altered the story to one in which he was killed in the war. But she hid the true facts of his arrest. As a result, Olga did not pursue her education, took odd jobs such as elevator operator, and later housekeeper. From 1946 onward, her work involved janitorial duties at the typesetting department of a Moscow newspaper. She recalls this period in the following way:

> Very few people were fired. Well, one was arrested, but otherwise, the attitude toward us was good. But everyone was afraid. I was checked and checked again. Both the editor and the deputy editor respected me. I cleaned very well. If I found money or documents, I would always pile them nicely and give them back. Maybe they checked on me that way. I was poor, but I never took anything. I never even had glasses because I was so poor, and I always had bad vision. And they respected me. They knew I was a Jew. I didn't hide it. Why bother? After all, I looked like a Jew. Everyone respected me. I worked well, never had any problem. I became a skilled worker [later], at the bindery. I only hid that I was the widow of an enemy of the people. And I didn't become a Party member.[42]

Though Olga worried much more about her status as a widow of an arrested Communist—"an enemy of the people"—she did talk about being Jewish (after being prompted). Like almost all interviewees, independent of their profession, she felt it was important to emphasize the "respect" that she enjoyed, despite her Jewish nationality. The assertion that "everyone knew she was a Jew" is contradictory, because it starts as a statement of bravery and honesty (she did not hide it out of cowardice), but ends up as an inevitability (she looked like a Jew, so there had been no point hiding it). Being Jewish also did not matter as much because she had a much more dangerous secret to hide—a foreign-born, convicted, "enemy of the people" husband. In this sense, Olga's testimony is quite typical for this group of interviewees; they worried less about being Jewish than about their other secrets.

Olga speaks of her honesty, work ethic, and poverty, all as part of the antithesis to her disadvantage of being born a Jew. It is also important that at the very beginning she speaks about *all* Jews being worried about arrests in 1948, as opposed to only those who were in positions of power. In fact, stories about being Jewish as an asset in 1948–53 are not rare, but they are more typical among interviewees without higher education. While German-based narrators fill their stories with more miracles and unexpected twists than those who now reside in Russia or the United States, the message was uniformly clear: government-run antisemitism affected those with education more than "simple people." This belief probably reflects the historical reality of the time, and certainly presents an important sign that the Russian-speaking Jewish community did not see itself as a uniform victim of antisemitic policies. Instead, many told stories of how they found ways not to be seen as Jews, and used these stories to illustrate their resilience and, ironically, their ability to survive as Jews in a hostile environment.

Although Olga attempts to dissociate herself and her behavior from the negative stereotypes of Jews, which she felt she needed to defy throughout her life story, she still stressed the unity of all Jews and spoke of Jewish suffering. This is juxtaposed against her personal, secret suffering, that of being the widow of an enemy of the Soviet state.

Some members of this group spoke, quite unexpectedly, about how being Jewish had helped them avoid persecution and prison. The guilty parties were neither arrested, persecuted, nor charged with any crimes, because they were Jews. Vladimir Y., for example, was born in 1921 in Leningrad. His father was a devoted Zionist and was involved in collecting funds for a new Jewish settlement in Palestine. In 1922, when the authorities began seriously persecuting Zionist activities, Vladimir's father was arrested, and he died (or was killed) in 1924. The family moved to a small town, Purkhov, where Vladimir's grandparents lived. Sometime during the early 1930s, Vladimir's grandfather's little store, which had been opened during the NEP era, was shut down. His grandfather was dekulakized, and his property was confiscated. Vladimir's mother did not have a source of income, and Vladimir does not know how they managed to survive.

One of his earliest memories came from the early 1930s, when he, the youngest of ten children, went to the forest along two older siblings to pick berries and mushrooms. His other brothers and sisters were much older, and by that time all of them had left for Moscow, Leningrad, and other large cities. He barely saw them later in life. Throughout his childhood, he was instructed not to say anything about his father's arrest, even though many of his classmates' parents had been arrested, too. Vladimir Y. was drafted into the army in 1939, served throughout the war, was wounded, and served again after his recovery. Miraculously, his mother survived the war, but died in 1946. Eventually he was discharged and went to Leningrad in 1948. A war buddy helped him get a job at a jewelry factory. Vladimir Y. found a bed in a dorm. Skilled, young, and enthusiastic, he continued to keep his father's arrest a secret and wholeheartedly believed in unlimited opportunities for his career. But things did not go smoothly:

My real name is not Volodya [the nickname for Vladimir]. My name on my passport was Wolf. During the war, the head of my company called me, I was still in the ski battalion, and told me, "What kind of a son of a bitch are you, Wolf? Wolfs are bombing us, your brothers are bombing us. Get your documents out, I'll tear them apart now, and I'll give you a new soldier's book." That's how I became Volodya.

A.S.: What about your last name?
V.Y.: No! He asked me to change it, but I refused. But many people changed theirs.
A.S.: Didn't you want to change it?
V.Y.: No.
A.S.: Why not?
V.Y.: It would have been an insult. I thought it was conniving, cowardly. It would have been a betrayal of the Jewish people to change it. You can say or write that you're Russian, the hell with that, but to change your last name is something completely different.

Even during the war, when an antisemite, some colonel, harassed me, I never even allowed myself to think that I could hide the fact I was a Jew.

After the war, I went to work at a jewelry-making factory. I had some friends there. Their director was Fradkin, Boris Mikhailovich Fradkin. The head of the tool workshop was Lapitskii, a Jew. The chief engineer was Rofalson. The head of the galvanizing plant was also a Jew. I came to apply for work as a jewelry maker there. They suggested that I should work with clocks instead, as they were planning to begin producing gold watches. They asked me to get a team of good watchmakers, and added my skills, and the work began. A year after, I was made the head of the watch-making workshop.

Then, the boss called me and said, "We want to make you the head of the quality control team. You need to check everything."

I said, "Boris Mikhailovich, why me? I have my own work. I'm busy all day." "Don't talk!" he said. "I need to make sure everything is done right."

I spent three days going through the books. I come in and reported that I had found eighteen kilos of extra gold. "Are you crazy?" he asked me. "How can we have eighteen extra kilos of gold? Find out what's happening."

How could I find out? I looked at the documents, and saw that there was extra gold at the warehouse.

He said to me, "What shall we do?"

I said, "We have to steal that gold away!"

He said, "Are you crazy, how can we steal it?!"

I said, "Maybe not steal, but at least hide it somewhere. In case we don't have enough, we could use it later. Instead of waiting for another month to get more gold."

It turns out that some Ivanov, the brigade leader, had been covering each watch with five microns of gold instead of twenty (as required by standard). That was how he had saved eighteen extra kilos of gold.

My boss did not agree with me that we had to hide it, but instead reported it to his bosses. The OBHSS (Soviet Financial Police)[43] came, revealed that he was not putting enough gold on the watches, and we were all fired, all Jews. It was in 1953. So fired is fired, the hell with that. I should have said, "Thank God they didn't put us in jail." But instead I said, "No, I'll go to the boss of OBHSS."

I showed up and said to the colonel, "Comrade Colonel, allow me to report. I am a senior lieutenant in reserve, winner of eighteen medals and orders, why was I fired?"

He said, "Where are you coming from?"

I said, "From the jewelry factory."

He laughed and said, "Say thank you that you were only fired. We got a special order to spare you a criminal investigation. Had I opened the investigation, you would have all been jailed. How do we know it was just eighteen kilos? Maybe it was thirty kilos, and you took the rest away. I should have arrested you, and tortured you in prison. But my bosses told me not to get involved with Jews. They said it would be seen as an antisemitic affair. So we let it slide."

In this story, Vladimir essentially suggests that being Jewish saved him from much bigger trouble. The tale is not a lament, a quest for justice, but instead a miracle story with unexpected twists and, ultimately, a happy ending. In fact, the narrative tells a story of Jewish power, as opposed to an expression of government antisemitism.

The hero in this story is Vladimir, who decided to stick to his Jewish ethnicity by rejecting the immediate potential rewards for changing it during the war. According to his account, he refused to do so because he did not want to betray, as he put it, his last name; he preferred to keep his integrity and Jewish pride. The postwar part of the story becomes a reward for his bravery.

When Vladimir fights the unjust decision to fire him, he appeals to the financial police officer. He emphasizes his war heroism, and demands justice: it was wrong to be fired for something that he did not do. The officer refuses to reinstate him, and instead points out that Vladimir is lucky that he and his bosses were not charged with a crime. His Jewish nationality, explains the officer, is something that "saved" Vladimir from prison and torture, because the officers' bosses did not want to be accused of antisemitism. This final part of the dialogue is the unexpected twist, so typical for German-based stories. It speaks about *luck* being associated with being Jewish and the weakness of Soviet authority in the face of Jews. In other words, such a tale implies that had the workers in question not been Jewish, they would certainly have been persecuted.

I did not find any specific records regarding the change of leadership at the Leningrad Jewelry Factory, where Vladimir worked, during this time, but arrests, firings, and restructurings of major factories were common, especially in Leningrad, home of the infamous Leningrad Affair, a series of fabricated criminal cases against prominent politicians,[44] which resulted in the deaths of all major leaders of the Communist Party in 1950, including some Jews.[45]

People of different professional backgrounds spoke in various ways about how they warded off antisemitism. They were proud to be Jews and knew that the hostilities would pass. Mikhail P. (born in the village Yanovo, now Ivanovo, in the Vinnitsa region of Ukraine, in 1929), was a tractor driver on a collective farm and recalls his life in 1948–53 in the following terms:

> Right before the war, I finished seven classes. We were evacuated to Uzbekistan. I worked there as a tractor driver during the war. After the war, we returned to Ukraine, to Yanovo. I was a brigade leader. I worked hard, and everyone respected me. These people, tractor drivers, mechanics, they were always drunk. And I was their brigade leader, and I had to punish them. But I didn't feel any of that.
>
> A.S. : You didn't feel any antisemitism?
> M.P. : No, no. Even when I had to fine or punish drivers, they were good-natured about it. . .
>
> Once I went to Kyiv to a meeting of all the mechanics in Ukraine. No other Jew worked as a tractor driver on a collective farm. I was the only Jew. I received the order "Sign of Honor," for good work. During the Doctors' Plot, people began to point at us, saying, "Jews, Jews, Jews." Whenever I went to a store, or to a street, I would hear, "A Yid, a Yid, you poisoned people. . ."
>
> A.S. : What did you answer?
> M.P. : What would I answer? I would say, "Were you there? Do you know what happened? Maybe it's a lie. You don't know the truth. And some-one might have invented a lie. It could be done against anybody." This was a time when attitudes toward us were bad. But after it was all sorted out, it became good again.[46]

Taking pride in maintaining good relationships with their non-Jewish neighbors, enjoying their respect, and even being the only Jew among tractor-drivers in Ukraine, are all part of a positive account of being Jewish. Once again, Mikhail does not present being Jewish as a disadvantage, but instead talks about the positive characteristics of being Jewish, even during the hardest times (the Doctors' Plot of 1953). In fact, the story does not associate antisemitism with persecution, difficulties, or discrimination in the workplace but rather with mild harassment in everyday life. Moreover, in describing the dialogue with neighbors, he does not recount uncertainty or humiliation, but instead portrays himself as morally superior. In fact, for Yuri, living through the black years gave him the right to be called a Jew, a word that he perceived and wore as a badge of honor.

## And Then I Hit Him: Stories of Violent Responses to Antisemitic Comments

Semyon D. (born in Moscow in 1923) lost his parents when they were arrested in 1937. First his father was arrested, then his mother. He ended up in an orphanage at the age of 14, along with his 12-year old brother and nine-year-old sister. He attempted to escape the orphanage three times, but was unsuccessful each time. He was drafted into the army right before the war began. He pretended to lose his documents, and never mentioned anywhere that his parents had been arrested. Instead, he said they had died from starvation. He served in the infantry until 1944, when he was transferred to the NKVD special forces. After he was released from the army, he worked as a guard in the Gulag. In 1949, he moved to Moscow and began work as a taxi driver. He recalled how the number of antisemitic comments from his passengers skyrocketed in this period, culminating in 1953. A decorated war veteran, he refused to listen quietly, and frequently engaged in fistfights with luggage carriers and other drivers. He also spoke about numerous incidents where he dropped passengers in the middle of the road, or even punched them on the nose for antisemitic remarks. Here is one episode that took place in 1953:

> Once I drove past the Rizhskii Railway Station, I was finishing my shift. Two young men and a girl flagged me:
>     They said, "Chief, we need to go there."
>     I said, "All right, sit down."
>     One of them sat next to me, another one with the girl on the back seat. They were all drunk. But the [unwritten] law was that if the passengers were drunk, I should take them to the militia, I had no obligation to drive them, because I risked not being paid.

I said to them, "Here's the thing. You guys are drunk, pay in advance."

They said, "No, only when you get us there."

I said, "No!"

They said, "You Yid!"

And I kicked him. I didn't want to damage my hands; I wasn't wearing gloves. He flew through the door of the car.

I told them, "Get out."

He flew out. The others ran out of the car. I wasn't going to take it.[47]

Later in life, Semyon worked as a bus driver, and in that capacity too, he admitted, he punched people for antisemitic remarks. (Buses, trams, and trolleys are uniformly mentioned as places where antisemitic statements could be frequently heard in public.) Whether or not the punches actually flew, it was important to Semyon to stress that he defended the honor of Jews and physically struck people for the words that hurt. Not only did hitting punish the offender, it was also supposed to destroy the stereotype of a powerless, physically weak and feeble Jewish male, unable to defend himself and his people. Semyon took pride in being a Jew who could not be accused of letting bigots get away with making such remarks. He presented his ability to successfully use his fists as something that separated him from other Jews, but also as a quality that made him a better Jew. On another level, he viewed his physical strength as a way to prove to antisemites that their condescending remarks about Jewish weakness were wrong.

## Most Honest and Most Resourceful: Stories
## of Work in the Soviet Luxury Trade

All 27 interviewees who worked in trade were employed in Soviet luxury enterprises–exotic foods, clothes, china, furniture, and chandeliers.[48] Theoretically, government stores were required to offer all these goods at standard (quite low) prices. In practice, most of these products were only available through special "closed" (to the general public) stores. Getting a position at such a store meant more than access to a good job. It meant that the person would become an important part of his or her acquaintances' network (a desirable part of any microworld), thus a person of significance and, at least potentially, significant influence. The fact that *all* of my interviewees employed in trade worked at such places speaks, once again, to the nonrepresentative nature of this sample. Yet it also provides an opportunity to analyze a large number of stories from this understudied sector of the Soviet and Soviet Jewish population.

The backgrounds of narrators from this group were not that different from others lacking a higher education; most of them had lost their parents in the Great Terror and survived through the support of extended family members. But they often spoke about topics that others did not cover: the gray economy, including reselling goods on the black market, and using their veterans' benefits for obtaining and reselling Soviet luxury foods, such as caviar, salami, and smoked fish.[49]

There were two types of stories associated with their work and the gray economy. One emphasized their honesty and integrity, which did not allow them to take advantage of their position. A typical example is the story of Faina M. (born in Proskurov, Ukraine, in 1918). After Faina's mother and father were arrested in 1937, a friend found her a job as a sales clerk at a local grocery store. She spent the war in Central Asia, where she worked as a seller of groceries, a highly lucrative position, which was key to her survival. She remembers having a gun at her side. Upon her return to Proskurov in 1946, her sister-in-law managed to help her secure a job selling bread. She held on to this position during the famine of 1947. Because bread was distributed only through ration cards during the postwar years, the job implied a high level of responsibility (and unlimited access to vital goods scarcely available to consumers).[50] Faina insists that she never took or sold anything that did not belong to her. Her honesty and toughness, as she recalled, landed her a promotion, as she was appointed to a Regional Party Committee special store that sold luxury foods. She was a member of the Communist Party, dealt with the local elite, and does not recall experiencing antisemitism a single time in her life, because "there was nothing people could hate me for: I was honest, reliable, and hard-working."[51]

Faina's story, recorded in the United States, reiterates a version of the American Dream, in which her hard work is rewarded by respect, a desirable position, and, above all, avoiding arrest or firing during the late 1940s. The straightforward flow of the story is also quite typical for American interviewees, and so is the happy ending. Less typical, but not rare either, is the implication that Jews who suffered from antisemitism somehow deserved it, because they were less honest, reliable, or hard-working than the interviewee. These types of assertions typically came from narrators living in

Germany or Russia, but not from those living in the United States, where people tended to emphasize Jewish solidarity. But interviewees involved in the luxury trade (eight of them were interviewed in United States) all tended to express this point of view: while others stole, they maintained honesty and integrity, and thus did not suffer from antisemitism. Those narrators also did not talk about wealth as an asset (as did those who lived in Germany or Russia). We can speculate that this group constructed their stories in such a way in order to deal with the ambiguities associated with how other immigrants perceive their occupation (similar to how German-based interviewees create complex stories to deal with the ambiguities of living in Germany). That is the only explanation, other than coincidence, for the fact that all eight American-based interviewees presented their work in this trade as Faina did, while nineteen others, interviewed in Germany and Russia, presented their lives differently.

These narrators admitted to using their access to *defitsit* (rare, hard to obtain goods) to their advantage. They spoke unapologetically about "getting" desirable goods to others through unofficial channels. They justified it as helping people: their families, their friends, and their communities. A typical example is a story by Moyshe B. (born in Riga, Latvia, in 1926), who began his career in trade in 1951. By 1953, he was a manager in a store that sold china, glass, and crystal, which were all in great demand and in severe short supply in the Soviet Union. He recalls enjoying "doing well" for people, especially his wife, who never had to work. When asked whether being Jewish affected him throughout his career, he replied:

It didn't concern me. I have a great background, my father was a Bolshevik. I was a Party member. They almost didn't take me, because they said I had an aunt abroad. I didn't know about the aunt, but they did! They took me anyway, and I led lots of activities in the Party.

There were very few Jews working in the store; we had an internationalist staff—Poles, Jews, Latvians, Russians, everybody.

Everyone knew I was a Jew. I never hid it. They were good to me, and I was good to them. I have awards, medals for hard work.

A.S.: Could you comment on antisemitism during the Soviet period?

M.B.: There was antisemitism, but you have to be a good human being, then it will be good. If you aren't human, everywhere is bad. I was never called a Yid. And I never hid that I was a Jew. Once, a drunk worker blurted out, "I don't want to take orders from Yids." I fired him, and I was right, the higher-ups backed me up.[52]

Though Moyshe contradicts his own assertion that if one is a good person one would not be called a Yid, literally in the same sentence, he still insists that antisemitism is something that one can combat with honesty and good behavior.

In Soviet society, cheating the state was not seen as a crime,[53] but Moyshe elevates it to the virtue of helping friends. He does not present his activities as an expression of anti-Soviet ideology. In fact, quite the opposite is true. He emphasizes his membership in the Communist Party (as Faina did), and he is unapologetic about it. Moyshe and Faina both stress their loyalty to the Soviet regime and to their families and take pride in having been able to "work the system" to their advantage, which meant, among other things, being able to avoid antisemitism. To them, this ability constitutes the core of their pride in being Jewish.

# 10

## Jewish Doctors and the Doctors' Plot

Every single person interviewed knew exactly where he or she was on January 13, 1953, the day *Pravda* published a front-page editorial revealing that nine doctors (six of them Jewish) had been arrested and accused of trying to murder members of the Soviet government, including Joseph Stalin himself. The editorial launched the infamous "Doctors' Plot." The arrested doctors were brutally interrogated, and were about to go on public trial, but Stalin's death rescued them from almost imminent death sentences. In April 1953, Lavrentii Beria, then the general secretary of the Communist Party, announced that the plot was fabricated and that the doctors had been found innocent. The arrested physicians were released. However, the impact of this short affair was felt well beyond the individuals imprisoned and released, and well beyond the few months during which it took place.

During the Doctor's Plot, physicians, patients, Soviet society at large, all seemed to be discussing Jews—usually from a negative perspective, but often defending them too.[1] Jewish doctors, who constituted between 3 and 5 percent of all Soviet physicians, were on the front lines of these discussions.[2] Of the 58 physicians interviewed for this project, 41 were practicing medicine in 1953 (the others were still medical students). Of them, 11 were fired from their positions, all in Ukraine. Fifteen were professionally demoted and had their salaries decreased. The other 15 continued to hold their posts, but they all were at the perceived mercy of their superiors and the chiefs of staff who managed to keep their jobs intact. Ilya Sh. (born in Voznesensk, Ukraine, in 1913) recalls:

In 1953, I was working in a clinic [in Moscow]. Things were brewing. Once, at a staff meeting, the chief of staff, who was Russian, said, "You know, there are many things being said right now about nationalities. Don't pay any attention to them. We wouldn't let anything happen to you. Work as you always work. No one will be fired or excluded." That was the end of it. Of course, there were also some unpleasant people. They used to say, "Don't refer me to that Jewish doctor. I want another doctor." But those were rare cases, and no one seemed to pay attention to them.[3]

Ilya Sh.'s story is by far the most optimistic account of the "Doctors' Plot" recorded for this project. However, even he mentions patients' fears about Jewish doctors, which every doctor interviewed for this project pointed out. Not all their colleagues, however, were portrayed as being as supportive as Ilya's were.

All the interviewees who worked at the more prestigious centers, such as medical research institutes or clinics attached to certain ministries, spoke of an atmosphere of fear, both of being fired and imprisoned. Fira G. (born in 1925 in Efingar, in the Nikolaev region of Ukraine), a newly appointed medical research assistant at the Nikolaev Medical Research Institute, recalls:

> The Doctors' Plot was a horror story. Many doctors in my institute slept with dried bread nearby. I was still a young doctor, so I wasn't in any danger. I was already respected, but I was young. But the older surgeons, other specialists, many were preparing dried bread.* In 1953, Jews were sent to jail without any cause.[4]

Fira suggests that the older, more experienced, and at times foreign-trained doctors (of whom many were still practicing in the 1950s) were the ones who were in more danger compared to the younger, Soviet-trained ones. I heard this sentiment often. Almost all narrators, but especially doctors, emphasized that in their minds, doctors trained before 1917 did not represent the same profession as Soviet-trained doctors. In the 1920s and 1930s, patients and doctors alike were in awe of older (and old-school) doctors; in 1953, being such a doctor (or being perceived as such) became a liability, largely because these doctors held more senior positions and had contacts with foreign colleagues, both hugely dangerous during the Plot.

---

* "Preparing dried bread" is a euphemism for getting ready for prison.

In 1951, during the height of the propaganda fight against cosmopolitanism (which was a code word for "Jewish"), the Soviet media often published the names of cultural activists accompanied by their alternate "Jewish-sounding" names in brackets, like Mikhoels (Vovsi). Sometimes these were indeed their real names, but most of the time they were either the names of their relatives or, even more often, simply made up. In addition to names, which were harder to identify as Jewish, the press often revealed the patronymics, which are commonly used in Russian and which often identified Jewish nationality better than a last name or passport registration.

Many interviewees remembered that the act of hiding a Jewish patronymic was perceived as an attempt to conspire against their patients, other doctors, and the Soviet government in general. Semyon Sh. (born in 1918 in Kuty, Ukraine), a decorated war veteran, recalls:

> When I was a student, right before the war, I worked as a paramedic at a mental hospital in Stavropol. There was another paramedic there, Luka Matveevich Galushka. When I came to report for duty, he asked for my last name and registered it, then asked for my name and patronymic. I said "Zunya Peysakhovich." He said, "What? What?" He didn't like the sound of it. He wrote me down as Semyon Petrovich. Since then I have kept that name.
>
> After the war, I worked at a hospital in the city of Vladimir. There was a boss there, Khasov, an Ossetian. He didn't like me. In 1953, he used to gather all the nurses and doctors together and read to them out loud the satirical pieces from newspapers about Jewish doctors.
>
> He did it once, twice, three times. The third time, I got outraged. I was sitting there, like a dummy. I let him finish, and then I said, "I don't want to see such meetings here. If you want to read these humorous pieces, read them in a recreation room, the Lenin corner. Go there during the lunch break and read it there. This is a doctor's station, a workplace."

A.S.: How did he react to that?

S.Sh.: He didn't say anything special. He was friendly with the head of SMERSH [Death to Spies Department].[5] Once I met that head of SMERSH, a lieutenant colonel. It was a week, maybe a few days, before the doctors were arrested for the Doctors' Plot.

> He asked me, "What was the name of your father?"
> I said, "Peysakh."

He asked, "Why then are you Semen Petrovich?"

I couldn't stand it anymore, and told him boldly, "Go ask the head of the hospital. I won't answer that question."

It was my luck that the doctors were acquitted a few days later, and my tormentor was fired, and there was no continuation of that behavior.[6]

Like Vladimir, Semyon was advised to change his Jewish sounding name and patronymic by a well-meaning, non-Jewish Soviet official. It was important for Semyon to emphasize two things: first, that he was not the one who made the decision to change the name recorded in his document, and second, that he suffered for doing it. Meanwhile, there is an additional story here as well, and it has less to do with 1953 and more with the late 1980s, when the Semyon's children decided to immigrate to the United States. With Russian-sounding names and the word "Russian" recording their ethnicity in their internal passports, Soviet Jews often had a difficult time proving that they were indeed Jewish. Still, it is significant that most, if not all, Jewish doctors chose to speak about 1953 as the time when they were harassed for being Jewish, and incidentally, the time when they started to think about the negative meaning of their Jewish identity.

In his interview, Semyon emphasized a few times, and even asked for affirmation from the interviewer, that he was a daredevil. In other words, he did not want to be seen as someone who listened passively to antisemitic remarks. Instead, he spoke of starting a fight against the person who was reading antisemitic slurs from Soviet newspapers in the common room. In the story, he almost paid for it, because a government official from the NKVD started to take an interest in him, which signaled a clear danger. Only Stalin's death saved Semyon from getting into real trouble.

Like many men interviewed, Semyon appealed to his wartime heroism and emphasized the respect he received from their patients. Women, even those with backgrounds similar to the men's, tended to appeal to the compassion of the people in charge: they asked for pity for their dependents (children and parents). Both men and women spoke about threatening to complain, and many indeed complained to higher Party authorities about the *proizvol* (arbitrariness) of officials in misinterpreting government policies, and indeed, exercising personal antisemitism. Astonishingly, even today most interviewees attribute their problems in 1953 to the personal views of people in charge, as opposed to the government's policies.

Irena S. (born in 1909 in Freiburg, Germany), who worked as a doctor at a sanitary-epidemiological station in Kyiv, recalls:

My boss fired me on April 6, 1953. I was left with my elderly mother and my school-age daughter, without anything. I started fighting. When someone pushes me too hard, I get initiative and bravery, and I will stop at nothing. Someone suggested I should go to the first secretary of the Party, because the sanitary-epidemiological station couldn't do anything, they were worried for themselves. So I went to the first secretary in my district, where I lived in Leningrad. He was also a good person, [coming] from workers who had risen on the political career ladder. I didn't know whether he knew me or about me, but I had heard from a colleague that he was a good person. He saw me, and described our chief of staff as a bad person and a coward.

They fired me just because they could, I wasn't even a Party member. He called her [the chief of staff] and asked her, in a demanding tone, "I'm asking you. Dr. S. is unemployed, she is supporting her daughter and her mother, she has no other means." My mother didn't have a pension. The chief took me back, but only to the lab. The atmosphere was bad there. My coworkers looked at me as they look at a new student in a class where everyone has known each other for a long time. I suffered there. I also never had a vacation, because it was a new job. But gradually I got used to it. I did my work. After Stalin died, the doctors were rehired, and I was rehired back to my old job.[7]

Despite a few possible mistakes in the interview (Irena says she was fired in April 1953 but rehired after Stalin's death, which took place in March 1953), the story presents a rather detailed and consistent account both of the process of firing and the process of fighting back. Irena understood that she needed to go to a Party official for help. Even though she was aware that doctors were being fired everywhere, she still assumed that the initiative came from local bosses rather than from Community Party organs.

Directives and instructions to "cut Jews" came directly through the Party's highest institutions, detailed enough to specify the number of Jews.[8] Yet in accounts of their personal stories, interviewees rarely suggested that their own job losses were the consequences of anything but the personal antisemitism of their immediate superiors. The reason for this discrepancy is that interviewees want to tell a story about how their initiative, wit, energy, and creativity helped them to survive in difficult times. Just as Holocaust survivors speak about their decisions and how they took charge in situations that were completely beyond their control,[9] Jewish doctors preferred to speak of individual circumstances and personal victories during the Doctors' Plot period.

Structured as a survivor narrative, Irena's story is a quest for justice, where the hero overcomes her own weaknesses (shyness and a reserved personality) in order to save her loved ones. It is not an accident that she refers to the chief of staff doctor as a "coward." After all, heroes in quests are the complete opposite of cowards, and the hero wins by defeating cowardly enemies. Most interviewees refer to people who fire them as both cowardly and personally antisemitic. In Irena's story, the party boss is portrayed positively, as having risen from a working-class background with knowledge and connections with people "from below," as opposed to being a Party elitist from the start. Such positive traits represent clichés from Soviet newspapers, ones that were never internalized by the educated strata of Soviet society. Instead, a working-class background was often mentioned as proof of a person's lack of culture and *intelligentnost'* (intelligence and sensitivity). Yet, in Irena's story, which generally displayed hostility toward clichés of the Soviet media, a working-class background is the only positive characteristic given to her protector and savior. There is no apparent explanation for this disposition except to say that Irena could not understand the logical reasons why the official decided to help her.

Usually, interviewees stressed that they were helped because officials knew them personally and respected their professional achievements. Irena implied in her testimony that if the First Secretary had known her personally, she would have felt more confident. Yet she went to ask for help anyway, without personal connections, because she understood that the only chance of her reinstatement at work could come from the Communist Party, even though she herself was not a member. Ironically, the fact that the Party official helped her, as opposed to a colleague, who she believed dismissed her on his own initiative, is her tribute to the Soviet regime, which eventually granted her justice. Her story, therefore, does not really challenge the Soviet regime and its policy, because it credits it with the restoration of justice. The local bureaucrats are shown as antisemitic, whereas those in official power were the agents of justice.

Irena and countless other interviewees shared their anger at the system that forced them to sacrifice their career aspirations, but they rarely expressed anything but sympathy for the heads of the local Party committees who helped them to obtain better jobs. This mode of presentation is explained by the process of life review, which softens the internal conflicts and contradictions of the past. In addition, the interviewees did not want to portray their lives as stories of victimhood. Instead, they liked to see themselves as people able to make independent decisions and navigate the difficult Soviet system. The ability to find support among Soviet apparatchiks is one of the most often quoted types of evidence of interviewees' personal strength. Ironically, that also explains the frequency of quotations of antisemitic remarks of colleagues and immediate bosses. My narrators apparently believe that without antisemitism, there are no Jewish heroes.

## Medical Science Research during the Doctors' Plot (and Its Aftermath)

Jewish doctors working in prestigious research institutions were the group whose careers collectively suffered the most as a result of discrimination in the wake of the Doctors' Plot. Every single medical scientist working in a lab in 1953 had a story about what happened to his or her research during that year. Because the oldest research doctor among my interviewees was 32 back in 1953, and most of them just had begun their careers at that time, their narratives often shared concerns about other (often more senior) scientists. Although the details of problems at the workplace vary, most interviewees spoke of being reduced in rank (from a primary investigator to a secondary one), non-Jewish superiors taking credit for their work, losing their research position altogether, or going into another sphere of medicine, usually a less prestigious one. Many even spoke of the Doctors' Plot as a specific attack against medical research, as opposed to an attack on all doctors.

Irina (Fira) G. graduated from a medical institute in 1948, began work as an epidemiologist in Nikolaev, and decided to engage in scientific research. But it turned out not to be such an easy venture:

After the war, antisemitism was a lot worse than before the war. When I got the position as an epidemiologist, I was forbidden to engage in science. The head of the department, Bolkanenko, didn't let me use the typewriter. I didn't have my own, and he wouldn't let me use the institutional one. I went to type at night, and they would kick me out at midnight. I studied like that for many, many years.

I got into the field accidentally. I graduated from the medical institute and was planning to be a general practitioner. When I arrived in Nikolaev, they told me they needed a parasitologist. They told me people were arriving from all over the country and had been bringing parasites, but general practitioners and surgeons couldn't help. I saw my first patients with the textbook on my knees, just to diagnose them. Later I studied with Professor Shulman in Kharkov, then in Leningrad, and it got easier. Then I set up my own lab and conducted research on echinococcosis. Eventually, I finished a monograph on the condition. And then they decided to steal it from me—the people from the Institute of Medical Professionalism at Adrianovskaya 20. Their logic was—how could it be that some doctor from Nikolaev was ahead of them in her research? I wanted to use this monograph as my dissertation, but they conspired to not let me pass.

The problem was that Moscow did not allow studying on that topic. Echinococcosis was a secret, and was referred to as classified topic number 6. But I studied it anyway. My father was in jail, so my husband helped, and I had a nanny for my two kids. I worked all day and all night.

I arrived at the [dissertation] defense. Elenka Leykina, my senior colleague told me, whispering, "They're going to fail you. We were sent tricky questions to ask you so that you wouldn't pass." . . . At the defense, they indeed challenged everything that I said, and at the end, they didn't pass me.

When they failed me, I ripped up all my visual [aids], left the room, and began crying. Professor Shulman, my advisor, followed me, and so did Leykina. Shulman was the best specialist in parasitology in the country. He told me, "Ira [short for Irina], don't cry. When they failed my doctoral [post-*kandidat*] dissertation, I didn't cry." These people were out of control. You could see that you had been failed for no good reason.

Then I decided to visit Academician Skriabin. He lived in the academic sanatorium "Uzkoe." I got there the next day at 9 a.m. I gave him my dissertation. He asked me if I could stay in Moscow for three more days. I said I didn't have any money, but I would try. Three days later, I came back. He typed a memo with a letterhead which said, "Academician Skriabin, Hero of Socialist Labor."[10] Then he outlined all the innovations of my approach, and stated that in his opinion the work met all the requirements of the *kandidat* degree. But it didn't help.

I think I encountered those problems both because I was a Jew and because my father was in jail.[11]

My interview with Fira G. (this is how she preferred to be addressed in New York, not Irina, as she was called during her life in the Soviet Union) took place two years after she suffered a stroke and experienced some memory loss, but the story was relatively fluid and articulate. Though some dates and names seem to be confused, she described her tribulations in significant detail, and all of them had to do with restrictions that she faced in her medical career.

First she was diverted from her original topic of interest into epidemiology, which seemed like a less desirable field than infectious disease, her preferred field. Then she was sent to a second-rate institution, outside the more desirable places to work, Moscow and Leningrad. Fira's testimony mentions Professor Evgenii Shulman (1899–1990), who was head of the department of helminthology at the Parasitology Institute (later the Institute of Medical Parasitology) in Kharkov until 1964. He received his Doctor of Science in 1948. One of the leading parasitologists in the Soviet Union, he moved to Moscow in 1964 to assume the position of a senior research scientist at the First Moscow Central Institute of Tropical Disease and Medical Parasitology.[12]

Fira's dialogue with Shulman about his difficulties in obtaining a doctoral degree in 1948 is detailed enough to seem trustworthy. The story of a warning from another senior colleague, Elenka Leikina, a Bulgarian parasitologist who worked in Moscow during that time, is significant. Leikina was not Jewish, but her dark hair and ambivalent-sounding last name deceived Fira into thinking that Leikina's sympathy to her cause stemmed from Jewish origins. In other words, the story of Fira's individual failure to successfully defend her dissertation turns into a story of both collective punishment and Jewish solidarity in the face of persecution. All the Jewish doctors in the story are victims of the system. Therefore, it is not surprising that a non-Jew, Academician Skriabin, delivers the ultimate accolade. It is his superior (almost supernatural) power that allows him to rise above bigotry and to praise the true achievement of a Jew. But even he, the most powerful scientist in the field, is powerless in face of the machinery that suppresses Jews and Jewish doctors.

Narratives of the persecution of Jewish doctors often mention fellow Jews who suffered from similar ordeals, but rarely speak of Jews in power who helped or tried to help them. Fira G.'s story is no exception. Even Evgenii Shulman, a high-powered Jewish scientist, a rare Doctor of Science back in 1948 (later the degree became more common), her former advisor from Kharkov working at a senior position in Moscow, is presented as a fellow sufferer. He was in the same boat as she was—an unsuccessful graduate student from a second-tier research institute. The initiative to seek help from Skriabin is presented as Fira's own, for which she is rewarded with a rare, important endorsement. Not only is Skriabin the world's leading expert in the field, he is also a non-Jew who testifies to Fira's professional ability, which is no less important in the story than the reiteration of the atmosphere of general antisemitism.[13]

What most likely happened was that it was Shulman, a former student of Skriabin, who contacted Skriabin (and found his whereabouts in a government-protected sanatorium) and advised Fira G. to follow up. If this is so, it was essentially Shulman's connections that ultimately helped Fira to receive the endorsement. Yet she does not present it that way. For the story of Jewish persecution in the Soviet Union which she wants to tell the interviewer, this detail would not fit. Instead, it would present a story of Jewish mutual aid, or worse, the younger colleague receiving the help of a Jew at a senior position, which could be perceived negatively, as it could suggest that Jews benefited from favoritism.

Doctors working outside Moscow or Leningrad had more freedom than those employed at larger research centers, even in Ukraine, where antisemitic attitudes were mentioned more frequently compared to other parts of the Soviet Union. Yet obstacles to research were prominent and caused numerous complications for the interviewees. Sometimes, their wartime past came up in dangerous way. Semyon Sh. (born in 1921 in Kuty, Ukraine) recalls the course of his career in medical research. Semyon worked at a small Vladimir-based hospital throughout the Doctors' Plot:

> I had been trying experimental procedures ever since the time I worked as a military surgeon. You had to be crazy to do these things. I conducted lots of surgeries. Once, when I visited Vinnitsa, a colleague consulted with me about two patients. They both displayed symptoms of schizophrenia. But something seemed off. It turned out that they both had infectious

intoxication in their brains. It resulted in similar symptoms. I performed surgeries, and they both recovered.

I decided to write up the cases. I believed that my contribution was in double-checking their neurological status. Such a case had been described in literature, but only theoretically. Epshtein wrote about the possibility, but he didn't have a practical case to back up his theory. Together with a colleague, I published an article in a leading Moscow journal. Then some time passed. I was reading the medical journal *Vestnik*, and saw that a woman from Arkhangelsk had defended a *kandidat* dissertation about infection-induced psychosis, but she copied my article word for word.

I wrote to her supervisor, the professor, to let him know. I said, "It is embarrassing for your clinic for a degree to be awarded to someone who 'borrowed' all her research materials." She wrote back to me, but nothing changed.

I knew my contribution was original, I had read the German and Soviet literature. I went to Moscow specifically to do research on the subject. These are my articles. [Shows the published offprints]. "The Question of Late Metastases of Lymphoepithelial Tumors." I used the Moscow Central Library. This article is about Henoch-Schönlein purpura, a complication of adenoidectomy. I didn't sleep after operating on patients with that condition. They always bled out. I came up with special measures to help them, and they were effective. I kept records of these child patients. Gradually, doctors from all over the region were sending patients to me because I had good results.

All my topics of research were original. I published quite a bit. I read the foreign literature, and used it in my work. I studied German, but I didn't know English, because it was forbidden.

[His wife, present at the interview, added:]

My husband is very meticulous. He was an impeccable doctor. He was famous. He risked surgeries that others didn't dare do, such as an urgent adenoidectomy for a six-month-old baby. No doctor wanted to do it, but he did it. His patients never had any complications. [Semyon nods.]

A.S.: Were you a *kandidat* of science?

S. Sh.: No, I never assembled a dissertation, or even applied to become a graduate student.

Wife: After the war, he considered going to Leningrad, but his career
would have been impossible there, because he'd been in a ghetto, so he
couldn't go to Leningrad.

Semyon to the interviewer : Please, eat.

Nothing in the course of the interview predicted this turn in the discussion.
I was not able to get Semyon to elaborate on how he was rejected for a position in Leningrad, or about his time in a ghetto. In fact, had his wife not
mentioned the ghetto, I would have not known that he had been in one. He
spoke about his career as a military surgeon, but discussed his story only
beginning in 1942. As I reread the transcript of the interview, I found nothing about 1941. When I discovered the gap, I called Semyon to ask, but he
did not want to talk about it and changed the topic to current affairs in the
Jewish world.

The Russian archives verify Semyon's military and postwar medical career,
and there are offprints of his publications in the Central Medical Library in
Moscow. The military record states that Semyon was drafted at the end of
1941 from Stavropol. In 1941, Semyon was a student at the Vinnitsa Medical
Institute, which was not evacuated when German troops invaded Vinnitsa
in July 1941.[14] Many of the Jews of Vinnitsa were immediately shot, others
ended up in ghettos, and still others, possibly including Semyon, ran away
on foot, either before the Germans invaded or soon after. Given that all his
family members were killed in Vinnitsa, Semyon managed to escape alone.
None of this information came from the interview. Eloquent and consistent,
equipped with an enviable memory and attention to detail, Semyon did
not speak about the first few months of war, despite being asked. In fact,
the harassment during the Doctors' Plot found its way into the testimony,
whereas the ghetto experience was mentioned only by his wife, and only in
the context of postwar limitations on Jewish medical scientists. But Semyon
did not deny being in a ghetto when his wife mentioned it, and I assumed
that he indeed had been there, managed to escape sometime early in the
war, and ended up in the city of Stavropol in the southern region of Russia,
where he was drafted into the military. His military record states Stavropol
as the place where he was drafted, but his presence in a ghetto is not mentioned. In fact, the form clearly states that Semyon was never in occupied
territory during the war. Such a discrepancy can only mean that Semyon, like
many other escapees or survivors from ghettos, was hiding his experience

from the Soviet government in fear of further persecutions, which were usually imposed on those who had spent any time in German-occupied territory. In this context, his earlier story about changing his patronymic from the decidedly Jewish-sounding "Peysakhovich" into the Russian "Petrovich" gains additional significance, because he was worried not only about being accused of concealing his Jewish nationality but about his wartime past.

Semyon does not blame antisemitism for his inability to obtain the *kandidat* degree. Instead, he portrays his life as a series of his own choices and successes: in practical medicine, rather than theoretical; in publishing his case studies, often with the help of those with advanced medical degrees, rather than difficulties obtaining a medical degree or other persecutions he endured; his outstanding record in patient care rather than harassment and fear from higher-ups. But even Semyon's positive outlook cannot hide the fact that his professional successes would have been greater had he not been a Jew. Although Semyon does not articulate this thought, and perhaps even suppresses it, his testimony cannot but highlight the fact that he, a doctor with unusual initiative, a creative mind and real talent, and a decorated war hero, who worked in a poorly equipped hospital, without access to the newest and latest technology or even up-to-date literature, was unable to train a new generation of Soviet doctors and unable to contribute fully to the field of medical science, all because he happened to be a Jew.

## Loss of Networks

Almost all interviewees formerly employed in medicine emphasized their ability to make friends in their places of work and to find a common language and sympathy from people in various positions of power. Indeed, the significance of microworlds—informal relationships in the Soviet Union— was critical during this period. The quality of life in Soviet society depended significantly on the ability to build and maintain support networks at work and at school, with local governments and with food store managers. In fact, achieving success in a professional career and in family life was impossible without being able to navigate those formal and informal relationships.

Medicine and medical services were vital parts of everyone's microworld. Despite the free medical care that was theoretically available to all Soviet citizens, getting proper treatment in the Soviet Union was often a matter of luck. Problems such as poor quality of training, shortages of medicine and hospital space, and generally insensitive attitudes toward patients among

Soviet medical professionals led to a situation in which getting proper medical care depended significantly on personal connections that family members may have had in the medical field.[15]

Many interviewees discussed the connection between the loss of their positions in the medical profession (demotions or general loss of authority and respect at the workplace) and the inability to provide better (or adequate) medical care for their family members. Sara K. (born in Artemovsk, in the Donetsk Region of Ukraine, in 1924) recalls:

> The Jewish question began for me on January 13, 1953. I lived through a lot as a doctor. I always said, "It's great luck that my father didn't live to see all this." It's impossible to describe. The humiliation was unbearable. I can only tell you that I worked at a very large military hospital. It was a huge deal for a young doctor. I received incredible training there from the old-school doctors. My mother got sick: her lung collapsed. I managed to admit her to this military hospital. When the Jewish question arose, my mother was discharged immediately. I was still working there, as a staff member. It's impossible to talk about this.[16]

We may speculate extensively about the reason for Sara's mother's discharge (assuming that it was in fact done against better medical judgment). It is possible that the chief of staff of the hospital was worried about the accusation of *semeistvennost'*, here meaning family-based corruption at the workplace—a word that quickly began to refer specifically to Jews. Perhaps discharging the mother allowed Sara to keep her job as a young doctor in a very prestigious hospital. The fact that Sara does not blame specific individuals who decided to discharge her mother suggests that perhaps she understood, even then, that the choice was between her career and her ailing mother's quality of life. She did blame the system for forcing her to make this choice.

In Soviet microworlds, it was close to impossible to achieve any professional success without help from friends and family, usually from echelons higher up within the Communist Party. But interviewees almost never directly acknowledged such help in their own careers. In fact, I have almost never heard a story of a Jew in power helping a fellow Jew. Quite to the contrary, numerous stories speak about how such help was expected, or even assumed on the interviewee's part, but never obtained. The son of Evgenii

Shulman (the parasitologist from Fira G.'s story), Gennady Shulman, who was also a medical scientist, published memoirs about himself and his father. He wrote about his difficulties obtaining a job in 1953:

> After I graduated from the university [in 1953], I was faced with a difficult life. Though I was one of the best students, it was obvious I could not stay at the university [as a scientific worker] or work in my specialty. I remember printing about a hundred application letters in which I suggested that I was ready to work in any area of science, even as a technician in a lab. . . . What else could I do? I was surprised that all my letters were answered. Though the form of each response was different, the content was identical: "For you, we have no vacancies." Even my current place of work, the Institute of Biology of the South Seas, where I have been working for forty years, rejected me then. Only one person wanted to hire me. It was Nikolai Evgenyevich Salnikov, who was the director of the Institute of Sea Fishing and Oceanography at the time. I worked there for twelve years.[17]

Gennady Shulman never mentions that he asked for his father's help or even if his father offered it to him. His father, an important doctor and scientist who had name recognition across the Soviet Union, could have made a call, but probably could not have helped his son anyway. My interviewees who held higher positions in medicine all spoke of their inability to hire Jews or to help their relatives find work because of fear of being accused of "creating a synagogue."

One should not be misled, however, into thinking that Jews were fully excluded from informal Soviet networks. Interviewees' stories discuss numerous instances of how they were helped or were able to help others through their positions as working doctors in hospitals and clinics by providing prescriptions for necessary medications and acquiring necessary medicines via hospitals, as opposed to pharmacies, which were always short of supplies. The informal networks also helped in negotiating better care in hospitals, arranging special consultations with the best surgeons and other specialists, allowing extra visitations by family members, and many other unofficial services that were unavailable through official channels, yet often vital. Although being a Jew had an effect on what could be achieved through these networks, it did not prevent or disturb the functionality of many of them.

The mechanism of work in postwar Soviet society, when knowing the "right people" was not a privilege but a necessity for successful social mobility. That Jews were not able to help each other out of fear of being accused of nationalism—even though everyone else was doing so—was a serious disadvantage, which could stop or seriously delay one's professional success.

A third context is the perception of non-Jews. Many of them believed that Jews helped each other, and characterized them as a nation whose members stand up for one another. Even sympathetic scholars have suggested that Jewish mutual help on a higher level was a way for a minority to survive in a larger, generally hostile society.[18] Though the perception of Jews enjoying comfortable positions within the Soviet economic system was prevalent, the perceptions of my interviewees did not concur. Instead, many complained of their inability to use the help of a higher-ranking family member or to help in advancing the career of a relative in need because of the fear of being accused of helping other Jews. In fact, it seems it was easier for a non-Jew to help a Jew, and vice versa, than for Jews to support each other. Essentially, studying experiences of Jewish doctors during the Doctors' Plot reveals how Jewish communal settings were destroyed on three levels: the first occurred on a religious level in the 1920s and 1930s, the second on a physical level in the early 1940s, and the third on a cultural one in the late 1940s. Person-to-person relationships were then crushed in 1953.

# 11

## The Happiest Memories

### Life in the World of Soviet Yiddish Culture

Exactly five years before the Doctor's Plot, on January 13, 1948, the tragic death of Solomon Mikhoels (born Shloyme Vovsi in 1890) shook the world of Soviet Yiddish speakers.[1] Many Jews as well as non-Jews saw the charismatic Solomon Mikhoels, actor, director of the Moscow State Yiddish Theater, and chairman of the Soviet Jewish Anti-Fascist Committee during the war, as the unofficial leader of Soviet Jews. Even at the time of his death, many believed the government secret service had organized the murder. Soon after Mikhoels' death, his colleagues in the Jewish Anti-Fascist Committee and the theater, along with many others, were arrested. On August 12, 1952, twelve of them were secretly shot.[2] Their families found out only four years later, in 1956. During 1949–56, the once thriving Soviet Yiddish public culture was effectively shut down.

But what happened to the thousands of actors, accountants, typists, secretaries, costume designers, directors, cleaning staff, part-time actors, students, and teachers employed by the Yiddish public culture system? How did they survive the period 1948–53, when their bosses, colleagues, and friends were arrested, lost their jobs, and disappeared? How do they remember and talk about this experience?

Because this project takes a special interest in Yiddish language and culture, I specifically sought and found living members of the Soviet Yiddish public sphere. I interviewed four teachers from Soviet Yiddish schools (born between 1900 and 1910), three former actors in regional Yiddish theaters, four students of the Soviet Jewish drama school affiliated with the Moscow State Yiddish Theater, two typists from Soviet Yiddish periodicals, and three Yiddish writers. I expected to hear trauma stories, tales of disillusionment, disappointment, and above all, fear.

Instead, the former Yiddish professionals accounted for the most cheerful and optimistic, and least bitter, narratives. Unlike most other narrators, they did not speak much about antisemitism (unless their children experienced it). They did not see their Jewish ethnicity as a liability or disability. Instead, they told stories of Jewish culture empowering and protecting them and giving them pride. For example, they referred to Yiddish theaters of the 1930s as institutions that provided employment and other support for dekulakized Jews.[3] Interviewees who chose to work in the field of Yiddish culture before 1948 are the only ones who spoke about interests and preferences that influenced their professional choices (rather than circumstances alone). Maya D. (born in Chervonnoye, in the Zhitomir region of Ukraine, in 1928) described how she decided between studying at a medical institute or the drama school at the Moscow State Yiddish Theater:

The war was over, I was discharged [from the army]. In Moscow, on Pirogovka Street, there was a large billboard of announcements. Open for admission. . . I saw calls for students at the First Medical Institute and at the Jewish Drama School. I had the right to enter any institute without an exam because I was discharged from the military.

I came home and told my papa about the situation. He said, "You know, you have a lot in you of all that." But we sang a lot at home. Papa played piano well, he had a beautiful voice, which he got from his father. He sang lots of Jewish songs and opera songs. He said, "If your heart wants it, go there."

My mother was completely against it. She said, "Go to medical school, you were born a doctor." Indeed, when my father was sick, I took care of him and gave him injections.

But I chose the Jewish theater school. I entered, I couldn't read or speak well. The male students surrounded me. I was dressed in a military uniform, my waist wrapped in a belt. They took me to their dorm and wrote down Sholem Aleichem's story "Di Gens (The Geese)" with Russian letters. I learned it by heart. I also prepared a poem by Krylov and a Hebrew lullaby, *Ben Yakir* [dear son], I knew that song from home. The students suggested to me, "You know, you should sing it, because this is of value now, no one knows the ancient Jewish language now." No one knew Hebrew there, but I knew that song because my father used to always sing me that Hebrew lullaby.

Then, in Sholem Aleichem's story "Di Gens," there is a passage, which is translated as, "Do you think this is a bald spot? But this is a bald patch!" And my examiners were both bald. I had no idea who they were, but I improvised and pointed at them. Later, I realized these were Mikhoels and [Venyomin] Zuskin [an actor at the Moscow State Yiddish Theater, a film actor, a celebrity][4]. All the students and all the people in the audience laughed and applauded. In short, I passed, and Mikhoels accepted me into his master class.[5]

Many details of this testimony are hard to verify (or believe). First, entrance exams were not conducted in front of an audience of students. Therefore, the comment could not have provoked laughter from students in the audience. Second, Maya D. herself explained that she simply memorized the pronunciation of the Yiddish language story *Di Gens* (Geese, written by Sholem Aleichem in 1902) by writing it down with Russian letters. Therefore, her knowledge of Yiddish was not sufficient to internalize the text and improvise with an audience of her examiners. On the other hand, she quoted accurately from the Yiddish text during the interview, and it is clear she did not read the story recently. Therefore, the quoted segment probably includes some imagined narrative, one that Maya (correctly) thought would impress an interviewer interested in Yiddish culture.

Considering this, it is even more significant that she does not mention her Jewish ethnicity in the story of choosing a career in Yiddish theater. Instead what she spoke about were her personal preferences and the advice from her family that had to do with her personal skills. After the drama school was closed, Maya held odd jobs, playing minor parts in Moscow theaters, and finally becoming a dry cleaning clerk in Moscow. In the testimony, she repeatedly discussed her friendship with Soviet celebrities, including those from her theater days. During the conversation, she repeatedly presented herself as idealistic, not pragmatic, and also not materialistic. Her choice of telling a story about Yiddish theaters illustrated these qualities, as opposed to emphasizing her involvement or interest in Judaism.

Yet all speculation aside, this testimony contributes to our understanding of the processes of career choices in 1946–48. She had to decide between a Jewish drama school and a medical school, and her choice was quite valid in 1946; in 1948, she would most likely have picked medical school.

Yiddish theaters had essentially replaced synagogues in their roles as community centers for Jews.[6] During the war, the situation changed, as theaters became centers of hope for the survival of Jews in the midst of destruction. But in 1948–49, professional association with Yiddish theaters became quite dangerous. Mariya Kotliarova (born in Ekaterinopol, Ukraine, in 1918), a Moscow State Yiddish Theater actress, wrote about the period between the death of Solomon Mikhoels and the theater's official closure in 1949:

> After Mikhoels' funeral, quietness arrived. We still played the shows, but there was some sort of a dark quiet in the theater. Even people who liked to talk were silent. People understood that all this was not an accident. Only the bravest still attended the essentially empty theater.
>
> Contrary to what people thought, it was not simply destruction. It was worse, and scarier—innocent people were sentenced to a slow extermination. Salaries weren't paid. Infrequently, we were paid five or ten rubles. Led by Zuskin, the administration decided to attract the public with subscriptions. We sold them among our friends and acquaintances. But after buying the subscriptions, people didn't show up in the theater. How could they? The rumor was that the theater was being monitored, and everyone who attended was recorded for future imprisonment. Who would risk it?[7]

Kotliarova identifies the situation of uncertainty for theater workers, combined with financial strains, fears, and isolation from her closest friends as the difficulties of 1948. However, her writing does not mention expressions of antisemitism. In fact, in both her memoirs and a personal interview, she focused on fear, jealousy, and the bravery and generosity of her colleagues (all of whom were Jews) and of her superiors (also Jews). She did not spend any time on the antisemitic remarks of friends, neighbors, tram conductors, or people standing in line, stories that are common in other testimonies. For Kotliarova, her work in the Yiddish world was not associated with fighting with non-Jews for equality and recognition. Instead, her career is a story of the fight for survival of Yiddish culture among Jews.

Unlike people who worked in non-Jewish environments, the workers in Yiddish theaters do not associate the "black years" with the painful discovery of their own ethnic identity. Ironically, they were the only interviewees who did not speak of 1948–53 as the darkest chapter in Soviet Jewish history. Instead, they spoke of the aftermath of Stalin's death as the time when they began to experience antisemitism. Consider a testimony by Vera L. (born in 1925 in Kyiv, Ukraine), a performer of Yiddish songs and the widow of Moisei Shulman (1911–1994), a Yiddish and Hebrew linguist. In 1948, Moisei (Monia) Shulman worked for the Jewish Anti-Fascist Committee, while Vera was a student at the Jewish theater studio, studying under Solomon Mikhoels. This is how she chose to speak about this period:

My husband spent four years fighting in the war. In 1947, he came to work at the Anti-Fascist Committee, in *Eynikayt*. This was after he finished fighting the Japanese war.[8] When I was in my fourth year of studying in *Eynikayt*, they often held concerts. I performed there a few times.

Once I got a phone call, and they asked me to come and pick up a newspaper where my picture had been published from one of the concerts. I arrived and met Monia. He was twelve years older than me. I was already dating someone else, but I really liked him. In addition to being very handsome, he was also very smart, intellectually developed, well read, he attracted people. You remember, right?[9] Young people liked him very much. We lived together for forty-seven years. He had very weak bones for the last three years, and suffered a lot.

How much we worried during the arrests... When *Eynikayt* was closed, he had no place to work. He stayed at home. He joined the [Anti-Fascist] committee late, only in 1947. In 1948, the arrests began. Also, he didn't have an easygoing personality. He argued with someone there and gave notice to leave his position in the Committee. He got a phone call on a Sunday. They asked him to come to the office. They never called on Sundays. He and someone else, [Misha] Lev, I think, went into the office. They came and saw a search going on. Later, when it was all over, they locked the doors, and announced, "That's it. No one is working here anymore." That's how he became unemployed. Later, he found a job as a proofreader. By the way, he was an expert not only in Yiddish, but also in Russian.

During sessions of the Supreme Council, or a Party Congress, he was always invited to proofread scripts, because he was the most literate person there.

After some time, he was hired by a Builders Union for their magazine. One Russian journalist said, "Finally, our magazine speaks Russian." That was because Monia was hired.

As for me, in 1948, I was in possession of a Mikhoels diploma. The theater was closed; everyone was arrested. But before that, the theater flourished. Why? Stalin was so mad when all the foreigners, Jews and non-Jews, asked to see the theater before any other sites. In our school, we had a wonderful atmosphere. We experienced nothing short of a renaissance. It was in both Jewish culture and Russian culture. [Evgenii] Evtushenko, [Andrei] Voznesenskii, [Robert] Rozhdestvenskii, [Yulia] Drunina, there were many wonderful poets who came to read for us.

I decided to go to Shchepkin's [Drama] School at the Malyi Theater. [Mikhail] Tsarev[10] was not there, Shashkova[11] was conducting exams. I know this is for the record, and her daughter can hear me say it, but Shashkova was an antisemite. She said to me, "Yes, we will admit you, but we won't pay you a stipend."

I said, "My husband is out of work. How will we survive?" So I was accepted without a stipend. I was of course disappointed, especially since I heard that someone said I had read the best. Then I met Tsarev. I was very shy, but it was an impossible situation. I approached him and said, "Mikhail Ivanovich, I graduated from Jewish Theater school." People say he was an antisemite, but he wasn't. Not to me, anyway.

So, he said, "Let me hear you." And I read my repertoire to him, *Mtsyri* by Lermontov, *Barbarians* by Gorky, all of it. He asked me to step out. I stepped out and waited.

Then his students who were there, came out, surrounded me, and told me, "You know, Mikhail Ivanovich really liked you."

He said, "I will make a reader [performer] out of her." And then I was accepted with the largest stipend. And I finished graduate school with the largest stipend too. It was very rare then. What helped me was that everyone knew Mikhoels and Zuskin, and respected their acting. I was their student, and it was all a breeze.

When I graduated from the institute [in 1951], I got an "unrestricted placement." Do what you want. But that was a horrific time. Antisemitism became wild, literally wild. It was impossible to get [a job] anywhere. In general, it was hard for actors to find work, even during normal times. When I came to the office of the minister [of culture] for help, he told me,

"There are as many of you as stray dogs." I remembered that phrase my entire life. I was terrified.

In 1953, I got lucky, as I somehow registered with the Soviet Bureau of Traveling Artists.[12] One day—I had just came back from a gig—I got a phone call inviting me to go to another one. Usually, I got one or two days of rest, so I said I was tired and refused. But then I was curious and asked, "Who's the artist?" "Lidiya Ruslanova."[13] "A-ah, then I'll go." "We want to warn you, she doesn't like anyone, so she might just send you away." I said, "Fine." I loved Ruslanova. No, I adored her. When I was little, I loved her singing, and try to imitate her. I knew all her songs by heart. . . .

We became friends. We talked every evening. She had been interrogated in jail every day until 3 a.m., so she got used to not sleeping. And she liked company when she was up. She kept me up too, with stories. The stories were so interesting that I simply couldn't leave. She would shame me: "You don't know what Passover is? You don't know how to celebrate? Aren't you ashamed of yourself?"

I'd say, "Lidiya Andreevna, no one celebrated with us, no one believed. God forbid, if someone had found out. They'd get us." She would say, "Yes, of course." But she was Garkavi's wife.[14] Garkavi's father was an Orthodox Jew, and he would teach them [during Passover]: you sit on the left, you sit on the right. She would tell me about how they got the *kashes* [were asked the Four Questions], and all those other things. She also learned a little Yiddish. When Shulman met me after work, she'd ask him questions in Yiddish. Can you imagine? Nobody would believe that.

Instead, I hear people saying that she was an antisemite. What antisemite? How can they? She told me that even though she loved Kryukov[15] madly, but no one understood her better than Garkavi, no one. And who helped her? Another Jew. Victor Ardov.[16] He sent her money. He wasn't scared. Garkavi was scared to help her when she was in jail, but he wasn't. He sent money and books to her in jail.

I never experienced that. I was blonde. I had a long nose, but Russians can also have long noses. But you know, I've never looked like one. I had grey eyes. When I heard those conversations, I would jump and people would apologize, say they didn't know. I had something Jewish inside me. I always felt I was a Jew, but I didn't feel I had been oppressed.[17]

This story deals with the termination of the Jewish Anti-Fascist Committee, the closing of the Jewish Theater School, and subsequent unemployment. However, it mentions antisemitism only in connection with looking for a job as an actor in a Russian theater in 1951. Moreover, involvement in the Yiddish industry is presented as an important asset even in those difficult circumstances. Vera emphasized how respected Mikhoels and Zuskin were and how their authority helped her in a career outside of the Yiddish world.

When Vera spoke of her husband's work at the Jewish Anti-Fascist Committee, she mentioned his "difficult personality," but not the stigma that could have surrounded a career in a Jewish organization in the 1940s. Moreover, like Kotliarova in speaking about Mikhoels' impeccable command of Russian, Vera discusses at length her husband's knowledge of Russian, his ability to proofread Russian texts, and his authority in the field of Russian philology. This emphasis is a signal to the listener that working in Yiddish culture and with the Yiddish language was a choice, not a necessity. The story contradicts the stigma of Yiddish actors being accused of "shtetl-like," vulgar, low-culture performances, and of being "borderline amateurs." The prestige associated with being a Yiddish actor was much lower than that of actors performing in Russian. However, none of these difficulties appeared in the testimonies of former Yiddish actors. Instead, they present Yiddish as a choice; they emphasized their versatility in both mainstream and Jewish spheres.

In Vera's story, antisemitism plays an important role. She attributes her problems in getting into Russian drama school to the antisemitism of V. S. Shashkova, the director of the school. At the same time, she praises Mikhail Tsarev (the director of the Malyi Theater in the 1950s) for going against the system and admitting her on merit with a scholarship. She also mentions rumors of Tsarev's antisemitism, and in showing that those rumors were false, she stresses that he was not hostile to her personally. Importantly, even though the testimony acknowledges the existence of an atmosphere and actual policies of discrimination, she attributes the real harm or good done to her to actions by individuals, out of their individual convictions, rather than following (or not following) the system itself.

In this context, the question of the Jewish reaction to discrimination, both perceived and real, deserves attention. Neither Vera nor any other interviewees, even those from the field of Yiddish professional work, spoke about instances when Jews helped other Jews in trouble (with the exception of Mikhoels and Zuskin admitting her to the drama school). Instead, they spoke about heroic and unusual non-Jews, who risked a great deal to help them as they suffered from antisemitism. Full of fascinating anecdotes of Soviet life of the 1950s, the story of Vera's work with Lidiya Ruslanova, one of the most important singers in the Soviet Union, provides a detailed narrative that suggests that Jews in power were able to help other people in trouble. Victor Ardov, a Russian writer of Jewish origin, was not afraid to send parcels to Ruslanova when she was in prison. Mikhail Garkavi, Ruslanova's first husband, understood her better than the Russian general Kryukov, her second husband. It is just that the Jewish characters in testimonies never seem to help each other.

Significantly, Vera presents her Jewishness positively. Despite stories of antisemitism, which affected both her career and her husband's, Vera did not talk about being Jewish as a misfortune, but instead characterized it as something to be proud of. In fact, Ruslanova, the "mentor" of the story, shames her for not being *more* Jewish. The non-Jewish singer celebrity teaches the young Jewish woman how to celebrate Jewish holidays and speak Yiddish and discusses Jewish solidarity and self-support. In other words, she instills positive feelings about being a Jew, as opposed to all the other non-Jewish mentors, who usually advised their colleagues to hide their Jewish nationality. Jewish culture is presented as a source of inspiration, resilience, courage, and even resistance to the Soviet regime.

Having said that, Vera still operates in the ecosystem of Soviet perceptions of Jews. She does speak about her non-Jewish looks as an asset, for example, but rather often refers to antisemitism as "that." She also talks about people being falsely accused of being antisemites (similarly to the testimony about other "mentors"). Presumably, such an accusation can only come from other Jews, and it is important for her to prove them wrong. In other words, she speaks positively of Jewishness, but somewhat negatively of other Jews.

Why were the former Yiddish activists the most optimistic and happy of all interviewees, independent of the country where they were interviewed? Perhaps because all of them were in demand at the time of the interview, despite their advanced age: Maria Kotliarova regularly worked as a consultant for major music shows, a university lecturer, and a performer until her final days, in 2008. Shimon Sandler worked on revisions of his textbook on Yiddish language and lectured around Moscow. In fact, he gave a detailed interview just two weeks before his death in 2002. Vera L. frequently performed in Russian and Yiddish, gave many interviews, and consulted for Hillel and other Jewish organizations. Ida V. ran her own Russian Jewish and Yiddish theater in Philadelphia, where she also performed major roles. Maya D. organized evenings of Jewish songs in Berlin. Maria Ch. was a consultant for Yiddish performances in New York. Among all the interviewees, the former Yiddish professionals were the only ones earning an income. Their professional involvement in Soviet Yiddish culture enabled them to be "authority holders" in the world of Yiddish, and their cultural currency was still in use.

## Being Jewish at Work: A Disability, an Obstacle, and an Asset

Independent of their profession, each interviewee emphasized that their abilities to find common ground with people and earn their respect, which helped them to survive. "*Ko mne horosho khorosho otnosilis'*" (People liked me) is a phrase used by almost everyone, and it usually appears for the first time in the context of a workplace in the late 1940s. I found it striking that despite being aware of Soviet policies that discriminated against Jews, narrators uniformly blamed personal antisemitic behavior by their potential and actual employers, when discussing being fired or not being able to obtain a job. It remains to be seen whether this phenomenon illustrates an overall belief in the "good" Soviet system with "bad individuals" making unfair decisions, or if it illustrates the process of how people speak talk about surviving a traumatic situation for over which they had no control (similar to how Holocaust survivors recall a sequence of events in which they could not take responsibility for their actions, but present them as if they did).[18]

Within professional occupations, certain patterns appeared as well. Teachers especially wanted to spend the most time speaking talking about the compromises and unfair choices of other Jews, hinting at their own uncomfortable decisions. Medical doctors presented a less controversial version of the late 1940s. They recalled patients who were afraid of them, and bosses who fired or harassed them, but they also remembered their own successes to a larger extent than teachers, and importantly, did not bad-mouth their senior colleagues, but instead spoke of them with awe and respect. This difference can be explained by the fact that doctors stood on a relatively high level in microworlds and personal networks. Even the limitations of the Doctors' Plot did not decrease their self-esteem and the way they understood their role in Soviet society.

Teachers, on the other hand, enjoyed very little professional respect in Soviet society and were usually on the lowest level of these informal networks. The only exception consisted of teachers who sat on admission committees of universities. However, I did not interview any of them, so I cannot test the hypothesis by comparing to their stories. The stories of Yiddish cultural workers, the only interviewees whom I actively solicited, are, ironically, the least useful in a historical context, because they are so influenced by their successful and exciting present work, that their testimonies do not provide information on discrimination that they might have experienced in the Soviet society. Were people afraid of them? Did they receive help in secret? These questions remain unanswered, and probably await a different approach or another angle.

People working in the trade and manual skilled manual labor suffered almost as much as academics in the humanities, but tended to be cheerful and spoke of this time with a larger greater degree of nostalgia than others. This was probably happened because they had disproportionally lost their parents in the Great Terror, or survived the Holocaust in ghettos, so to them, these events represented a lesser trauma. And their hierarchy in microworlds was even higher than that of doctors, as they had access to goods that everyone wanted, and were able to trade those goods for almost any service that they needed.

Overall, all interviewees who started their careers in the 1930s were more traumatized by the arrests of their family members in 1937–1939 than by the discrimination of 1948–1953, because the latter was more about involved verbal abuse, or firing, but not jail. However, the people who began working in the late 1940s remember 1948-1953 as their largest greatest trauma, the one that continued to influence them throughout their professional lives, and affected how they related to colleagues and professional contacts.

In the realm of Soviet Jewish daily life, oral histories uncover the evolution of the Jewish role in microworlds and networks in the 1940s and early 1950s. By the mid-1930s, traditional Jewish networks based on religious institutions, such as schools and mutual aid societies, were destroyed and stopped playing a role in the lives of a majority of Jews. New Soviet Jewish institutions, such as Yiddish schools, theaters, trade unions, and the press, did not help to maintain the community, but were designed to educate Yiddish-speaking Jews about the Soviet regime. The identity and culture that they fostered did not encourage group solidarity, but instead aimed to instill pride in belonging to a larger "family" of Soviet people.

In the early 1940s, the Jewish Anti-Fascist Committee was not created to help the domestic Jewish community in crisis, but instead was designed to raise money and awareness for the Soviet fight against Nazi Germany among the Western Jewish population. And while some surviving Yiddish theaters remained de- facto community centers until the mid-1940s, they did not consolidate Jews into working professional and personal networks. Even when the Jewish Anti-Fascist Committee was destroyed in 1948, that event did not affect the personal lives of most Jews. However, the government-sponsored discrimination policies that followed did. Already severely damaged by the war, with 2.7 million of Jewish dead, the Jewish community received a strong blow in 1953, during the Doctors' Plot, when mutual help among Jews was labeled *semeistvennost'*, and became an object of ridicule and persecution. In effect, the events of that year had a tremendous impact on Jewish life for the next forty 40 years, because even though the doctors were acquitted and released, the fear and stigma of Jewish *semeistvennost'* prevailed in Soviet society until the very collapse of the Soviet Union.

Interviewees of all professions living in all countries involved in the study did not speak often about the help they received from other Jews in their professional lives, and did not speak about the help that they themselves provided for other Jews. Instead, they spoke of failed attempts to do so in the 1950s, and how these attempts taught them about the dangers of remaining part of a Jewish community in the Soviet Union. The interviewees internalized this idea to such an extent that many are still suspicious of any organized Jewish groups, even in the United States, where they benefit from such support to the largest greatest extent.

The second impact of the events of the early 1950s is that interviewees became mistrustful of other Jews. Having experienced many restrictions in their careers, and having had to compromise their integrity and values in order to obtain necessities or luxury objects, they instantly began to understand that a person who has had all these privileges *despite* being a Jew must have done something to betray others or take advantage of them. Instead of expressing pride in the successes of other Soviet Jews, many speculated on what terrible things they or their parents had to do in order to achieve this level of success. In other words, Jewish solidarity ceased to become a part of Soviet Jewish culture and subjectivity.

# Epilogue

## Soviet Jewish Oral Histories:
## Past and Future

Human memory tends to preserve the details of most significant decisions, and the process of life review helps them talking about these choices. Falling in love, starting a career, giving birth to children, succeeding professionally are exciting and memorable moments for anyone. Later in life, they translate into a captivating story of coming of age, making decisions, overcoming obstacles, and becoming a mature and successful individual. Soviet Jews born in the 1920s went through these milestones when their country went through difficult social and political upheavals: the bloodiest war and a traumatic postwar transition filled with openly antisemitic legislation and practices.

The personal stories of Russian Jews do not answer many questions about their personalities. Did their experiences make them stronger or weaker? Kinder or tougher? We will probably never know for sure. But one thing the accounts prove with a degree of certainty is that the personal successes and failures of interviewees strongly depended on their being born Jewish, or, more specifically, on their not being able to hide their Jewish origins because of the mandatory record of nationality in their internal passports. Stories of being Jewish can be described as quests or wonder tales of overcoming Jewishness as an obstacle, beating it as one beats a disease, succeeding despite being burdened by misfortune. Only Yiddish cultural workers were unapologetically proud of their ethnicity, but even they could not avoid pointing out instances of being victims to oppression, restrictions, and hardships.

In fact, over and over interviewees seem to provide thick narratives of adaptation in their lives in Canada, United States, Germany, and post-Soviet Russia. Former engineers interviewed in New York spoke at length of the Jewish leadership in their workplace, those in Berlin stressed the unexpected "synagogue-like" nature of their research institute, those interviewed in Canada focused on antisemitism, and those interviewed in Moscow elaborated on their contributions to Soviet society. Similarly, doctors interviewed in Moscow tended to downplay the popular effect of the Doctors' Plot, whereas those interviewed in Germany talked about the cowardliness of their Jewish and non-Jewish colleagues; those interviewed in the United States emphasized their personal ability to overcome the difficulties and hostile atmosphere of the Doctors' Plot. Overall, it is safe to say that an experienced oral historian can link almost everything that interviewees say to their current circumstances. In fact, I believe that my study will help to increase our knowledge of how older people perceive immigration and the change of political regime.[1]

But is this enough? Does a close textual reading of these testimonies, combined with contextual analysis, preclude their potential to contribute to our understanding of the historical processes described in these accounts? And if it does not, can the information from testimonies be used more broadly than self-representation or even the creation and evolution of the ethnic identity of the interviewees?

There are no easy answers to these questions. However, why dismiss a wealth of knowledge provided by people who lived through a historical period which left so few reliable documents? To use an example from a closely related field, where would Holocaust history be today without utilizing testimonies? Would we be at all aware of the experiences of the victims? Similarly, in the context of Soviet Jewish history, the limitations of the oral history sources can actually increase their value for historians. If one can verify historical facts and scrutinize interviewees' contemporary situations, as all responsible oral historians do, it is possible to uncover details of the daily life of the past that are simply unavailable in other sources, and it is a professional responsibility to preserve and analyze these sources at a time when it is still possible to verify this information.

In studying Soviet Jewish history, it is impossible to separate family stories from stories of work life, especially in discussing the period of the mid-1940s to the mid-1950s. In fact, stories of family lives and choosing a life partner usually have an equal amount of information related to professional lives, and stories devoted to work deal as much if not more with families. The nature of interdependency shifted a few times during the 1930s and early 1950s, but the connection between the two was never broken or weakened.

In the 1930s, being Jewish played a less significant role in choosing both a spouse and a place to study or work. The generation that come of age during this time dealt with bigger problems—loss of their parents in the Great Terror, famine, poverty, changes in socioeconomic positions, a shortage of living space, and more. Those who had a strong extended family network— aunts, uncles, grandparents, and cousins who lived in larger cities—fared better than those who had to rely on government institutions alone. Those with stronger family networks had the luxury of choosing an occupation that they wanted, rather than what was available, but even in their cases, they tended to think of starting their careers based on convenient circumstances rather than callings.

Similarly, getting married in the 1930s did not involve a wedding or, often, even parental consent. Jewish tradition, discrimination against Jews, or even the very word "Jew" did not enter wedding stories when discussing the 1930s unless interviewees were prompted. When they were, all they could talk about was their grandparents' attempts to retain their lifestyle associated with Jewish tradition. For my interviewees, who were young in the late 1930s, to be Jewish meant to be "old," even backward and outmoded.

Between 1941 and 1945, Jewish families became much smaller. Grandparents were the first to go, more reluctant to evacuate and more likely to be left behind. They were starved in ghettos, sunk in wells, shot in ravines, and otherwise murdered. So was almost everyone else who stayed behind, those not eligible for the draft or who could not make it to an evacuation train. Those who served in the army spent a great deal of their waking moments looking for family members, writing letters, and sending formal requests and informal inquiries, more often than not, destined to find out the devastating truth: they had lost their immediate and extended family members, who helped them live and survive in the 1930s.[2]

The luckiest Soviet Jews spent those years in Central Asia and Siberia. Most often, they were too young to serve in the army, or too valuable alive to be drafted. They too did not have it easy: starvation, disease, and difficult living conditions accompanied their lives in evacuation. Most worked extremely long hours, often under duress. However, some had opportunities to benefit from the unprecedented concentration of evacuated factories, research institutes, cultural institutions, and human resources, all grouped in small areas which welcomed evacuees and refugees. The presence of a family member evacuated to the same area as the desired place of work or study was an important factor in choosing a professional career, but not as important as in the 1930s. Still, family ties remained strong, and the grief for the loss of the family even stronger.

When the war was over, Jewish family and work values began to change again, and once more, not on their own initiative. Broken by the war and the loss of their families, Jewish army veterans were perceived to be less desirable as husbands, both male and female Jewish Holocaust survivors hid their past, and former evacuees tended to stick with each other. Mutual trust among Jews was shattered, which created difficulties in choosing a spouse and building families. Still euphoric from the Soviet victory, a little drunk from the sheer fact of survival, yet devastated by the loss of their families, Soviet Jews born in the 1920s rushed into work and study. Educated specialists were in huge demand, universities accepted war veterans without exams, and opportunities seemed unlimited. The future promised to be better.

In 1948, things changed again, almost radically. The government's discriminatory policies, which first concerned workers in Jewish cultural institutions, then elite physicians, gradually spread into every Soviet workplace. Some people dealt with this stoically, others complained, and still others protested and resisted. But none, not even the most powerful, were able to accomplish what their relatives had done for them in the 1930s: help find jobs for their own children, let alone nephews and nieces. Family connections, so treasured after the war, became useless in professional worlds and ultimately put Jews at a disadvantage. The compensation came from family's private lives. Celebrations of Jewish milestones, such as weddings, made an unexpected comeback, with people organizing quiet religious ceremonies, hosting celebratory dinners with Jewish food and Yiddish music. These weddings marked the creation of Jewish families where the word "Jewish" would not be spoken out loud and where every effort would be made to diminish the trauma of being born Jewish, something that these children were destined to experience at their workplaces.

The circle closed. In the 1930s, without family support one could not leave the shtetl and succeed in jumping into the next socioeconomic level. Being Jewish did not seem significant, either in the creation of one's own family or in choosing an appealing career path. By the early 1950s, being Jewish had become a professional liability, and using family connections became a crime. Out of this juxtaposition grew a new Jewish identity, one that began to associate being born Jewish with misfortune.

Can this identity live without antisemitism? Can it live without communism? Can it be meaningful as Jewish?[3] These are the questions that sociologists, social scientists, historians, and literary scholars ask, but so do Jewish activists all over the world. Unexpectedly for scholars, and inconveniently for Western Jewish community leaders, the answer is unapologetically "yes." Not only did the Soviet Jewish identity not disappear after the collapse of the Soviet Union, it became stronger and developed into a culture, fully equipped with markers of thick identity, complete with its language (Russian), foods (Russian and Jewish, but not kosher), rituals (which combine Judaism, Christianity, and the Soviet legacy), and notions of a shared past and values. Soviet-born Russian Jewish identity is alive and well, more than two decades after the collapse of the Soviet Union and 25 years after Russian Jews began to settle around the globe.

Moreover, as the results of the 2013 PEW Survey of Judaism and Jewish Identity in the United States suggest, American Jews define themselves increasingly similarly to how Soviet-born Jews do, with a decreased emphasis on religion and an increased attention on awareness of one's roots. Zvi Gitelman, the author of the Russian Jewish "thin identity" concept, published an article in the *Forward* with the title "Are We All Russian Jews Now?"[4] In other words, it looks as if Russian Jewish identity, which seemed marginal and "thin" twenty years ago, is quickly becoming a mainstream way of how Jews understand being Jewish in the United States.

The stories of my interviewees therefore constitute the foundational myth of this new identity, and should be studied as such: as unexpected, but valid, narratives of the birth of new definitions of what it means to be a Jew. In a few decades, it will probably be impossible to speak about Jewish history without mentioning Soviet Jewish survival of the Stalin years, just as we cannot imagine today's Jewish history without mentioning the expulsion of Jews from Spain in 1492, the pogroms in tsarist Russia, the Holocaust, or the creation of the state of Israel. Soviet Jewish participation in World War II is already on its way to becoming part of mainstream culture in Israel, with a special permanent exhibit devoted to it in the Yad Vashem Museum.[5] In the United States and Canada, serious efforts are being made to preserve, commemorate, and honor Soviet Jewish war veterans.[6] The story of the postwar Soviet persecutions of Jews will eventually be considered a story of Jewish resistance and will attain ritualistic thickness.

The process is not a smooth one and is certainly still fluid. In fact, the Russian Jewish community has not yet worked out an acceptable narrative for the Soviet Jewish story. Some things are still only mentioned in private and cannot be repeated to larger audiences. I want to illustrate this point with two concluding anecdotes, both glimpses into the future.

In June 2014, I was invited to speak at Bar Ilan University to members of Soviet Jewish veterans' organizations, including memorial museums, whose members were born in the 1930s (most of them were not actual veterans, but they belonged to the organization anyway). During the lecture, I read some parts of my interviews that discussed dealing with Jews serving in the army and a little about the antisemitic oppressions of 1948–53. After I finished (reading the quote, not my lecture), many members of the audience began shouting, "What a bunch of lies!" "It wasn't so!" "It didn't happen!" I was barely able to finish the talk. After the lecture, angry listeners lined up to explain what was wrong with the quotes, how they remembered things differently, and how their parents told them completely different stories about that same period. These stories did not include narratives of compromise, adjustment, playing the system, and making the best out of it. Instead these were stories of integrity, refusal to compromise, and almost uniform suffering. It became very clear to me during that exchange that the narratives from my interviews were not ready-made foundational myths of the new culture. They needed to be adjusted and transformed to become a legacy.

After my return to Canada, I had a glimpse into this transformation. On August 12, 2014, I was invited to give a lecture at an event commemorating the anniversary of the murders of Soviet Yiddish writers in 1952. The event took place at a Russian restaurant in the northern part of Toronto, in a neighborhood heavily populated by Russian speakers. The audience was mixed; I recognized some of my interviewees, accompanied by their grown children and grandchildren. Also in attendance were local, non-Russian politicians: the city councilman from my district, a local MP, the deputy mayor of Vaughan (a Toronto suburb), and representatives of the Israeli consulate. Some leaders of the Toronto Jewish community came, too. The food served was unapologetically Russian (buckets with caviar), but also Israeli (feta and watermelon salad) and Jewish (gefilte fish).

The event started with a minute of silence to commemorate the murdered Yiddish writers, followed by my lecture, in which I spoke about postwar antisemitism (I toned it down, after the experience in Bar Ilan so that no one would yell at me). After the lecture, there was a musical program of Yiddish oldies performed by a group of Soviet Jewish retirees, followed by a violinist playing music from *Fiddler on the Roof* and a young singer performing Israeli favorites, including "Jerusalem of Gold." All members of the audience could relate to something in this event—they felt the sense of belonging and community of which they spoke when interviewed by journalists from both Russian- and English-language Jewish newspapers. It occurred to me then that I was witnessing the process of integration of Soviet Jewish heritage into Canadian Jewish culture, and that the public versions of the stories of my interviewees, sitting in this room, surrounded by both their families and their new Canadian neighbors, are becoming the stories of the global Jewish community and identity, and I have learned (and now my readers have too) about how this came to be.

# Appendix 1: Methodology

I began looking for interviewees in New York by contacting relatives and friends of people I knew and asking them if they had grandparents who suited my criteria—people needed to be born before 1928 and identify themselves as Jews. After that, I contacted friends and relatives of these interviewees, a way of accumulating data known as the snowball method. In order to diversify the pool of interviewees, I participated in a few events organized by and for elderly Russian Jews and invited them personally to tell their stories. I then sat with random people on benches in Brighton Beach in Brooklyn, New York, and approached strangers walking in Brooklyn parks if they looked the right age and spoke Russian. I camped out in the building of the Russian Jewish Community Center at the Shorefront Community Center in Brooklyn and sat in synagogues which I knew were popular among the Russian elderly. But the most enthusiastic narrators came through the Russian-language announcements I placed in local newspapers, which invited any Yiddish speaker born in the Soviet Union before 1928 to tell me about their life so that they could help me write a book on Soviet Jewish culture. I also told them they would receive a copy of the transcript for them to give to their children. Eager responses to the ad filled my voicemail, and kept it full to the limit for months. It led to about a hundred interviews with random strangers, all willing to tell their story.

In Moscow, I approached people with requests for interviews while I worked with a charity kitchen sponsored by the Joint Distribution Committee. In addition, one of the organizations that provided medical help to the Jewish elderly shared its client list with me, and I called each person to request an interview (approximately three-quarters wanted to talk to me). In Berlin, I worked with a nursing home that catered to elderly Russian Jews, as well as with the Jewish Community Center. Its social worker, Ella Shakhnikova, personally called people and asked whether they wanted to be interviewed (about 90 percent wanted to tell me the story of their lives). After that, I used the snowball method again with each interviewee.

Shakhnikova's personal endorsement of the project played a crucial role in the success of the German-based part of the interview project. I also attended events run by the local Soviet World War II veterans' association in Potsdam, where I met both leaders and participants of the movement. The activities of this organization inspired a long article on the topic,[1] but as usual, the most interesting information came from in-depth interviews with the members, which were conducted in their homes.

Finally, in Toronto, where I live, I put an announcement in a local Russian newspaper, where I invited people who survived the war in the Soviet interior to tell me their life story. Although I originally collected these interviews for my forthcoming book on Soviet Jewish wartime experiences, I used the material for this book as well, because most of the interviews came from members of the generation born in the 1920s or earlier in the Soviet Union.

Only 68 of the interviewees could handle the entire interview in Yiddish. Still, many others spoke in Yiddish for more than half of the interview. In addition, many people with a weaker knowledge of the language chose to speak about some issues in Yiddish, and many inserted Yiddish words and expressions where they thought it necessary. Inspired by the experience of Yiddish ethnographers such as Rakhmiel Peltz, I encouraged interviewees to speak as much Yiddish as possible, sometimes asking them questions in Yiddish, in hopes that the sound of the language would trigger memories associated with their childhood, and thus with the period that most interested me.[2] This technique probably prompted my interviewees to speak about Jewish aspects of their lives in more detail than if they had been questioned in Russian.[3]

The transnational approach, the fact that it took ten years to conduct all of the interviews, as well as evolving interests and agendas, could not but affect the nature of the data. In 1999, the initial goal was to find out whether the respondents could remember anything from Yiddish popular culture of the 1930s. In 2001, when I travelled to Germany and Russia, I revised my expectations and approaches, matured in interviewing techniques, and added broader, more open-ended questions that concerned Jewish daily life during the entire span of respondents' memories. By 2008, when I began interviewing in Canada, I had generally given up on asking specific questions, opting instead to simply ask people to speak to what *they* thought was relevant to Jewish life in the Soviet Union. Occasionally, I directed them, but only when I felt that would help me to understand the gaps in their testimonies.

# Appendix 2: Statistical Distribution of Interviewees

**Table 1** Statistical Distribution of Interviewees

| Place of Residence | Total | Gender | | Place of Birth | | | | Education | | Yiddish | |
|---|---|---|---|---|---|---|---|---|---|---|---|
| | | Men | Women | Ukraine | Belorussia | Russia | Poland & Lithuania | Higher Education | No Higher Education | Speaker | Non-speaker |
| New York | 157 (33%) | 81 (52%) | 76 (48%) | 76 (48%) | 52 (33%) | 11 (7%) | 18 (11%) | 72 (46%) | 85 (54%) | 87 (55%) | 70 (45%) |
| Toronto | 99 (21%) | 41 (41%) | 58 (59%) | 48 (48%) | 23 (23%) | 19 (19%) | 9 (9%) | 56 (57%) | 43 (43%) | 36 (36%) | 63 (64%) |
| Philadelphia | 64 (14%) | 31 (48%) | 33 (52%) | 31 (48%) | 9 (14%) | 11 (17%) | 13 (20%) | 28 (44%) | 36 (56%) | 41 (64%) | 23 (36%) |
| Berlin (incl. Potsdam) | 102 (22%) | 61 (60%) | 41 (40%) | 55 (54%) | 27 (26%) | 12 (12%) | 8 (8%) | 60 (59%) | 42 (41%) | 25 (25%) | 77 (75%) |
| Moscow | 52 (11%) | 19 (37%) | 33 (63%) | 39 (75%) | 3 (6%) | 10 (19%) | 0 (0%) | 43 (83%) | 9 (17%) | 18 (35%) | 34 (65%) |
| Total | 474 (100%) | 233 (49%) | 241 (51%) | 249 (53%) | 114 (24%) | 63 (13%) | 48 (10%) | 259 (55%) | 215 (45%) | 207 (44%) | 267 (56%) |

**Table 2** Professional and Gender Distribution among Interviewees

| Profession | Total | Gender | | Place of Birth | | | |
|---|---|---|---|---|---|---|---|
| | | Men | Women | Ukraine | Belorussia | Russia | Non-Soviet |
| Engineers | 66 (14%) | 32 (48%) | 34 (52%) | 29 (44%) | 22 (33%) | 10 (15%) | 5 (8%) |
| Blue-Collar Workers | 65 (14%) | 29 (45%) | 36 (55%) | 33 (51%) | 12 (18%) | 11 (17%) | 9 (14%) |
| Medical Doctors | 58 (12%) | 26 (45%) | 32 (55%) | 34 (59%) | 12 (21%) | 8 (14%) | 4 (7%) |
| Teachers | 49 (10%) | 4 (8%) | 45 (92%) | 25 (51%) | 9 (18%) | 7 (14%) | 8 (16%) |
| Military | 43 (9%) | 43 (100%) | 0 (0%) | 25 (58%) | 12 (28%) | 6 (14%) | 0 (0%) |
| Accountants | 34 (7%) | 13 (38%) | 21 (62%) | 21 (62%) | 10 (29%) | 0 (0%) | 3 (9%) |
| Management Personnel | 33 (7%) | 27 (82%) | 6 (18%) | 20 (61%) | 7 (21%) | 6 (18%) | 0 (0%) |
| Trade | 27 (6%) | 5 (19%) | 22 (81%) | 15 (56%) | 9 (33%) | 0 (0%) | 3 (11%) |
| Academics and Professors | 21 (4%) | 16 (76%) | 5 (24%) | 12 (57%) | 5 (24%) | 3 (14%) | 1 (5%) |
| Yiddish Professionals | 19 (4%) | 6 (32%) | 13 (68%) | 8 (42%) | 3 (16%) | 0 (0%) | 8 (42%) |
| Lawyers | 17 (4%) | 12 (71%) | 5 (29%) | 6 (35%) | 3 (18%) | 7 (41%) | 1 (6%) |
| Athletes | 9 (2%) | 9 (100%) | 0 (0%) | 3 (33%) | 1 (11%) | 4 (44%) | 1 (11%) |
| Artists (Painters) | 8 (2%) | 8 (100%) | 0 (0%) | 4 (50%) | 2 (25%) | 1 (12%) | 1 (12%) |
| Other | 25 (5%) | 3 (12%) | 22 (88%) | 14 (56%) | 7 (28%) | 0 (0%) | 4 (16%) |
| Total | 474 (100%) | 233 (49%) | 241 (51%) | 249 (53%) | 114 (24%) | 63 (13%) | 48 (10%) |

# Notes

## Chapter 1

1. The latest scholarship on Soviet Jews addresses their creative and destructive role in the Soviet system. Igor Krupnik suggests that they benefited from the Revolution: "Soviet Cultural and Ethnic Policies Toward Jews: A Legacy Reassessed," in Yaacov Ro'i, ed., *Jews and Jewish Life in Russia and the Soviet Union* (Ilford: Frank Cass, 1995). Ken Moss, David Shneer, Gennady Estraikh, Jeffrey Veidlinger, and Harriet Murav deal with the Yiddish intelligentsia and the start that it got with the Revolution. See David Shneer, *Yiddish and the Creation of Soviet Jewish Culture, 1918–1930* (Cambridge: Cambridge University Press, 2004); Kenneth B. Moss, *Jewish Renaissance in the Russian Revolution* (Cambridge: Harvard University Press, 2009); Gennady Estraikh, *In Harness: Yiddish Writers' Romance with Communism* (Syracuse: Syracuse University Press, 2005); Jeffrey Veidlinger, *The Moscow State Yiddish Theater: Jewish Culture on the Soviet Stage* (Bloomington: Indiana University Press, 2000); and Harriet Murav, *Music from a Speeding Train: Jewish Literature in Post-Revolution Russia* (Stanford: Stanford University Press, 2011). Zvi Gitelman discussed the inherited ambiguity of the Soviet Jewish experience in Zvi Y. Gitelman, *A Century of Ambivalence: The Jews of Russia and the Soviet Union, 1881 to the Present* (Bloomington: Indiana University Press, 2001). Very few studies have been done on rural Soviet Jews and their perceptions of Soviet policies. The first study in the field is by Deborah Hope Yalen, "Red Kasrilevke: Ethnographies of Economic Transformation in the Soviet Shtetl, 1917–1939" (PhD diss., University of California, Berkeley, 2007).

2. In the past two decades, scholars of the Soviet system have begun to widely employ the "generation" category. See Alexei Yurchak, *Everything Was Forever, Until It Was No More: The Last Soviet Generation* (Princeton: Princeton University Press, 2005); Masha Gessen, *Ester and Ruzya: How My Grandmothers Survived Hitler's War and Stalin's Peace* (New York: Dial Press, 2004); Catherine Merridale, *Ivan's War: Life and Death in the Red Army, 1939–1945* (London: Macmillan, 2007); Anna Shternshis, *Soviet and Kosher: Jewish Popular Culture in the Soviet Union, 1923–1939* (Bloomington: Indiana University Press, 2006); and David Ransel, *Village Mothers: Three Generations of Change in Russia and Tataria* (Bloomington: Indiana University Press, 2000). The category makes sense in analyzing social, ideological, and cultural developments, as people born at different times experienced the Soviet system differently, and, of course, the system changed often during the country's seventy-four years of existence.

3. For a general study, see Gitelman, *A Century of Ambivalence*. The 1920s and 1930s have been addressed. Arkadii Zeltser, *Evrei Sovetskoi provintsii: Vitebsk i mestechki, 1917–1941* (Moscow: ROSSPEN, 2006); Elissa Bemporad, *Becoming Soviet Jews: The Bolshevik Experiment in Minsk* (Bloomington: Indiana University Press, 2013); M. Beizer, *Evrei Leningrada: 1917–1939: Natsional'naia zhizn' i sovetizatsiia* (Moscow: Mosty kul'tury, 1999).

4. Jeffrey Veidlinger, *In the Shadow of the Shtetl: Small Town Jewish Life in Soviet Ukraine* (Bloomington: Indiana University Press, 2013).

5. Mordechai Altshuler, *Soviet Jewry since the Second World War: Population and Social Structure* (New York: Greenwood Press, 1987) and *Soviet Jewry on the Eve of the Holocaust: A Social and Demographic Profile* (Jerusalem: Centre for Research of East European Jewry, Hebrew University of Jerusalem, 1998). See also Vyacheslav Konstantinov, *Evreiskoe naselenie byvshego SSSR v XX veke (sotsialno-demograficheskii analiz)* (Jerusalem: Lira, 2007).

6. Sheila Fitzpatrick, "Lives and Times," in *In the Shadow of Revolution*, ed. Sheila Fitzpatrick and Yuri Slezkine, 3–18 (New Jersey: Princeton University Press, 2000), 4.

7. Benjamin Pinkus, *The Jews of the Soviet Union: The History of a National Minority* (Cambridge: Cambridge University Press, 1990), p. 89. Poland, the Baltic states, and Bessarabia had been cut off from what was, after 1924, the Soviet Union.

8. John Klier, "Pogroms," in YIVO Encyclopedia of Jews in Eastern Europe (2010), http://www.yivoencyclopedia.org/article.aspx/Pogroms (accessed January 2, 2016).

9. These were the Jewish sections of the Communist Party (*Evsektsii*), which functioned until 1930, and the more short-lived Jewish Commissariat (*Evkom*), which operated until 1924. Zvi Gitelman, *Jewish Nationality and Soviet Politics: The Jewish Sections of the CPSU, 1917–1930* (Princeton: Princeton University Press, 1972), 121–44.

10. Gitelman, *Century of Ambivalence*, 92.

11. According to Jonathan Dekel Chen, we do not have the numbers of Jewish "dekulakized," but Jewish peasants from old Jewish farm colonies were not specifically targeted by this measure. Peasants from the German colonies suffered significantly more (Jonathan Dekel Chen, personal correspondence, September 2, 2014).

12. For more on Stalin's great terror, see *The Anatomy of Terror: Political Violence under Stalin*, edited by James R. Harris (Oxford: Oxford University Press, 2013); *Writing the Stalin Era: Sheila Fitzpatrick and Soviet Historiography*, edited by Kiril Tomoff, Julie Hessler, Sheila Fitzpatrick, et al. (New York: Palgrave Macmillan, 2011); *Contending with Stalinism: Soviet Power & Popular Resistance in the 1930s*, edited by Lynne Viola (Ithaca: Cornell University Press, 2002); Robert Conquest, *The Great Terror: Stalin's Purge of the Thirties* (New York: Macmillan, 1968); Hiroaki Kuromiya, *The Voices of the Dead: Stalin's Great Terror in the 1930s* (New Haven: Yale University Press, 2007); Norman M. Naimark, *Stalin's Genocides* (Princeton: Princeton University Press, 2010); and Peter Whitewood, *The Red Army and the Great Terror: Stalin's Purge of the Soviet Military* (Lawrence: University Press of Kansas, 2015).

13. Altshuler, *Soviet Jewry on the Eve of the Holocaust*, 89.

14. Yaacov Ro'i, "Union of Soviet Socialist Republics," in *YIVO Encyclopedia of Jews in Eastern Europe* (2010), http://www.yivoencyclopedia.org/article.aspx/Union_of_Soviet_Socialist_Republics (accessed June 25, 2013).

15. Zvi Gitelman, "History, Memory and Politics: The Holocaust in the Soviet Union," *Holocaust and Genocide Studies* 5.1 (1990): 23–37, Mordechai Altshuler, *Soviet Jewry on the Eve of the Holocaust* (Jerusalem: Ahva Press, 1998), p. 190.

16. Yitzhak Arad, *In the Shadow of the Red Banner: Soviet Jews in the War Against Nazi Germany* (Jerusalem: Yad Vashem, The International Institute for Holocaust Research, 2010), p. 9 and p. 126 (on losses).

17. Yitzhak Arad, *Katastrofa evreev na territorii Sovetskogo Soiuza (1941–1945)* (Dnepropetrovsk and Moscow, 2007), p. 154. M. N. Potemkina, "Evakuatsiia i natsional'nye otnosheniia v sovetskom tylu v gody Velikoi Otechestvennoi voiny (na materialakh Urala)," *Otechestvennaia istoriia* 3 (2002). For Polish-Jewish refugees, see

Yosef Litvak, *Plitim yehudim mi- polin be-brit ha-moatsot: 1939–1946[Jewish Refugees from Poland in the Soviet Union, 1939–1946]* (Jerusalem: ha-Universitah ha-Ivrit bi-Yerushalayim, ha-Makhon le-Yahadut zemanenu, 1988); and Shlomo Kless, Pe'ilut ziyonit shel plitim yehudiim bivrit hamo'azot bashanim 1941–1945 vekesher hayishuv hayehudi beerz yisrael imahem "Zionist Activities of Jewish Refugees in the USSR in 1941–1945 and the Relations of the Yishuv in the Land of Israel with Them] (PhD Diss., Hebrew University, Jerusalem, 1985).

18. S. D. Dodik, "Sud'ba evreev Transnistrii," *Korni* 24 (Oct.–Dec. 2004). For more on the Holocaust in Transnistria, see Diana Dumitru and Carter Johnson, "Constructing Interethnic Conflict and Cooperation: Why Some People Harmed Jews and Others Helped Them During the Holocaust in Romania," *World Politics* 63,1 (2011): 1–42.

19. Mordechai Altshuler, *Soviet Jewry on the Eve of the Holocaust* (Jerusalem: Ahva Press, 1998), p. 190. For more on evacuation, see Rebecca Manley, *To the Tashkent Station: Evacuation and Survival in the Soviet Union at War* (Ithaca: Cornell University Press, 2009).

20. Konstantinov, p. 17.

21. Benjamin Pinkus, *The Soviet Government and the Jews, 1948–1967* (Cambridge: Cambridge University Press, 1984). Mordechai Altshuler, *Religion and Jewish Identity in the Soviet Union, 1941–1964* (Waltham: Brandeis University Press, 2012); Yaacov Ro'i, *The Struggle for Soviet Jewish Emigration, 1948–1967* (Cambridge: Cambridge University Press, 1991).

22. G. Kostyrchenko, *Gosudarstvennyĭ Antisemitizm v SSSR ot nachala do kul'minatsii: 1938–1953* (Moscow: Mezhdunar. fond "Demokratiia," 2005); Joshua Rubenstein and Vladimir P. Naumov, *Stalin's Secret Pogrom: The Postwar Inquisition of the Jewish Anti-Fascist Committee* (New Haven: Yale University Press, 2005).

23. Ya. L. Rapoport, *The Doctors' Plot of 1953* (Cambridge: Harvard University Press, 1991); Rubenstein and Naumov, *Stalin's Secret Pogrom.*

24. The term "black years" was coined by Y. Gilboa in Jehoshua A. Gilboa, *The Black Years of Soviet Jewry, 1939–1953* (Boston: Little, Brown, 1971). See also Benjamin Pinkus, *Me-ambivalenṭiyut li-verit bilti-ketuvah: Yi'sra'el, Tsarfat vi-Yehude Tsarfat 1947–1957* ([Israel]: Mekhon Ben-Guryon le-heker Yi'sra'el, ha-Tsiyonut u-moreshet Ben-Guryon, Kiryat 'Sedeh Boker, Hotsa'at ha-sefarim shel Universitat Ben Guryon ba-Negev, 2005). Among the most recent publications that focus on state policies toward Jews in the Soviet Union during the last years of Stalin's rule is Jonathan Brent and Vladimir Naumov, *Stalin's Last Crime* (New Haven: Yale University Press, 2002).

25. Gitelman, *Century of Ambivalence,* 157.

26. Pinkus, *The Soviet Government and the Jews.* See also G. Kostyrchenko, *Tainaia politika Khrushcheva: Vlast', intelligentsiia, evreiskii vopros* (Moscow: Mezhdunarodnye otnosheniia, 2012).

27. For the pre-Revolutionary Jewish migration, see Shaul Stampfer, "Patterns of Internal Jewish Migration in the Russian Empire," in Yaacov Ro'i, ed., *Jews and Jewish Life in Russia and the Soviet Union* (London: Frank Cass, 1995), pp. 28–51.

28. Yaacov Ro'i, "Union of Soviet Socialist Republics," in *YIVO Encyclopedia of Jews in Eastern Europe* (2010), accessed December 8, 2014.

## Chapter 2

1. All of these interviews are in my possession. Some are translated into English, some are not. All are typed and transcribed. I have also read 229 interviews that were

conducted in Kyiv by Kyiv Judaica Institute sociologists. But because I rely significantly on body language, intonation, and other nonverbal elements in the understanding and analysis of testimonies, I used the Kyiv interviews only occasionally.

2. The "great wave" of Soviet and post-Soviet Jewish immigration that brought approximately 1.8 million Jews out of the former Soviet Union to Israel (1 million), United States (500,000), Germany (300,000), Canada, and Australia between 1988 and 2012 was enabled by the newly open Soviet borders, but galvanized by the unstable economic, social, and political situation, as well as the explosion of the Chernobyl nuclear power plant in 1986. For more on Russian Jewish diaspora, see Larissa I. Remennick, *Russian Jews on Three Continents: Identity, Integration, and Conflict* (New Brunswick: Transaction, 2007), and Mark Tolts, "Demography of the Contemporary Russian-Speaking Jewish Diaspora" (paper presented at the conference on the Contemporary Russian-speaking Jewish Diaspora, Harvard University, November 13–15, 2011). See also Dina Siegel, *The Great Immigration: Russian Jews in Israel* (New York: Berghahn, 1998).

3. For a detailed description of how interviewees were found, please see Appendix 1 (methodology).

4. Those who were younger usually did not remember the prewar time sufficiently.

5. OGPU—Joint State Political Directorate (also translated as the All-Union State Political Administration)—Soviet secret police between 1923 and 1934.

6. Interviewees call these arrests "dekulakization," whereas historians use this term to describe the expropriation of property and deportation of 1.8 million peasants which took place in 1929–1930. For more on dekulakization, see Lynne Viola, *The Role of the OGPU in Dekulakization, Mass Deportations, and Special Resettlement in 1930* (Pittsburgh: University of Pittsburgh Press, 2000), and Lynne Viola, ed., *The War Against the Peasantry, 1927–1930: The Tragedy of the Soviet Countryside* (New Haven: Yale University Press, 2005). For deportation, see Lynne Viola, *The Unknown Gulag: The Lost World of Stalin's Special Settlements* (New York: Oxford University Press, 2007). Some 6–8 percent of Jews in old Jewish agricultural colonies were dekulakized. Jonathan L. Dekel-Chen, *Farming the Red Land: Jewish Agricultural Colonization and Local Soviet Power, 1924–1941* (New Haven: Yale University Press, 2005), 159.

7. According to Mordechai Altshuler, Jews constituted over 1.5 percent of the Gulag population before 1939 (half the proportion of Jews in the Soviet population, which was about 3 percent): Altshuler, *Soviet Jewry on the Eve of the Holocaust*, p. 27.

8. For more on how the Great Terror affected the Jewish population, see Bemporad, *Becoming Soviet Jews*, pp. 176–210. Also, Orlando Figes discusses a number of Jewish victims of the Great Terror; see Figes, *The Whisperers*.

9. Yitzhak Arad, *The Holocaust in the Soviet Union* (Lincoln: University of Nebraska Press, 2009), pp. 520–21.

10. NKVD Order № 001683, issued on December 12, 1941, "About operative-emergency service of places liberated from the troops of the enemy," and Order of NKVD and NKGB № 494/94 issued on October 11, 1943, about the arrests and verifying of military collaborationist formations (Приказ НКВД СССР № 001683 от 12 декабря 1941 года «Об оперативно-чекистском обслуживании местностей, освобожденных от войск противника», Приказ НКВД СССР и НКГБ СССР № 494/94 от 11 октября 1943 года о порядке арестов и проверки военнослужащих коллаборационистских формирований, № 494/94, 11 октября 1943 года), Central FSB Archive, ЦА ФСБ. Ф. 66. Оп. 1. Д. 734. Л. 53–54, both can be found at http://reibert.info/threads/chistka-territorij-osvobozhdennyx-ot-okkupacii.97721/,

retrieved on August 31, 2014. My sincere thanks to Gennady Kostyrchenko for finding and sending these documents to me.

11. Esther Iecovich et al., "Social Support Networks and Loneliness among Elderly Jews in Russia and Ukraine," *Journal of Marriage and Family* 66, no. 2 (May 2004): 306–17.

12. For a full table with professional distribution among interviewees, see table 2 in the appendix.

13. Michael Beizer estimates, for example, that 69 percent of all dentists in Leningrad in 1939 were Jewish. Michael Beizer, "The Jews of a Soviet Metropolis in the Interwar Period: The Case of Leningrad," in *Revolution, Repression, and Revival: The Soviet Jewish Experience*, ed. Zvi Y. Gitelman and Yaacov Ro'i (Lanham, MD: Rowman & Littlefield, 2007), pp. 113–30.

14. Bertaux, Rotkirch, and Thompson, *Surviving the Soviet System*, 5–6. See also Anna Kushkova, "Surviving in the Time of Deficit and the Narrative Construction of a 'Soviet Identity,'" in *Soviet and Post-Soviet Identities*, ed. Mark Bassin and Catriona Kelly (Cambridge: Cambridge University Press, 2012), pp. 278–96.

15. For an exemplary reading of Holocaust survivor narratives as post-traumatic stories, see Sarah Carney, "Transcendent Stories and Counter-narratives in Holocaust Survivor Life Histories: Searching for Meaning in Video-testimony Archives," in *Narrative Analysis: Studying the Development of Individuals in Society*, ed. Colette Daiute and Cynthia Lightfoot (Thousand Oaks, CA: Sage, 2004), pp. 201–22.

16. Trauma: Z. Harel, "Jewish Aged: Diversity in Need and Care Solutions," in *Age through the Ethnic Lenses*, ed. L. K. Olson (Lanham, MD: Rowman & Littlefield, 2001), pp. 145–59. Depression: ibid. and T. Fitzpatrick, "Elderly Russian Jewish Immigrants," in *Therapeutic Interventions with Ethnic Elders: Health and Social Issues*, ed. S. Alemán, T. Fitzpatrick, T. V. Tran, and E. W. Gonzalez (Binghamton, NY: Haworth Press, 2000), pp. 55–78.

17. United Jewish Communities, *A United Jewish Communities Report* (New York: United Jewish Communities, 2004).

18. R. N. Butler, "The Life Review: An Interpretation of Reminiscence in the Aged," *Psychiatry* 26 (1963): 65–75.

19. Ibid., 66.

20. Gay Becker, Yewoubdar Beyene, and Leilani Cuizon Canalita, "Immigrating for Status in Late Life: Effects of Globalization on Filipino American Veterans," *Journal of Aging Studies* 14, no. 3: 273–91. Daniel Lai and Wendy Leonenko, "Correlates of Living Alone among Single Elderly Chinese Immigrants in Canada," *International Journal of Aging and Human Development* 65, no. 2 (2007): 121–48; David Ip, Chi Wai Lui, and Wing Hong Chui, "Veiled Entrapment: A Study of Social Isolation of Older Chinese Migrants in Brisbane, Queensland," *Ageing & Society* 27 (2007): 719–38; Ruth Mccaffrey, "The Lived Experience of Haitian Older Adults' Integration Into a Senior Center in Southeast Florida," *Journal of Transcultural Nursing* 19 (2008): 33.

21. For more on theoretical discussion on life review, reminiscence, and oral history, see Joanna Bornat, "Remembering in Later Life: Generating Individual and Social Change," *Oxford Handbooks Online* 2012-09-18 (Oxford University Press).

22. Jean-Marie Robine, *Longevity: To the Limits and Beyond* (Berlin: Springer, 1997).

23. James W. Vaupel, "Demographic Analysis of Aging and Longevity," *American Economic Review* 88, no. 2 (May 1998): 242–47.

24. Deborah D. Danner, David A. Snowdon, and Wallace V. Friesen, "Positive Emotions in Early Life and Longevity: Findings from the Nun Study," *Journal of Personality and Social Psychology* 80, no. 5 (May 2001): 804–13.

25. Becca R. Levy, Martin D. Slade, Suzanne R. Kunkel, and Stanislav V. Kasl, "Longevity Increased by Positive Self-Perceptions of Aging," *Journal of Personality and Social Psychology* 83, no. 2 (August 2002): 261–70.

26. Some studies show that nonverbal communication is responsible for over 70 percent of the information received by the human brain. Mark L. Knapp and Judith A. Hall, *Nonverbal Communication in Human Interaction* (Boston: Wadsworth, 2009).

27. One of the best fictional portrayals of this generation's dilemmas of immigration is in David Bezmozgis, *The Free World* (Toronto: HarperCollins, 2011).

28. George Herbert Mead, "The Nature of the Past," in *Essays in Honor of J. Dewey*, ed. John Coss (New York: Henry Holt, 1929), pp. 235–42; George Mead, *The Philosophy of the Present* (La Salle, IL: Open Court, 1959).

29. For more on this, see Anna Shternshis, "Between the Red and Yellow Stars: Ethnic and Religious Identity of Soviet Jewish World War II Veterans in New York, Toronto, and Berlin," *Journal of Jewish Identities* 4, no. 1 (2011): 43–64. For the role of Russian media among Russian-speaking migrants, see Nelly Elias, *Coming Home: Media and Returning Diaspora in Israel and Germany* (New York: State University of New York Press, 2008). See also Olena Bagno, "The Price of Fear: Israel Beiteinu in 2009," in *The Elections in Israel—2009*, ed. A. Arian and M. Shamir (New Brunswick: Transaction Publishers, 2011), pp. 19–41.

30. Anelise Orelick, *The Soviet Jewish Americans* (Westport: Greenwood, 1999), pp. 149–63.

31. Once established in Canada, skilled workers can sponsor their family members if they can provide for them for ten years. Upon the completion of the ten-year term, these individuals are eligible for all benefits paid to the elderly in Canada. Until then, the elderly migrants are solely dependent on their children. For the details of the skilled labor program, see http://www.cic.gc.ca/english/immigrate/skilled/apply-who.asp, retrieved on August 22, 2016.

32. Gitelman, *Century of Ambivalence*, 115–43.

33. For an overview of second country migrants in Toronto, see Remennick, *Russian Jews on Three Continents*, 279–312; Robert Brym "Jewish Immigrants from the Former Soviet Union in Canada, 1996," *East European Jewish Affairs* 31, no. 2 (2001): 36–43; and Dina Roginsky, "Israelis in Toronto: From Stigmatization to Self-Organization" (paper presented at the annual meeting of the American Association for Jewish Studies, Toronto, December 16, 2007).

34. Larissa I. Remennick, *Russian Jews on Three Continents: Identity, Integration, and Conflict* (New Brunswick: Transaction Publishers, 2007), p. 316.

35. In Germany, Jewish community centers are government-sponsored agencies responsible for organizing and distributing social services, welfare, language courses, and cultural initiatives among their members. Individual communities are governed by the Central Council of Jews in Germany, which represents 107 communities. Since 2003, the federal government and the Central Council have signed a national agreement according to which the council receives funds to support its programs on integration of Jews from the former Soviet Union. The policy of membership in Jewish community centers has been a controversial matter for a number of years.

36. Anna Shternshis, "Kaddish in a Church: Perceptions of Orthodox Christianity among Moscow Elderly Jews in the Early Twenty-First Century," *Russian Review* 66, no. 2 (2007): 273–94.

37. For a study that analyzes stories of antisemitism among post-Soviet Jewish students in Israel and Germany, see Tamar Rapoport, Edna Lomsky-Feder, and Angelika Heider, "Recollection and Relocation in Immigration: Russian-Jewish

Immigrants 'Normalize' Their Anti-Semitic Experiences," *Symbolic Interaction* 25, no. 2 (2002): 175–98. See also J. Lerner, T. Rapoport, and E. Lomsky-Feder, "The 'Ethnic Script' in Action: The Re-grounding of Russian-Jewish Immigrants in Israel," *Ethos* 35, no. 2 (2007): 168–95.

38. Paperno, *Stories of the Soviet Experience*, xiii.

39. The only book that has used a similar approach is L. L. Fialkova and Maria N. Yelenevskaya, *Ex-Soviets in Israel: From Personal Narratives to a Group Portrait* (Detroit: Wayne State University Press, 2007). However, the book is focused on Israel and does not exclusively deal with the older generation. My book does not discuss post-Soviet Jews based in Israel.

40. Lisa A. Kirschenbaum, *The Legacy of the Siege of Leningrad, 1941–1995: Myth, Memories, and Monuments* (Cambridge: Cambridge University Press, 2006).

41. Daria Hubova, Andrei Ivankiev, and Tonia Sharova, "After Glasnost: Oral History in the Soviet Union," in Luisa Passerini, ed., *Memory & Totalitarianism* (New Brunswick: TransactionPublishers, 2005), 89–102 (89).

42. Quoted in Donald Raleigh, *Soviet Baby Boomers*, 5–6.

43. V. Ia. Propp and A. N. Afanas'ev, *Morfologiia skazki* (St. Petersburg: Nauka, 1995), originally published 1928; translated as V. Propp, *Morphology of the Folktale* (Bloomington: Research Center, Indiana University, 1958).

44. Rapoport, Lomsky-Feder, and Heider, "Recollection and Relocation in Immigration," 177.

45. Anna Shternshis, "Salo on Challah: Soviet Jews' Experience of Food in the 1920s–1950s," in *Jews and Their Foodways*, ed. Anat Helman (New York: Oxford University Press, 2015).

46. Colette Daiute and Cynthia Lightfoot, *Narrative Analysis: Studying the Development of Individuals in Society* (Thousand Oaks, CA: Sage, 2004), and especially Anna De Fina and Alexandra Georgakopoulou, *Analyzing Narrative: Discourse and Sociolinguistic Perspectives* (Cambridge: Cambridge University Press, 2012).

47. For a similar approach, though in a different geographical context, see Charles Van Onselen, *The Seed Is Mine: The Life of Kas Maine, a South African Sharecropper, 1894–1985* (New York: Hill and Wang, 1996).

## Chapter 3

1. Interview with Klara G., Brooklyn, New York, August 2000.

2. Interview with Klara G., Brooklyn, New York, August 2000.

3. Interview with Klara G., Brooklyn, New York, August 2000.

4. Interview with Klara G., Brooklyn, New York, August 2000.

5. There is an extensive literature on the nature of the Soviet family in Stalin's Russia. Selected titles include Lynne Attwood, *Gender and Housing in Soviet Russia: Private Life in a Public Space* (Manchester: Manchester University Press, 2010); Stephen Kotkin, *Magnetic Mountain: Stalinism as a Civilization* (Berkeley: University of California Press, 1997), pp. 157–97; H. Kent Geiger, *The Family in Soviet Russia* (Cambridge, MA: Harvard University Press, 1968); Cynthia Hooper, "Terror of Intimacy: Family Politics in the 1930s Soviet Union," in *Everyday Life in Early Soviet Russia: Taking the Revolution Inside*, ed. Christina Kiaer and Eric Naiman (Bloomington: Indiana University Press, 2006), pp. 61–91; Rudolf Schlesinger, *The Family in the U.S.S.R.* (London: Routledge, 1949); Susan M. Kingsbury and Mildred Fairchild, *Factory, Family, and Woman in the Soviet Union* (New York: G. P. Putnam's Sons, 1935); Bertaux, Thompson, and Rotkirch, *On Living through Soviet Russia*.

6. Altshuler suggests that Jewish families were the most unstable ones in the Soviet Union during the 1930s: Mordechai Altshuler, *Soviet Jewry on the Eve of the Holocaust: A Social and Demographic Profile* (Jerusalem: Yad Vashem, 1998), pp. 77–8.

7. Similarly to Klara, some women said that their parents were reluctant to send them to school in fear of losing domestic help. For example, Lilya Sh. (born in Cherkassy, Ukraine, 1909) recalled that because her parents needed her to work at home, she did not go to school, but managed to learn to read and write without any formal instruction, whereas her brothers studied in schools. Similarly, Esfir A. (born in Orsha, Byelorussia, 1908) recalls that her parents did not want to send her to school, and only the interference of local teachers helped her to obtain a primary education. Klara's and other mentioned testimonies are in line with how both Jewish and non-Jewish girls were treated in many families in early postrevolutionary Russia. Interview with Lilya Sh., Berlin, June 2002. Interview with Esfir A., Potsdam, June 2002.

8. Gorsuch, *Youth in Revolutionary Russia*, 32.

9. Douglas Taylor Northrop, *Veiled Empire: Gender & Power in Stalinist Central Asia* (Ithaca: Cornell University Press, 2004). For a special case, see Dan Healey, "Sexual and Gender Dissent: Homosexuality as Resistance in Stalin's Russia," in *Contending with Stalinism: Soviet Power & Popular Resistance in the 1930s*, ed. Lynne Viola (Ithaca: Cornell University Press, 2002), pp. 139–69.

10. For a comprehensive study on women and European Jewish history, see Paula Hyman, *Gender and Assimilation in Modern Jewish History: The Roles and Representation of Women* (Seattle: University of Washington Press, 1995). Specifically on Jewish education in tsarist Russia, see Eliyana R. Adler, *In Her Hands: The Education of Jewish Girls in Tsarist Russia* (Detroit: Wayne State University Press, 2011).

11. Anna Shternshis, *Soviet and Kosher: Jewish Popular Culture in the Soviet Union, 1923–1939* (Bloomington: Indiana University Press, 2006), and Veidlinger, *In the Shadow of the Shtetl*.

12. For an explanation of this phenomenon, see Rakhmiel Peltz, *From Immigrant to Ethnic Culture: American Yiddish in South Philadelphia* (Stanford: Stanford University Press, 1997), pp. 115–72.

13. Interview with Yurii P., Berlin, June 2002.

14. Interview with Maya D., Berlin, 2002.

15. For more on how the respondents speak about food, see Shternshis, "Salo on Challah."

16. Shternshis, "Salo on Challah."

17. Esfir A. (born in Orsha, Byelorussia, 1908), for example, asserted that she did not know any non-Jews until she was sixteen years old (which did not stop her from marrying a non-Jew just a few years later). Interview with Esfir A., Potsdam, June 2002.

18. Interview with Etya G., Brooklyn, New York, January 1999. Leon Dennen, an American journalist who visited Jewish collective farms in Russia in 1932, also observed that dancing was extremely popular among young Jewish women. Leon Dennen, *Where the Ghetto Ends* (New York: King Alfred, 1934).

19. Interview with Ilya F., Berlin, June 2002.

20. Interview with Ilya and Sima F., Berlin, June 2002.

## Chapter 4

1. For more on the specificity of Soviet oral histories and gender, see Daniel Bertaux, Paul Richard Thompson, and Anna Rotkirch, "Introduction," in *On Living through Soviet Russia*, ed. Bertaux, Thompson, and Rotkirch, pp. 1–24.

2. Interview with Yosef V., Berlin, June 2002.

3. Interview with Ilya Sh., Moscow, June 2001.

4. Interview with Olga K., Moscow, June 2001.

5. Ibid.

6. For women in industry during this time, see Wendy Z. Goldman, *Women at the Gates: Gender and Industry in Stalin's Russia* (Cambridge: Cambridge University Press, 2002).

7. Altshuler, *Soviet Jewry since the Second World War*, p. 73.

8. Interview with Grigorii B., Berlin, June 2002.

9. Interview with Veniamin Sh., Moscow, June 2001.

10. Interview with Ilya Sh., Moscow, June 2001.

11. Interview with Lilya Sh., Berlin, June 2002.

12. Interview with Esfir A., Berlin, June 2002.

13. Arkady Zeltser, personal correspondence, September 25, 2014. Altshuler's data comes from Altshuler, *Soviet Jewry on the Eve of the Holocaust*, pp. 74–6.

14. Altshuler, *Soviet Jewry on the Eve of the Holocaust*, p. 76.

15. Ibid., p. 74.

16. For an overview of a wedding ritual in Eastern Europe as well as an important bibliography on the topic, see Barbara Kirshenblatt-Gimblett, "Weddings," *YIVO Encyclopedia of Jews in Eastern Europe*, <http://www.yivoencyclopedia.org/article. aspx/Weddings>. Retrieved October 18, 2013.

17. The most important collector of East European Jewish folklore was Shloyme Zaynvl Rappoport (1863–1920), known as S. Ansky. Because of his initiative of collecting folklore from Jewish communities affected by World War I, we currently have a large ethnographic collection of Jewish culture, with a specific emphasis on weddings. For more on the nature of his expedition, see Benyamin Lukin, "An-ski Ethnographic Expedition and Museum," *YIVO Encyclopedia of Jews in Eastern Europe*, http://www.yivoencyclopedia.org/article.aspx/An-ski_Ethnographic_Expedition_ and_Museum. Retrieved August 22, 2013.

18. Freeze, *Jewish Marriage and Divorce in Imperial Russia*, p. 49.

19. Veidlinger, *In the Shadow of the Shtetl*.

20. For more on Jewish middle class in the Imperial Russia, see Natan M. Meir, *Kyiv, Jewish Metropolis: A History, 1859–1914* (Bloomington: Indiana University Press, 2010); Benjamin Nathans, *Beyond the Pale: The Jewish Encounter with Late Imperial Russia* (Berkeley: University of California Press, 2002); and Jeffrey Veidlinger, *Jewish Public Culture in the Late Russian Empire* (Bloomington: Indiana University Press, 2009).

21. Freeze, *Jewish Marriage and Divorce in Imperial Russia*, 44.

22. Altshuler, *Soviet Jewry on the Eve of the Holocaust*, 64.

23. Interview with Fira G., New York, March 1999.

24. Interview with Ilya Sh., Moscow, June 2001.

25. Interview with Olga K., Moscow, June 2001.

26. Interview with David Sh., Moscow, June 2001. Esfir A. (born in Orsha, Byelorussia, 1908), who got married in 1932, had a similar experience: "We did not have a wedding. Neither I nor my husband had money. My father bought a big bottle

of beer, my mother fried a goose, and that was our wedding." Interview with Esfir A., Moscow, June 2001.

27. Rozaliya U. (born in Cherkassy, 1907) elaborated on additional reasons for the lack of her own wedding ceremony, and explained that it was because of poverty. A.S. "Did you have a wedding?" R.U. "People gathered; a cake was baked. During that time, there were no big weddings. Only rich people like policemen or noblemen had them. If simple people had big celebrations, others would look funny at them. Ordinary people didn't do that." Interview with Rozaliya U., Moscow, June 2001.

28. Ransel, *Village Mothers*, 88.

29. Interview with Grigorii B., New York, April 1999.

30. Veidlinger, *In the Shadow of the Shtetl*, p. 104.

31. Interview with Mariya K., Moscow, June 2001.

32. Veidlinger, *In the Shadow of the Shtetl*, p. 104.

33. Interview with Fira F., Berlin, June 2002.

34. Interview with Iona K., Potsdam, June 2002.

## Chapter 5

1. Nicholas Timasheff, *The Great Retreat: The Growth and Decline of Communism in Russia* (New York: E. P. Dutton, 1946). Timasheff has been criticized for suggesting the retreat by many historians (Jeffrey Brooks, Evgenii Dobrenko, and others), yet most scholars of Soviet social history have found confirmation of his hypothesis in archival sources. See Matthew Lenoe, "In Defense of Timasheff's Great Retreat," *Kritika: Explorations in Russian and Eurasian History* 5, no. 4 (2004): 721–30. See also David L. Hoffmann, *Stalinist Values: The Cultural Norms of Soviet Modernity, 1917–1941* (Ithaca, NY: Cornell University Press, 2003), and Elena Zubkova, *Russia after the War: Hopes, Illusions, and Disappointments, 1945–1957* (Armonk, NY: M. E. Sharpe, 1998).

2. Konstantinov, p. 61.

3. For more on gender relations in the Soviet army, see Oleg Budnitski, "Muzhschiny i zhenschiny v Krasnoi Armii (1941–1945)," *Cahiers du monde russe* 52 (2011): 405–22.

4. SMERSH is an acronym formed from *Smert' Shpionam* ("death to spies"), which was an umbrella name for three independent counterintelligence agencies in the Red Army formed in late 1942 or even earlier, but officially founded on April 14, 1943.

5. Interview with Anna M., Moscow, June 2001.

6. For a collection of memoirs on *Umanskaya Yama*, see http://www.sdivizia-141. narod.ru/umanskaya_jama.htm, retrieved on June 21, 2013.

7. Interview with Mira G., Philadelphia, February 2001.

8. For pregnancy among inmates of concentration camps, see Myrna Goldenberg, "Memoirs of Auschwitz Survivors: The Burden of Gender," in *Women in the Holocaust*, ed. Dalie Ofer and Lenore J. Weitzman (New Haven: Yale University Press, 1998), pp. 327–39. See also Na'ama Shik, "Sexual Abuse of Jewish Women in Auschwitz-Birkenau," in Dagmar Herzog (ed.), *Brutality and Desire: War and Sexuality in Europe's Twentieth Century* (New York: Palgrave Macmillan, 2009), pp. 221–46.

9. I. A. Al'tman, ed., *Kholokost na territorii SSSR: Entsiklopediia*, 2nd ed. (Moscow: ROSSPEN, 2011), pp. 1004–5.

10. For strategies of coping among women during the Holocaust, see Ofer and Weitzman, *Women in the Holocaust*.

11. For Russian-language memoirs of the women who went through the war, see http://www.liveinternet.ru/users/liebkind37/post268650565/, retrieved on

June 21, 2013. For more on "field wives," see Barbara Engel, "The Womanly Face of War: Soviet Women Remember World War II," in *Women and War in the Twentieth Century: Enlisted with or Without Consent*, ed. Nicole Dombrowski Risser (New York: Garland, 1999), pp. 102–19. For a diary/memoir of a woman translator at SMERSH, see I. M. Dunaevskaia, *Ot Leningrada do Kenigsberga: Dnevnik voennoi perevodchitsy (1942–1945)* (Moscow: ROSSPEN , 2010).

12. Interview with David S., Brooklyn, New York, February 1999.

13. Interview with Semion Sh., Brooklyn, New York, August 1999.

14. Interview with Olga K., Brooklyn, New York, March 1999.

15. Evgeniia B. was born in the Vinnitsa region, Ukraine, and was in high school when the war began. After the war, she studied history at the Vinnitsa Pedagogical Institute.

16. Interview with Evgeniia B., Brooklyn, New York, May 1999.

17. Interview with Bella G., Berlin, June 2002.

18. Interview with Liusia G. and Semion Sh., New York, August 1999.

19. Interview with Mariya P. and Mikhail P., Berlin, July 2002.

20. Interview with Liusia G., New York, August 1999.

21. Benjamin Pinkus, *The Soviet Government and the Jews, 1948–1967: A Documented Study*, ed. Jonathan Frankel (New York: Cambridge University Press, 1984), p. 28.

22. Interview with Mariya D., Berlin, June 2002.

23. Ibid.

24. Ibid.

25. Interview with Mariya K., Moscow, June 2001.

26. This characteristic has been noted by many oral historians working with the Soviet-born respondents of this generation. See Ingrid Oswald and Viktor Voronkov, "The 'Public–Private' Sphere in Soviet and Post-Soviet Society: Perception and Dynamics of 'Public' and 'Private' in Contemporary Russia," *European Societies* 6, no. 1 (2004): 97–117.

27. Interview with Mila Ch., New York, April 1999.

28. Katherine Jolluck, *Exile and Identity: Polish Women in the Soviet Union during World War II* (Pittsburgh: University of Pittsburgh Press, 2002), pp. 183–84.

29. Interview with Mila Ch., Brooklyn, New York, June 1999.

30. Interview with Mila Ch., Brooklyn, New York, June 1999.

31. Interview with Evgeniya B., Brooklyn, New York, May 1999.

32. Interview with Vladimir K., Potsdam, July 2002.

33. Interview with Lazar F., Moscow, June 2001.

34. Thanks to Lynne Viola for pointing this out. For some accounts of visiting Soviet prisons, see Adam Hochschild, *The Unquiet Ghost: Russians Remember Stalin* (New York: Viking, 1994), pp. 269–73.

35. Interview with Anonymous, Brighton Beach, New York, August 1999.

36. Interview with Lev G., New York, August 1999.

37. Interview with Lisa S., New York, May 1999.

38. Anna Shternshis, *Soviet and Kosher*, pp. 104–05.

39. Interview with Ava T., Potsdam, June 2002.

40. Interview with Mikhail B., Potsdam, June 2002.

41. Interview with Samuil G., New York, April 1999.

42. Some scholars, like Vyacheslav Konstantinov, consider this a decisive factor (Konstantinov, p. 51).

43. Interview with Vladimir Ya., Berlin, July 2002.

44. Interview with Yakov B., Moscow, June 2001.

45. Interview with Ilya Sh., Moscow, June 2001.
46. Interview with Sima F., Berlin, June 2002.
47. Interview with Semyon and Faina Ya., Berlin, June 2002.
48. Juliane Fürst, *Stalin's Last Generation: Soviet Post-war Youth and the Emergence of Mature Socialism* (Oxford: Oxford University Press, 2010), 200–49.
49. Juliane Fürst, "The Importance of Being Stylish: Youth, Culture and Identity in Late Stalinism," in *Late Stalinist Russia: Society between Reconstruction and Reinvention,* ed. Juliane Fürst (New York: Routledge, 2006), pp. 209–30, especially p. 224.
50. For more on production of luxury items, see Jukka Gronow, *Caviar with Champagne: Common Luxury and the Ideals of the Good Life in Stalin's Russia* (Oxford: Berg, 2003).
51. Interview with Ava T., Potsdam, June 2002.
52. Interview with Vera L., Moscow, June 2001.
53. Interview with Elizaveta Z., Berlin, June 2002.
54. Interview with Elizaveta K., Potsdam, June 2002.
55. A representative example is a collection of letters to Soviet writer Ilya Ehrenburg devoted to the last years of Stalin's rule (1946–1953), published in Mordechai Altshuler, Itskhak Arad, and Shmuel Krakovsky, eds., *Sovetskie evrei pishut Il'ye Erenburgu 1943–1966* (Jerusalem: Yad Vashem, 1993), pp. 255–352.
56. Interview with Bella G., Berlin, June 2002.
57. Interview with Klara R., Berlin, June 2002.
58. Interview with Lyubov B. Berlin, June 2002.

## Chapter 6

1. Alex Inkeles and Raymond Bauer, *The Soviet Citizen: Daily Life in a Totalitarian Society* (Cambridge: Harvard University Press, 1959), p. 228. For the text of the interviews and more on the resource, see http://hcl.harvard.edu/collections/hpsss/index.html, retrieved on December 18, 2015. For a critique of the Harvard project and its use, see Sam Prendergast, "Revisiting the Harvard Project on the Soviet Social System," in *Oral History Review,* forthcoming.
2. According to Inkeles, among the Harvard project respondents, 80 percent of those born between 1895 and 1904 had two or more siblings, but among those born in the next decade only 73 percent, in the next decade 63 percent, and in the youngest group, who were 25 or under in 1950, only 51 percent had two or more brothers and sisters. A similar pattern was manifested in the families of each level of the social class hierarchy. Inkeles and Bauer, *The Soviet Citizen,* 202.
3. Altshuler, *Soviet Jewry on the Eve of the Holocaust,* 84. According to Altshuler, in 1926 the ratio of Jewish women to children aged 0–8 was 720; by 1939, it had dropped to 529.
4. Altshuler, *Soviet Jewry since the Second World War,* p. 40.
5. Ibid., p. 41.
6. Ibid., p. 211.
7. Shlapentokh, *Love and Marriage,* p. 68.
8. Slezkine, *The Jewish Century,* pp. 204–373.
9. Shlapentokh, *Love and Marriage,* p. 73.
10. Interview with Dora Z., Moscow, June 2001.
11. Ibid.
12. Interview with Mariya D., Berlin, July 2002.
13. Shlapentokh, *Love and Marriage,* p. 149.

14. For an account on attribution bias, see Michael Eid and Randy J. Larsen, *The Science of Subjective Well-Being* (New York: Guilford Press, 2008). I am grateful to Olga Gershenson, who pointed out the connection to social psychology in the analysis.

15. For more on this, see Helen Carback, Yulia Gradskova, and Zhanna Kravchenko, eds., *And They Lived Happily Ever After: Norms and Everyday Practices of Family and Parenthood in Russia and Central Europe* (Budapest and New York: Central European University Press, 2012), and Goldman, *Women, the State, and Revolution.*

16. Interview with Sima F., Berlin, June 2001.

17. Interview with Fira F., Berlin, 2002.

18. Interview with Liza R., New York, August 1999.

19. Interview with Mila Ch., Brooklyn, New York, March 1999.

20. Interview with Elizaveta K., Philadelphia, March 2001.

21. Interview with Evgeniya R., Moscow, June 2001.

22. Interviews with Sima F., Berlin, June 2002.

23. Interviews with Dora Z., Moscow, June 2001, and Elizaveta K., Philadelphia, March 2001.

24. Interview with Elizaveta K., Brooklyn, New York, August 1999.

25. Interview with Semyon F., Moscow, June 2001.

26. Interview with Vladimir Ia., Berlin, June 2002.

27. Interview with Lev G., New York, June 2000.

28. Interview with Mila Ch, Brooklyn, New York, March 1999.

29. Interview with Vera L., Moscow, June 2001.

30. Interview with Klara G., Berlin, June 2002.

31. Interview with Elizaveta K., Philadelphia, March 2001.

32. Interviews with Ilya R., Moscow, June 2001; Evgeniya R., Moscow, June 2001; Lev L., Moscow, June 2001; Klara G., Philadelphia, March 2001; and others.

33. For a discussion of how spouses shared (or did not share) secret information with each other and the children, see Bertaux, Rotkirch, and Thompson, *On Living through Soviet Russia*, especially the introduction. For Gulag-related secrets, see Figes, *The Whisperers.*

34. Interview with Mariya S., Brooklyn, New York, March 1999.

35. Kiril Feferman, *Soviet Jewish Stepchild: The Holocaust in the Soviet Mindset, 1941–1964* (Saarbrücken, Germany: VDM Verlag Dr. Müller, 2009), and Zvi Y. Gitelman, *Bitter Legacy: Confronting the Holocaust in the USSR* (Bloomington: Indiana University Press, 1997).

36. Viola, Lynne. "Popular Resistance in the Stalinist 1930s: Soliloquy of a Devil's Advocate," *Kritika: Explorations in Russian and Eurasian History* 1, no. 1 (2000): 45–69.

37. Many interviewees from Moscow stated that their children lived in Israel or Germany as well.

38. Larissa Remennick has observed that these values retain importance for Russian-speaking Israelis decades after immigration. Larissa Remennick, "The 1.5 Generation of Russian Immigrants in Israel: Between Integration and Sociocultural Retention," *Diaspora: A Journal of Transnational Studies* 12, no. 1 (Spring 2003): 39–66.

39. Steven Martin Cohen and Arnold M. Eisen, *The Jew Within: Self, Family, and Community in America* (Bloomington: Indiana University Press, 2000), p. 116.

## Chapter 7

1. Gaysin is a town in the Vinnitsa region of Ukraine.

2. Interview with Victor Kh., New York, August 1999.

3. For more on the system of Soviet higher education and the admission requirements, see Richard Pipes, *Russia under the Bolshevik Regime* (New York: Vintage, 1995), pp. 321–36.

4. For living conditions of the 1930s, see Sheila Fitzpatrick, *Everyday Stalinism: Ordinary Life in Extraordinary Times; Soviet Russia in the 1930s* (New York: Oxford University Press, 1999). For living conditions and universities, as well as dorm policies, see Peter Konecny, *Builders and Deserters: Students, State, and Community in Leningrad, 1917–1941* , ed. Peter Konecny (Montreal: McGill-Queen's University Press, 1999). Also, M. B. Smith, *Property of Communists: The Urban Housing Program from Stalin to Khrushchev* (DeKalb: Northern Illinois University Press, 2010). For post-Stalin urban living conditions, see Steven E. Harris, *Communism on Tomorrow Street: Mass Housing and Everyday Life after Stalin* (Baltimore: Johns Hopkins University Press, 2013).

5. Altshuler, p. 124.

6. Interview with Ilya Sh., Moscow, 2001.

7. Interview with Olga K., Moscow, 2001.

8. Interview with Faina D., New York, 2001.

9. Larisa Remennick observed a similar situation among Russian Jews living in Israel. See Larisa Remennick, "Intergenerational Transfer in Israeli-Russian Immigrant Families: Parental Social Mobility and Children's Integration," *Journal of Ethnic and Migration Studies* 38 (2012): 1533–50, and Larisa Remennick, "Former Soviet Jews in the New/Old Homeland: Between Integration and Separatism," in Takeyuki Tsuda, ed., *Diasporic Homecomings: Ethnic Return Migrations of the Late 20th Century* (Stanford: Stanford University Press, 2009), chap. 8.

10. Yuri Slezkine, *The Jewish Century* (New Jersey: Princeton University Press, 2004), pp. 206–9.

11. Interview with Maria M., New York, August 2001.

12. Classic studies on Soviet values include Alex Inkeles, *The Soviet Citizen: Daily Life in a Totalitarian Society* (Cambridge: Harvard University Press, 1961), and Vera S. Dunham, *In Stalin's Time: Middleclass Values in Soviet Fiction* (Cambridge: Cambridge University Press, 1976). For a later period, see Vladimir Shlapentokh, *Public and Private Life of the Soviet People: Changing Values in Post-Stalin Russia* (New York: Oxford University Press, 1989); David L. Hoffmann, *Stalinist Values: The Cultural Norms of Soviet Modernity, 1917–1941* (Ithaca: Cornell University Press, 2003); and Mark Edele, *Stalinist Society, 1928–1953* (Oxford: Oxford University Press, 2011). Excellent collections of essays on the topic are *Writing the Stalin Era: Sheila Fitzpatrick and Soviet Historiography*, ed. Golfo Alexopoulos, Kiril Tomoff, and Julie Hessler (New York: Palgrave Macmillan, 2011), and *Soviet and Post-Soviet Identities*, ed. Mark Bassin and Catriona Kelly (New York: Cambridge University Press, 2012).

13. On the American dream and its evolution, see Lawrence R. Samuel, *The American Dream: A Cultural History* (Syracuse, NY: Syracuse University Press, 2012).

14. For more on Soviet higher education during World War II, see William Moskoff, "Soviet Higher Education Policy during World War II," *Soviet Studies* 38, No. 3 (1986): 406–15. On schools, see John Dunstan, *Soviet Schooling in the Second World War* (Basingstoke: Macmillan Press in association with Centre for Russian and East European Studies, Univ. of Birmingham, 1997).

15. Zh. A. Agapoga, "Deti i molodiozh' Prikam'ia v gody voiny" (2007), available at http://www.permgani.ru/publikatsii/stati/deti-i-molodezh-prikamya-v-gody-vojny.html. See also Dunstan, *Soviet Schooling in the Second World War*.

16. For more on bread cards and other rationing during World War II, see William Moskoff, *The Bread of Affliction: The Food Supply in the USSR During World War II* (Cambridge: Cambridge University Press, 1990), pp. 70–185.

17. Interview with Fira G., New York, August 2001.

18. Moscow State Geological Prospecting Institute (Московский государственный геологоразведочный институт) was the 1941–45 official name of the contemporary Russian State Geological Prospecting University named after Sergo Ordzhonikidze (Российский государственный геологоразведочный университет имени Серго Орджоникидзе).

19. Interview with Roza K., Philadelphia, 2001.

20. Katherine R. Jolluck, *Exile and Identity: Polish Women in the Soviet Union during World War II* (Pittsburgh: University of Pittsburgh Press, 2002), pp. 45–86.

21. For more on memories of the extreme weather during the process of evacuation see Tatiana Tsivyan, "Iz russkogo provintsial'nogo teksta: 'Tekst evakuatsii,'" *Russian Literature* 53 (2003): 127–41.

22. Konstantinov, p. 127.

23. Konstantinov, p. 128.

24. For more on policies on the admission of war veterans into Soviet institutions of higher education, see Mark Edele, *Soviet Veterans of the Second World War: A Popular Movement in an Authoritarian Society 1941–1991* (Oxford: Oxford University Press, 2008).

25. Interview with Mikhail B., Berlin, Germany, 2002.

26. Marita Eastmond, "Stories as Lived Experience: Narratives in Forced Migration Research," *Journal of Refugee Studies* 20 (2007): 248–64, esp. 254–56.

27. Konstantinov, p. 128.

28. Konstantinov, p. 128.

29. Konstantinov, p. 135.

30. Konstantinov, pp. 135–36.

31. Interview with Mila Ch., New York, 2000.

32. Interview with Nissan K., New York, 2001.

33. On Uzbekistan, see Semen Gitlin, *Natsional'nye men'shinstva v Uzbekistane: Proshloe i nastoiashchee*, Vol. 2: *Evrei v Uzbekistane* (Tel Aviv, 2004), pp. 623–727 (I am very grateful to Dr. Zeev Levin, Hebrew University, for this reference).

34. Konstantinov, p. 151.

## Chapter 8

1. According to the 1930 resolution of the Central Committee of the Communist Party and SNK SSSR, "O reogranizatsii vysshikh uchebnykh zavedenii, tekhnikumov i rabochikh fakultetov." The full text of the document is located at http://intellect-invest.org.ua/content/userfiles/files/social_history_pedagogic/official_documents/Postanovlenie_CIK_SNK_O_reorganiz_VUZov_1930.pdf, retrieved on August 18, 2014.

2. Benjamin Tromly, *Making the Soviet Intelligentsia: Universities and Intellectual Life Under Stalin and Khrushchev* (New York: Cambridge University Press, 2014); presents the oral histories of a slightly younger generation.

3. Interview with Boyarskii, Berlin, 2002.

4. Edele, *Soviet Veterans of the Second World War*. Female veterans often faced stigmatization and hid the fact of their participation in the war. For an in-depth analysis of the perception of women veterans, see Edele, pp. 73–78.

5. Bolshevo is a small town near Moscow.

6. Interview with Victor Kh., New York. 1999.

7. Personal correspondence with Esfir Slepakova, June 6, 2013.

8. A collection of primary sources documenting Soviet Jewish enthusiasm in 1948 is Mordechai Altshuler, Yitzhak Arad, and Shmuel Krakowski, *Sovetskie evrei pishut Il'e Ėrenburgu, 1943–1966* (Jerusalem,1993).

9. Jeffrey Veidlinger argues that secularization was a slower process in smaller Soviet shtetlakh, where Jews continued their religious lifestyle throughout the Soviet period. Veidlinger, *In the Shadow of the Shtetl*, xiv.

10. Interview with Froim B., New York, 1999.

11. Interview with Mariya, Toronto, 2010.

12. Lenore Layman, "Reticence in Oral History Interviews," *Oral History Review* 36.2 (2009): 207–30.

13. Shternshis, "Between the Red and Yellow Stars," pp. 49–50.

14. Interview with Roza K., Philadelphia, 2000.

15. Interview with Mikhail B., Berlin, Germany, 2002.

16. Moshe Lewin, *The Gorbachev Phenomenon: A Historical Interpretation*, rev. ed. (Berkeley: University of California Press, 1991), p. 66.

17. Interview with Esfir A., Berlin, 2001.

18. Interview with David B., Moscow, 2002.

19. Feodosia was in Russia until 1954, 1954–2014 in Ukraine, then from 2014 de facto in Russia.

20. Interview with Zhenya, Toronto, 2008.

21. For more on constructing the narrative of persecution, see Lynn Abrams, *Oral History Theory* (London: Routledge, 2010); John Martin Campbell, *Magnificent Failure: A Portrait of the Western Homestead Era* (Stanford: Stanford University Press, 2001); Michael K. Honey, *Black Workers Remember: An Oral History of Segregation, Unionism and the Freedom Struggle* (Berkeley: University of California Press, 2000); Mary Chamberlain and Paul Richard Thompson, eds., *Narrative and Genre* (New York: Routledge, 1998); Wendy Singer, *Creating Histories: Oral Narratives and the Politics of History-Making* (Delhi: Oxford University Press, 1997); Paul Howard Takemoto, *Nisei Memories: My Parents Talk about the War Years* (Seattle: University of Washington Press, 2006); Anne M. Valk and Leslie Brown, *Living with Jim Crow: African American Women and Memories of the Segregated South* (New York: Palgrave Macmillan, 2010); and Kathleen Wells, *Narrative Inquiry* (New York: Oxford University Press, 2011).

## Chapter 9

1. Konstantinov, p. 219.

2. Yuri Slezkine, *The Jewish Century*, pp. 302–03 (on "the Pushkin faith" and Russian Jewish affinity to Russian language and literature).

3. Interview with Evgeniya K., New York, 1999.

4. For the text of the law about the gold medal, see William B. Simons, *The Soviet Codes of Law* (The Hague: M. Nijhoff, 1984), p. 968.

5. The story of the "gold medal" and obtaining (or not obtaining) it is one of the most prevalent ones in the Soviet Jewish narratives; both autobiographies written by Russian Jews and memoirs written by American Jewish author of Russian origin mention its significance. See Melanie Ilic, *Life Stories of Soviet Women: The Interwar Generation* (New York: Routledge, 2013), and Maxim Shrayer, *Leaving Russia: A Jewish Story* (Syracuse, NY: Syracuse University Press, 2013).

6. *Raionnyi otdel narodnogo obrazovaniia*, District Department of People's Education.

7. Actually, his 200th birthday in 1949.

8. Interview with Lyusya G. (wife of Semyon Sh.), New York, August 2001.

9. Interview with Mariya Kh., Toronto, 2007.

10. One popular American writer writes about this quality as one of the driving forces behind the success of immigrants in the United States. Amy Chua, *The Triple Package: How Three Unlikely Traits Explain the Rise and Fall of Cultural Groups in America* (New York: Penguin, 2014).

11. Noah Efron, *A Chosen Calling: Jews in Science in the Twentieth Century* (Baltimore: John Hopkins University Press, 2014), p. 41.

12. Kherman Branover, *Rossiĭskaia evreĭskaia ėntsiklopediia* (Moscow: Rossiĭskaia akademiia estestvennykh nauk, 1994).

13. Sam Barnai, "Advanced/Inhibited Minority: Jews in the Soviet Educational-Occupational System, 1950s–1960s" (paper delivered at the New Directions in Russian Jewish Studies conference, Brandeis University, 2016).

14. Konstantinov, p. 175.

15. Konstantinov, pp. 175–76.

16. Konstantinov, pp. 175–76.

17. Stalin's personal interest in the development of scholarly doctrines, ranging from the humanities to political economy to philosophy to biology, led to the famous science wars, which could not but influence the dynamics of Soviet academic culture. Ethan Pollock, *Stalin and the Soviet Science Wars* (Princeton: Princeton University Press, 2006).

18. For more on universities of the late Stalin era, see Benjamin Tromly, *Making the Soviet Intelligentsia: Universities and Intellectual Life Under Stalin and Khrushchev* (New York: Cambridge University Press, 2014).

19. Interview with Yurii K., Berlin, 2001.

20. Vsesoiuznyi komitet po radiofikatsii i radioveshchaniiu pri SM SSSR.

21. It was divided into separate committees, one for Soviet listeners and one for foreigners.

22. In 1946, a two-step system for granting academic degrees was established in the Soviet Union. The first step was the *kandidat nauk* (*kandidat* in science), earned by completing coursework and a dissertation, similar to the Western PhD. The second step required a number of publications, including books, and a larger, more groundbreaking dissertation, which would earn the title of *doktor nauk*. The salary depended significantly on the degree, more than it did before the war. After 1965, an academic reform led to a large number of *kandidat*s; over 35 percent of all academics were *kandidat*s by 1987, and over 51 percent of Jewish academics were *kandidat*s. Konstantinov, p. 178.

23. Interview with Anna M., Moscow, June 2002.

24. Konstantinov, pp. 184–85.

25. Soviet engineers usually worked in "engineering groups," or bureaus, which by the end of the 1940s normally consisted of draftsmen, technicians, senior technicians, engineers, senior engineers, the heads of the group, senior constructionists, and the head of the department.

26. For more on worker-students, see Shelia Fitzpatrick, *Education and Social Mobility in the Soviet Union, 1921–1934* (Cambridge: Cambridge University Press, 1979), pp. 48–51.

27. For more on Soviet wood plane construction and the early Soviet aviation industry, see Reina Pennington, "From Chaos to the Eve of the Great Patriotic War,

1922-41," in Robin Higham, John T. Greenwood, and Von Hardesty, *Russian Aviation and Air Power in the Twentieth Century* (London: Frank Cass, 1998), pp. 37-61.

28. Dmitrii Ustinov (1908-84) was a defense minister in 1941-53. In 1976-84, he was a member of the Politburo of the Communist Party, the most important executive organ of the Soviet regime.

29. K. Gerasimov served as Ustinov's deputy until 1951; See http://www.vko.ru/biblioteka/glava-2-chast-3, retrieved on August 20, 2014.

30. Interview with Izrail N., Berlin, June 2001.

31. The best study of contemporary Russian Jewish life in Germany and its ambivalence is Sveta Roberman, *Sweet Burdens: Welfare and Communality among Russian Jews in Germany* (Albany: SUNY Press, 2015). See also Shternshis, "Between the Red and Yellow Stars."

32. For more on this, see Shternshis, "Between the Red and Yellow Stars."

33. M. V. Davydov, *D 13: Gody i lyudi: Iz istorii NIEMI* (Moscow: Radio and Sviaz, 2009), p. 89.

34. Davydov, *Gody i lyudi*, pp. 59-61.

35. Gennady Kostyrchenko, "Deportatsiia—mistifikatsiia: proshchanie s mifom Stalinskoi epokhi," *Lechaim* 9 (2002), available at http://www.lechaim.ru/ARHIV/125/kost.htm, retrieved on August 20, 2014.

36. For more, see Stefan Karner, *Im Archipel GUPVI: Kriegsgefangenschaft und Internierung in der Sowjetunion 1941–1956* (Vienna: Oldenbourg, 1995).

37. Interview with Grigorii B., Berlin, June 2001.

38. Interview with Esfir A. Berlin, June 2001.

39. Konstantinov, pp. 195-96.

40. Interview with Evgeniya R., Moscow, 2002,

41. Interview with Mikhail K., Moscow, 2002.

42. Interview with Olga K., Moscow, 2002.

43. *Otdel po bor'be s khishcheniiami sotsialisticheskoi sobstvennosti*, the Department against Misappropriation of Socialist Property.

44. The Leningrad Affair was a series of criminal cases fabricated in the late 1940s and early 1950s to accuse a number of prominent politicians and members of the Communist Party of treason because of their supposed attempt to create an anti-Soviet organization in Leningrad. For more, see David Brandenberger, "Stalin, the Leningrad Affair, and the Limits of Postwar Russocentrism," *Russian Review* 63, no. 2 (2004): 241-55; Blair A. Ruble, "The Leningrad Affair and the Provincialization of Leningrad," *Russian Review* 42, no. 3 (1983): 301-20; Benjamin Tromly, "The Leningrad Affair and Soviet Patronage Politics, 1949–1950," *Europe-Asia Studies* 56, no. 5 (2004): 707-29; and V. F. Mikheev, "'Leningradskoe delo' (po materialam sledstvennykh del) (chast' II)" ["'The Leningrad Affair' (on the Base of the Investigatory Files) (Part II)"], *Noveishaia istoriia Rossii = Modern history of Russia* 1 (2013): 178, available at http://cyberleninka.ru/article/n/leningradskoe-delo-po-materialam-sledstvennyh-del-chast-ii, retrieved July 9, 2016.

45. A few of those arrested were Jews, including some from the Moscow Factory named after Stalin (ZIS). In the affair of 1950, during which the Jewish leadership of the factory was arrested and shot, Jews from a number of auto-making and tractor-making factories and the Kuznetsk Metal Factory were fired, at times arrested, and at times shot. Kostyrchenko, *Stalin protiv "kosmopolitov": Vlast' i evreĭskaia intelligentsiia v SSSR* (Moscow: ROSSPÈN, 2009), pp. 232-40.

46. Interview with Mikhail P., Berlin, June 2002.

47. Interview with Semyon D., Moscow, 2002.

48. Jukka Gronow, *Caviar with Champagne: Common Luxury and the Ideals of the Good Life in Stalin's Russia* (Oxford: Berg, 2003).

49. For more on the inner workings of Soviet trade, see Gronow, *Caviar with Champagne*; Julie Hessler, *A Social History of Soviet Trade: Trade Policy, Retail Practices, and Consumption, 1917–1953* (Princeton: Princeton University Press, 2004); and Serguei Alex. Oushakine, "'Against the Cult of Things': On Soviet Productivism, Storage Economy, and Commodities with No Destination," *Russian Review* 73 (April 2014): 198–236.

50. For more on Soviet rationing and food policies in the aftermath of World War II, see M. Ellman, "The 1947 Soviet Famine and the Entitlement Approach to Famines," *Cambridge Journal of Economics* 24.5 (2000): 603–30.

51. Interview with Faina M., Philadelphia, 2000.

52. Interview with Moyshe B., Toronto. 2007.

53. For more on stories of criminality in interviews and their analysis, see Larisa Fialkova and Maria Yelenevskaya, *In Search of the Self: Reconciling the Past and the Present in Immigrants' Experience* (Tartu: ELM Scholarly Press, 2013), 83–146.

## Chapter 10

1. On public opinion during the Doctors' Plot, see Leonid Smilovitsky, "Byelorussian Jewry and the 'Doctors' Plot,'" *East European Jewish Affairs* 27.2 (1997): 39–52. For more on the Doctors' Plot in general, see Jonathan Brent and Vladimir P. Naumov, *Stalin's Last Crime: The Plot against the Jewish Doctors, 1948–1953* (New York: HarperCollins, 2003).

2. Konstantinov, p. 185.

3. Interview with Ilya Sh., Moscow, June 2002.

4. Interview with Fira G., Brooklyn, August 2000.

5. SMERSH (short for *Smert' Shpionam*, meaning "death to spies") was a counter-intelligence agency in the Red Army that existed between 1943 and 1946. In 1946, it was merged into the NKVD.

6. Interview with Semen Sh., Brooklyn, New York, 2001.

7. Interview with Irena S., October 1997, Kyiv, interviewer Leonid Finberg. Kyiv Interviews, file name sadynsk.

8. Kostyrchenko, *Stalin protiv kosmopolitov*, p. 212.

9. Doris Bergen, "No End in Sight? The Ongoing Challenge of Producing an Integrated History of the Holocaust," in Christian Wiese and Paul Betts, ed., *Years of Persecution, Years of Extermination: Saul Friedländer and the Future of Holocaust Studies* (London: Continuum, 2010), pp. 289–310.

10. Konstantin Skriabin (1878–1972) was a biologist, the founder of Soviet helminthology, a member of the Soviet Academy of Sciences, and winner of the Lenin and Stalin state prizes.

11. Interview with Fira G., New York, August 2001.

12. Georgii Shulman, "Ne puskaete na Blizhnii Vostok, budu ezdit' na Dal'nii," *Mishpokha* 12(2), 2002, http://mishpoha.org/nomer12/a24.php, retrieved on August 21, 2014.

13. My thanks to Arkady Zeltser for this observation; personal correspondence, October 9, 2014.

14. Faina A. Vinokurova, "The Holocaust in Vinnitsa Oblast," http://www.rtrfoundation.org/webart/UK-arch-d2.pdf, retrieved on August 21, 2014.

15. For more on doctors and Soviet daily life, see Katherine Bliss Eaton, *Daily Life in the Soviet Union* (New York: Greenwood, 2004), pp. 175–208.

16. Interview with Sara K., Toronto, June 2007.

17. Shulman, "Ne puskaete na Blizhnii Vostok, budu ezdit' na Dal'nii."

18. Gennady Kostyrchenko, *Tainaia politika Stalina* (Moscow: Mezhdunarodnye otnosheniia, 2003), pp. 508–15.

## Chapter 11

1. For a book-length study of his life, see Matvei Geizer, *Mikhoels* (Moscow: Molodaia gvardiia, 2004).

2. Shimon Redlich, *Propaganda and Nationalism in Wartime Russia: The Jewish Antifascist Committee in the USSR, 1941–1948* (Boulder: East European Quarterly, 1982). Shimon Redlich, *War, Holocaust and Stalinism: A Documented Study of the Jewish Anti-Fascist Committee in the USSR* (Luxembourg: Harwood Academic Publishers, 1995). Arno Lustiger and Roman Brackman, *Stalin and the Jews: The Red Book: The Tragedy of the Jewish Anti-Fascist Committee and the Soviet Jews* (New York: Enigma, 2003).

3. For example, Hasya (born in 1904 in Vinnitsa, Ukraine) recalls that her father, who was dekulakized, was able to get a job at the Kyiv Jewish theater, which saved them from starvation. Interview with Hasya, Philadelphia, 2001.

4. Veniamin Zuskin (1899–1952) was an actor and later the director of the Moscow State Yiddish Theatre, a laureate of the Stalin Prize in 1946. For more on Zuskin, see Alla Zuskina-Perel'man and Sharon Blass, *The Travels of Benjamin Zuskin* (Syracuse: Syracuse University Press, 2015).

5. Interview with Maria D., Berlin, 2001.

6. Anna Shternshis, *Soviet and Kosher*, pp. 70–105.

7. Mariya Kotliarova, *Plecho Mikhoelsa: Vospominaniya aktrisy GOSETa* (Moscow: Bibliotechka gazety Tarbut, 2003), p. 100.

8. Soviet-Japanese War of 1945 (May–September).

9. Monia Shulman was my instructor of Yiddish in 1993 at the Russian State University for the Humanities. I remember him as an extremely knowledgeable and kind professor, who had difficulty walking upstairs. Prior to the interview, I did not know that Vera was married to him, but after I found out, I told her he had been my teacher.

10. Mikhail Tsarev (1903–87), director-in-chief of the Maly Theater (1950–63).

11. V. S. Shashkova, director of the Shchepkin Higher Theater School in 1946–50.

12. Gastrol'byuro SSSR—the Traveling Artists Agency of the Soviet Union, the organization that coordinated all Soviet concert performances, especially by Moscow and Leningrad stars (replaced by Goskontsert in 1956).

13. Lidiya Ruslanova (1900–73) was a renowned performer of Russian folk music.

14. Mikhail Garkavi (1897–1964), a famous entertainer, was married to Ruslanova 1929–1942.

15. Vladimir Kryukov (1897–1959) was Ruslanova's second husband, a general in the Soviet Army, arrested in 1948, released and acquitted in 1953.

16. Viktor Ardov, pen name of Viktor Zigberman (1900–76), popular Russian writer of film scripts and humorous prose.

17. Interview with Vera L., Moscow, June 2002.

18. Bergen, "No End in Sight?" and Doris Bergen, "I Am (Not) to Blame: Intent and Agency in Personal Accounts of the Holocaust," forthcoming in *Lessons and Legacies* vol. XII (Evanston: Northwestern University Press).

## Epilogue

1. Most if not all studies of older immigrants focus on their physical and mental health, but barely deal with culture. Gay Becker, Yewoubdar Beyene, and Leilani Cuizon Canalita, "Immigrating for Status in Late Life: Effects of Globalization on Filipino American Veterans," *Journal of Aging Studies* 14, No. 3 (2000): 273–91. Daniel Lai and Wendy Leonenko, "Correlates of Living Alone Among Single Elderly Chinese Immigrants in Canada," *International Journal of Aging and Human Development* 65 (2007): 121–48. David Ip, Chi Wai Lui, and Wing Hong Chui, "Veiled Entrapment: A Study of Social Isolation of Older Chinese Migrants in Brisbane, Queensland," *Ageing & Society* 27 (2007): 719–38. Ruth Mccaffrey, "The Lived Experience of Haitian Older Adults' Integration into a Senior Center in Southeast Florida," *Journal of Transcultural Nursing* 19 (2008): 33. A notable exception is Sveta Roberman, "Fighting to Belong: Soviet WWII Veterans in Israel," *Ethos* 35, No. 4 (2007): 447–77.

2. Ilya Altman and Leonid Terushkin, *Sokhrani moi pis'ma. . .: Sbornik pisem i dnevnikov evreev perioda Velikoĭ Otechestvennoĭ voĭny* (Moscow: TSentr i Fond "Kholokost," 2007).

3. The characteristics addressed in Amy Chua's *The Triple Package*, with minor variations, apply also to Soviet Jews and their place in Soviet society. See note 10 to Chapter 9.

4. Zvi Gitelman, "Are We All Russian Jews Now?" *Forward*, November 8, 2013, available at http://forward.com/articles/186698/we-are-all-russian-jews-now/?p=all, retrieved August 27, 2014.

5. Sveta Roberman, "Commemorative Activities of the Great War and the Empowerment of Elderly Immigrant Soviet Veterans in Israel," *Anthropological Quarterly* 80.4 (2007): 1035–64, esp. p. 1056.

6. For example, in 2005 the Blavatnik Archive undertook a long-term project to record the personal testimonies of Jewish veterans who fought in the Soviet Red Army during World War II. With over 650 video-recorded testimonies from all over the world, supplemented with digitized photographs and documents, it is the Archive's mission to preserve the memories of the Jewish veterans and make available new materials for academic research and public inquiry. The interview phase of the project was expected to continue through 2009, with the ultimate goal of creating an online searchable database of the entire video collection. Julie Chervinski, executive director of the Blavatnik Foundation, e-mail message to author, May 1, 2009. For more on the Blavatnik Institute, see http://www.blavatnikarchive.org/mission-history/.

A similar project, though on a smaller scale, is conducted in Canada. Managed by Elen Steinberg, a Toronto-based philanthropist, the project aims to make the heritage of Soviet Jewish war veterans living in Canada known and public. For more on their work, see http://www.sovietjewishveterans.com/index.html.

## Appendix 1

1. Shternshis, "Between the Red and Yellow Stars."

2. Rakhmiel Peltz, *From Immigrant to Ethnic Culture: American Yiddish in South Philadelphia* (Stanford: Stanford University Press, 1998).

3. When Jeffrey Veidlinger compared the interviews given by the same respondents in Yiddish and in Russian, he noticed that they highlighted Jewish holidays and customs more in Yiddish, whereas the Russian-language ones emphasized the celebrations of Soviet holidays in Russian (*In the Shadow of the Shtetl*, Introduction).

# Bibliography

Abrams, Lynn. *Oral History Theory*. London: Routledge, 2010.

Adler, Eliyana R. *In Her Hands: The Education of Jewish Girls in Tsarist Russia.* Detroit: Wayne State University Press, 2011.

Alexopoulos, Golfo, Kiril Tomoff, and Julie Hessler, eds. *Writing the Stalin Era: Sheila Fitzpatrick and Soviet Historiography.* New York: Palgrave Macmillan, 2011.

Alexopoulos, Golfo, Kiril Tomoff, Julie Hessler, and Sheila Fitzpatrick. *Writing the Stalin Era: Sheila Fitzpatrick and Soviet Historiography.* New York: Palgrave Macmillan, 2011.

Al'tman, Ilya, and Leonid Terushkin. *Sokhrani moi pis'ma: Sbornik pisem i dnevnikov evreev perioda Velikoi Otechestvennoi voiny.* Moscow: TSentr i Fond "Kholokost," 2007.

Al'tman, Ilya, ed. *Kholokost na territorii SSSR: Entsiklopediia*, 2nd ed. Moscow: ROSSPEN, 2011.

Altshuler, Mordechai. *Religion and Jewish Identity in the Soviet Union, 1941–1964.* Waltham: Brandeis University Press, 2012.

Altshuler, Mordechai. *Soviet Jewry on the Eve of the Holocaust: A Social and Demographic Profile.* Jerusalem: Yad Vashem, 1998.

Altshuler, Mordechai. *Soviet Jewry since the Second World War: Population and Social Structure.* New York: Greenwood Press, 1987.

Altshuler, Mordechai, Itskhak Arad, and Shmuel Krakovsky, eds. *Sovetskie evrei pishut Il'ye Erenburgu 1943–1966.* Jerusalem: Yad Vashem, 1993.

Anderson, Barbara A. *The Life Course of Soviet Women Born 1905–1960.* Urbana: University of Illinois at Urbana-Champaign, 1986.

Arad, Yitzhak. *The Holocaust in the Soviet Union.* Lincoln: University of Nebraska Press, 2009.

Arad, Yitzhak. *In the Shadow of the Red Banner: Soviet Jews in the War Against Nazi Germany.* Jerusalem: Yad Vashem. The International Institute for Holocaust Research, 2010.

Attwood, Lynne. *Gender and Housing in Soviet Russia: Private Life in a Public Space.* Manchester: Manchester University Press, 2010.

Avgar, Amos, Miriam Barasch, Esther Iecovich, Roni Kaufman, Aliza Kol-Fogelson, and Julia Mirsky. "Social Support Networks and Loneliness among Elderly Jews in Russia and Ukraine." *Journal of Marriage and Family* 66, no. 2 (May 2004): 306–17.

Avrutin, Eugene M. *Jews and the Imperial State: Identification Politics in Tsarist Russia.* Ithaca: Cornell University Press, 2010.

Baader, Benjamin Maria. *Gender, Judaism, and Bourgeois Culture in Germany, 1800–1870.* Bloomington: Indiana University Press, 2006,

Bagno, Olena. "The Price of Fear: Israel Beiteinu in 2009." *The Elections in Israel—2009* (2011): 19–41.

Basin, Mark, and Catriona Kelly, eds. *Soviet and Post-Soviet Identities.* New York: Cambridge University Press, 2012.

Bauer, Raymond, and Alex Inkeles. *The Soviet Citizen: Daily Life in a Totalitarian Society.* Cambridge: Harvard University Press, 1959.

Becker, Gay, Yewoubdar Beyene, and Leilani Cuizon Canalita, "Immigrating for Status in Late Life: Effects of Globalization on Filipino American Veterans." *Journal of Aging Studies* 14, no. 3 (2000): 273–91.

Beizer, Mikhail. *Evrei Leningrada: 1917–1939: Natsional'naia zhizn' i sovetizatsiia.* Moscow: Mosty kul'tury, 1999.

Beizer, Michael. "The Jews of a Soviet Metropolis in the Interwar Period: The Case of Leningrad." In *Revolution, Repression, and Revival: The Soviet Jewish Experience,* edited by Zvi Y. Gitelman and Yaacov Ro'i, pp. 113–30. Lanham: Rowman & Littlefield, 2007.

Bemporad, Elissa. *Becoming Soviet Jews: The Bolshevik Experiment in Minsk.* Bloomington: Indiana University Press, 2013.

Bergen, Doris. "I Am (Not) to Blame: Intent and Agency in Personal Accounts of the Holocaust." *Lessons and Legacies,* vol. 12. Evanston: Northwestern University Press, forthcoming.

Bergen, Doris. "No End in Sight? The Ongoing Challenge of Producing an Integrated History of the Holocaust." In *Years of Persecution, Years of Extermination: Saul Friedländer and the Future of Holocaust Studies,* edited by Paul Betts and Christian Wiese, 289–310. London: Continuum, 2010.

Bertaux, Daniel, Anna Rotkirch, and Paul Thompson. *On Living through Soviet Russia.* New York: Routledge, 2004.

Bertaux, Daniel, Anna Rotkirch, and Paul Thompson, eds. *Surviving the Soviet System.* New Brunswick and London: Transaction Publishers, 2006.

Bezmozgis, David. *The Free World.* Toronto: HarperCollins, 2011.

Biale, David. "Eros and Enlightenment: Love against Marriage in the East European Jewish Enlightenment." *Polin* 1 (1986): 49–69.

Bornat, Joanna. "Remembering in Later Life: Generating Individual and Social Change." *Oxford Handbooks Online.* 2012-09-18. Oxford University Press.

Brackman, Roman, and Arno Lustiger. *Stalin and the Jews: The Red Book; The Tragedy of the Jewish Anti-Fascist Committee and the Soviet Jews.* New York: Enigma, 2003.

Brandenberger, David. "Stalin, the Leningrad Affair, and the Limits of Postwar Russocentrism." *Russian Review* 63, no. 2 (2004): 241–55.

Branover, Kherman. *Rossiiskaia evreiskaia ėntsiklopediia.* Moscow: Rossiiskaia akademiia estestvennykh nauk, 1994.

Brent, Jonathan, and Vladimir P. Naumov. *Stalin's Last Crime: The Plot against the Jewish Doctors, 1948–1953.* New York: HarperCollins, 2003.

Brym, Robert. "Jewish Immigrants from the Former Soviet Union in Canada, 1996." *East European Jewish Affairs* 31, no. 2 (2001): 36–43.

Budnitski, Oleg. "Muzhshchiny i zhenschiny v Krasnoi Armii (1941–1945)." *Cahiers du Monde Russe* 52 (2011): 405–22.

Butler, R. N. "The Life Review: An Interpretation of Reminiscence in the Aged." *Psychiatry* 26 (1963): 65–75.

Campbell, John Martin. *Magnificent Failure: A Portrait of the Western Homestead Era.* Stanford: Stanford University Press, 2001.

Carback, Helen, Yulia Gradskova, and Zhanna Kravchenko, eds. *And They Lived Happily Ever After: Norms and Everyday Practices of Family and Parenthood in*

*Russia and Central Europe.* Budapest and New York: Central European University Press, 2012.

Carney, Sarah. "Transcendent Stories and Counter-narratives in Holocaust Survivor Life Histories: Searching for Meaning in Video-testimony Archives." In *Narrative Analysis: Studying the Development of Individuals in Society,* ed. Colette Daiute and Cynthia Lightfoot, 201–22. Thousand Oaks, CA: Sage, 2004.

Chamberlain, Mary, and Paul Richard Thompson, eds. *Narrative and Genre.* New York: Routledge, 1998.

Chatterjee, Choi. *Celebrating Women: Gender, Festival Culture, and Bolshevik Ideology, 1910–1939.* Pittsburgh: University of Pittsburgh Press, 2002.

Chua, Amy. *The Triple Package: How Three Unlikely Traits Explain the Rise and Fall of Cultural Groups in America.* Edited by Jed Rubenfeld. New York: Penguin, 2014.

Clements, Barbara Evans. *Bolshevik Women.* New York: Cambridge University Press, 1997.

Clements, Barbara. *A History of Women in Russia: From Earliest Times to the Present.* Bloomington: Indiana University Press, 2012.

Clements, Barbara Evans, Barbara Alpern Engel, and Christine Worobec, eds. *Russia's Women: Accommodation, Resistance, Transformation.* Berkeley: University of California Press, 1991.

Cohen, Steven Martin, and Arnold M. Eisen. *The Jew Within: Self, Family, and Community in America.* Bloomington: Indiana University Press, 2000.

Conquest, Robert. *The Great Terror: Stalin's Purge of the Thirties.* New York: Macmillan, 1968.

Coser, Lewis. "Some Aspects of Soviet Family Policy." *American Journal of Sociology* 56, no. 5 (March 1951): 429.

Daiute, Colette, and Cynthia Lightfoot. *Narrative Analysis: Studying the Development of Individuals in Society.* Thousand Oaks, CA: Sage, 2004.

Danner, Deborah D., Wallace V. Friesen, and David A. Snowdon. "Positive Emotions in Early Life and Longevity: Findings from the Nun Study." *Journal of Personality and Social Psychology* 80, no. 5 (May 2001): 804–13.

David-Fox, Michael. "Whither Resistance," *Kritika* 1, no. 1 (2000): 161–65;

Davis, Sara. *Popular Opinion in Stalinist Russia: Terror, Rebels and Dissent, 1934–41.* Cambridge: Cambridge University Press, 1997.

Davydov, M. V. *Gody i lyudi: Iz istorii NIEMI.* Moscow: Radio and Sviaz, 2009.

De Fina, Anna, and Alexandra Georgakopoulou. *Analyzing Narrative: Discourse and Sociolinguistic Perspectives.* Cambridge: Cambridge University Press, 2012.

Dekel-Chen, Jonathan L. *Farming the Red Land: Jewish Agricultural Colonization and Local Soviet Power, 1924–1941.* New Haven: Yale University Press, 2005.

Denisova, L. N. *Rural Women in the Soviet Union and Post-Soviet Russia.* New York: Routledge, 2010.

Dennen, Leon. *Where the Ghetto Ends.* New York: King Alfred, 1934.

Dodik, S. D. "Sud'ba evreev Transnistrii." *Korni* 24 (Oct.–Dec. 2004).

Dumitru, Diana, and Carter Johnson. "Constructing Interethnic Conflict and Cooperation: Why Some People Harmed Jews and Others Helped Them During the Holocaust in Romania." *World Politics* 63, no. 1 (2011): 1–42.

Dunaevskaia, I. M. *Ot Leningrada do Kenigsberga: Dnevnik voennoi perevodchitsy (1942–1945).* Moscow: ROSSPEN, 2010.

Dunham, Vera S. *In Stalin's Time: Middleclass Values in Soviet Fiction.* Cambridge: Cambridge University Press, 1976.

Dunstan, John. *Soviet Schooling in the Second World War*. Basingstoke: Macmillan Press in association with Centre for Russian and East European Studies, University of Birmingham, 1997.

Eastmond, Marita. "Stories as Lived Experience: Narratives in Forced Migration Research." *Journal of Refugee Studies* 20.2 (2007): 248–64.

Eaton, Katherine Bliss. *Daily Life in the Soviet Union*. New York: Greenwood, 2004.

Edele, Mark. *Soviet Veterans of the Second World War: A Popular Movement in an Authoritarian Society 1941–1991*. Oxford: Oxford University Press, 2008.

Edele, Mark. *Stalinist Society, 1928–1953*. Oxford: Oxford University Press, 2011.

Efron, Noah. *A Chosen Calling: Jews in Science in the Twentieth Century*. Baltimore: John Hopkins University Press, 2014.

Eid, Michael, and Randy J. Larsen. *The Science of Subjective Well-Being*. New York: Guilford Press, 2008.

Elias, Nelly. *Coming Home: Media and Returning Diaspora in Israel and Germany*. New York: State University of New York Press, 2008.

Ellman, M. "The 1947 Soviet Famine and the Entitlement Approach to Famines." *Cambridge Journal of Economics* 24.5 (2000): 603–30.

Engel, Barbara. "The Womanly Face of War: Soviet Women Remember World War II." In *Women and War in the Twentieth Century: Enlisted with or without Consent*, edited by Nicole Dombrowski Risser, 102–19. New York: Garland, 1999.

Engel, Barbara A., Anastasia Posadskaya-Vanderbeck, and Sona S. Hoisington, *A Revolution of Their Own: Voices of Women in Soviet History*. Boulder, CO: Westview, 1998.

Engel, Barbara Alpern. *Mothers and Daughters: Women of the Intelligentsia in Nineteenth-Century Russia*. Evanston: Northwestern University Press, 2000.

Estraikh, Gennady. *In Harness: Yiddish Writers' Romance with Communism*. Syracuse: Syracuse University Press, 2005.

Estraikh, Gennady. *Soviet Yiddish: Language Planning and Linguistic Development*. Oxford: Oxford University Press, 1999.

Estraikh, Gennady, ed. *Yiddish in the Cold War*. London: Legenda/Modern Humanities Research Association and Maney Publishing, 2008.

Fairchild, Mildred, and Susan M. Kingsbury. *Factory, Family, and Woman in the Soviet Union*. New York: G. P. Putnam's Sons, 1935.

Fialkova, L. L., and Maria N. Yelenevskaya. *Ex-Soviets in Israel: From Personal Narratives to a Group Portrait*. Detroit: Wayne State University Press, 2007.

Fialkova, Larisa, and Maria Yelenevskaya. *In Search of the Self: Reconciling the Past and the Present in Immigrants' Experience*. Tartu: ELM Scholarly Press, 2013.

Field, Deborah A. *Private Life and Communist Morality in Khrushchev's Russia*. New York: Peter Lang, 2007.

Figes, Orlando. *The Whisperers: Private Life in Stalin's Russia*. London: Allen Lane, 2007.

Filtzer, Donald. *Soviet Workers and Late Stalinism: Labour and the Restoration of the Stalinist System after World War II*. Cambridge: Cambridge University Press, 2002.

Fitzpatrick, Sheila. *Education and Social Mobility in the Soviet Union, 1921–1934*. Cambridge: Cambridge University Press, 1979.

Fitzpatrick, Sheila. *Everyday Stalinism: Ordinary Life in Extraordinary Times: Soviet Russia in the 1930s*. New York: Oxford University Press, 1999.

Fitzpatrick, Sheila. "Lives and Times." In *In the Shadow of Revolution*, edited by Sheila Fitzpatrick and Yuri Slezkine, 3–18. Princeton: Princeton University Press, 2000.

Fitzpatrick, Sheila. *Stalinism: New Directions*. London: Routledge, 1999.

Fitzpatrick, Tanya. "Elderly Russian Jewish Immigrants." In *Therapeutic Interventions with Ethnic Elders: Health and Social Issues*, edited by S. Alemán, T. Fitzpatrick, E. W. Gonzalez, and T. V. Tran, 55–78. Binghamton: Haworth Press, 2000.

Freeze, ChaeRan. *Jewish Marriage and Divorce in Imperial Russia*. Hanover: University Press of New England for Brandeis University Press, 2002.

Freidenreich, Harriet Pass. *Female, Jewish, and Educated: The Lives of Central European University Women*. Bloomington: Indiana University Press, 2002.

Fürst, Juliane. *Stalin's Last Generation: Soviet Post-war Youth and the Emergence of Mature Socialism*. Oxford: Oxford University Press, 2010.

Geiger, H. Kent. *The Family in Soviet Russia*. Cambridge, MA: Harvard University Press, 1968.

Geizer, Matvei. *Mikhoels*. Moscow: Molodaia gvardiia, 2004.

Gershenson, Olga. *The Phantom Holocaust: Soviet Cinema and Jewish Catastrophe*. New Brunswick: Rutgers University Press, 2013.

Gershenson, Olga, and David Shneer, "Soviet Jewishness and Cultural Studies," *Journal of Jewish Identities* 4, no. 1 (2011): 129–46.

Gessen, Masha. *Ester and Ruzya: How My Grandmothers Survived Hitler's War and Stalin's Peace*. New York: Dial Press, 2004.

Gheith, Jehanne M., and Katherine R. Jolluck, *Gulag Voices: Oral Histories of Soviet Incarceration and Exile*. New York: Palgrave Macmillan, 2011.

Gilboa, Yehoshua. *The Black Years of Soviet Jewry, 1939–1953*. Boston: Little, Brown, 1971.

Gitelman, Zvi. "Are We All Russian Jews Now?" *Forward*, November 8, 2013. Available at http://forward.com/articles/186698/we-are-all-russian-jews-now/?p=all, accessed on August 27, 2014.

Gitelman, Zvi. *A Century of Ambivalence*. Bloomington: Indiana University Press, 2001.

Gitelman, Zvi. "History, Memory and Politics: The Holocaust in the Soviet Union." *Holocaust and Genocide Studies* 5, no. 1 (1990): 23–37.

Gitelman, Zvi. *Jewish Identity in Postcommunist Russia and Ukraine: An Uncertain Ethnicity*. Cambridge: Cambridge University Press, 2012.

Gitelman, Zvi. *Jewish Nationality and Soviet Politics: The Jewish Sections of the CPSU, 1917–1930*. Princeton: Princeton University Press, 1972.

Gitlin, Semyon. *Natsional'nye men'shinstva v Uzbekistane, proshloe i nastoiashchee*. Vol. 2: *Evrei v Uzbekistane*, 623–727. Tel-Aviv, 2004.

Goldenberg, Myrna. "Memoirs of Auschwitz Survivors: The Burden of Gender." In *Women in the Holocaust*, edited by Dalie Ofer and Lenore J. Weitzman, 327–39. New Haven: Yale University Press, 1998.

Goldman, Wendy Z. *Women, the State, and Revolution*. Cambridge and New York: Cambridge University Press, 1993.

Gorsuch, Anne E. *Youth in Revolutionary Russia*. Bloomington: Indiana University Press, 2000.

Gronow, Jukka. *Caviar with Champagne: Common Luxury and the Ideals of the Good Life in Stalin's Russia*. Oxford: Berg, 2003.

Gubrium, Jaber F., and James A. Holstein. *Analyzing Narrative Reality*. Thousand Oaks, CA: Sage Publications, 2009.

Hall, Judith A., and Mark L. Knapp. *Nonverbal Communication in Human Interaction*. Boston: Wadsworth, 2009.

Harel, Zev. "Jewish Aged: Diversity in Need and Care Solutions." In *Age through the Ethnic Lenses*, edited by L. K. Olson, 145–59. Lanham: Rowman & Littlefield, 2001.

Harris, James R., ed. *The Anatomy of Terror: Political Violence under Stalin.* Oxford: Oxford University Press, 2013.

Harris, Steven E. *Communism on Tomorrow Street: Mass Housing and Everyday Life After Stalin.* Baltimore: Johns Hopkins University Press, 2013.

Healey, Dan. "Sexual and Gender Dissent: Homosexuality as Resistance in Stalin's Russia." In *Contending with Stalinism: Soviet Power & Popular Resistance in the 1930s,* edited by Lynne Viola, 139–69. Ithaca: Cornell University Press, 2002.

Heider, Angelika, Edna Lomsky-Feder, and Tamar Rapoport. "Recollection and Relocation in Immigration: Russian-Jewish Immigrants 'Normalize' Their Antisemitic Experiences." *Symbolic Interaction* 25, no. 2 (2002): 175–98.

Hellbeck, Jochen. *Revolution on My Mind: Writing a Diary under Stalin.* Cambridge, MA: Harvard University Press, 2006.

Hessler, Julie. *A Social History of Soviet Trade: Trade Policy, Retail Practices, and Consumption, 1917–1953.* Princeton: Princeton University Press, 2004.

Hochschild, Adam. *The Unquiet Ghost: Russians Remember Stalin.* New York: Viking, 1994.

Hoffmann, David L. *Stalinist Values: The Cultural Norms of Soviet Modernity, 1917–1941.* Ithaca: Cornell University Press, 2003.

Honey, Michael K. *Black Workers Remember: An Oral History of Segregation, Unionism and the Freedom Struggle.* Berkeley: University of California Press, 2000.

Hooper, Cynthia. "Terror of Intimacy: Family Politics in the 1930s Soviet Union." In *Everyday Life in Early Soviet Russia: Taking the Revolution Inside,* edited by Christina Kiaer and Eric Naiman, 61–91. Bloomington: Indiana University Press, 2006.

Hyer, Janet. "Fertility Control in Soviet Russia, 1920–1936: A Case Study of Gender Regulation and Professionalization." PhD diss., University of Toronto, 2007.

Hyman, Paula E. *Gender and Assimilation in Modern Jewish History: The Roles and Representation of Women.* Seattle: University of Washington Press, 1995.

Ilic, Melanie. *Life Stories of Soviet Women: The Interwar Generation.* New York: Routledge, 2013.

Ilic, Melanie. *Women Workers in the Soviet Interwar Economy: From "Protection" to "Equality."* Basingstoke: Macmillan in association with Centre for Russian and East European Studies, 1999.

Inkeles, Alex. *The Soviet Citizen: Daily Life in a Totalitarian Society.* Cambridge: Harvard University Press, 1961.

Ip, David, Chi Wai Lui, and Wing Hong Chui, "Veiled Entrapment: A Study of Social Isolation of Older Chinese Migrants in Brisbane, Queensland." *Ageing & Society* 27 (2007): 719–38.

Johnson, Timothy. *Being Soviet: Identity, Rumour and Everyday Life under Stalin 1939–1953.* Oxford: Oxford University Press, 2011.

Jockusch, Laura, and Tamar Lewinsky. "Paradise Lost? Postwar Memory of Polish Jewish Survival in the Soviet Union." *Holocaust Genocide Studies* 24, no. 3 (2010): 373–99

Jolluck, Katherine R. *Exile and Identity: Polish Women in the Soviet Union During World War II.* Pittsburgh: University of Pittsburgh Press, 2002.

Kaplan, Marion A. *The Making of the Jewish Middle Class: Women, Family, and Identity in Imperial Germany.* New York: Oxford University Press, 1991.

Karner, Stefan. *Im Archipel GUPVI: Kriegsgefangenschaft und Internierung in der Sowjetunion 1941–1956.* Vienna: Oldenbourg, 1995.

Kelly, Catriona. "What Was Soviet Studies and What Came Next?" *Journal of Modern History* 85, no. 1 (March 2013): 109–49.

Kelly, John D. "Seeing Red: Mao Fetishism, Pax Americana, and the Moral Economy of War." In *Anthropology and Global Counterinsurgency*, edited by John D. Kelly, Beatrice Jauregui, Sean T. Mitchell, and Jeremy Walton, 67–83. Chicago: University of Chicago Press, 2010.

Kirschenbaum, Lisa A. *The Legacy of the Siege of Leningrad, 1941–1995: Myth, Memories, and Monuments.* Cambridge: Cambridge University Press, 2006.

Kirshenblatt-Gimblett, Barbara. "Weddings." *YIVO Encyclopedia of Jews in Eastern Europe.* Accessed on October 18, 2013.

Kless, Shlomo. "Zionist Activities of Jewish Refugees in the USSR in 1941–1945 and the Relations of the Yishuv in the Land of Israel with Them" PhD diss., Hebrew University, 1985.

Klier, John. "Pogroms." *YIVO Encyclopedia of Jews in Eastern Europe.* Accessed on January 2, 2016.

Konstantinov, Vyacheslav. *Evreiskoe naselenie byvshego SSSR v XX veke (sotsialno-demograficheskii analiz).* Jerusalem: Lira, 2007.

Kostyrchenko, G. *Gosudarstvennyi Antisemitizm v SSSR ot nachala do kul'minatsii: 1938–1953.* Moscow: Mezhdunar. fond "Demokratiia," 2005.

Kostyrchenko, G. *Tainaia politika Khrushcheva: Vlast', intelligentsiia, evreiskii vopros.* Moscow: Mezhdunarodnye otnosheniia, 2012.

Kostyrchenko, Gennady. *Deportatsiia—Mistifikatsiia: Proshchanie s mifom Stalinskoi epokhi.* Available at http://www.lechaim.ru/ARHIV/125/kost.htm, accessed on August 20, 2014.

Kostyrchenko, Gennady. *Stalin protiv "kosmopolitov": Vlast' i evreiskaia intelligentsiia v SSSR.* Moscow: ROSSPĖN, 2009.

Kostyrchenko, Gennady. *Tainaia politika Stalina.* Moscow: Mezhdunarodnye otnosheniia, 2003.

Kostyrchenko, Gennady. *V plenu u krasnogo faraona: Politicheskie presledovaniia evreev v SSSR v poslednee stalinskoe desiatiletie; dokumental'noe issledovanie.* Moscow: Mezhdunarodnye otnosheniia, 1994.

Kotkin, Stephen. *Magnetic Mountain: Stalinism as a Civilization.* Berkeley: University of California Press, 1997.

Kotlerman, Ber Boris. *In Search of Milk and Honey: The Theater of "Soviet Jewish Statehood" (1934–49).* Bloomington: Slavica, 2009.

Kotliarova, Maria. *Plecho Mikhoelsa: Vospominaniya aktrisy GOSETa.* Moscow: Bibliotechka gazety Tarbut, 2003.

Krupnik, Igor. "Soviet Cultural and Ethnic Policies Toward Jews: A Legacy Reassessed." In *Jews and Jewish Life in Russia and the Soviet Union*, edited by Yaacov Ro'i, 67–86. Ilford: Frank Cass, 1995.

Krutikov, Mikhail. *From Kabbalah to Class Struggle: Expressionism, Marxism, and Yiddish Literature in the Life and Work of Meir Wiener.* Stanford: Stanford University Press, 2011.

Kuromiya, Hiroaki. *The Voices of the Dead: Stalin's Great Terror in the 1930s.* New Haven: Yale University Press, 2007.

Lai, Daniel, and Wendy Leonenko. "Correlates of Living Alone Among Single Elderly Chinese Immigrants in Canada." *International Journal of Aging and Human Development* 65 (2007): 121–48.

Lapidus, Rina. *Jewish Women Writers in the Soviet Union.* Abingdon: Routledge, 2012.

Layman, Lenore. "Reticence in Oral History Interviews." *Oral History Review* 36.2 (2009): 207–30.

Lenoe, Matthew. "In Defense of Timasheff's Great Retreat." *Kritika: Explorations in Russian and Eurasian History* 5, no. 4 (2004): 721–30.

Lerner, J., E. Lomsky-Feder, and T. Rapoport. "The 'Ethnic Script' in Action: The Regrounding of Russian-Jewish Immigrants in Israel." *Ethos* 35, no. 2 (2007): 168–95.

Levitt, Laura. *Jews and Feminism: The Ambivalent Search for Home.* New York: Routledge, 1997.

Levy, Becca R., Martin D. Slade, Suzanne R. Kunkel, and Stanislav V. Kasl, "Longevity Increased by Positive Self-Perceptions of Aging." *Journal of Personality and Social Psychology* 83, no. 2 (August 2002): 261–70.

Lewin, Moshe. *The Gorbachev Phenomenon: A Historical Interpretation.* Rev. ed. Berkeley: University of California Press, 1991.

Litvak, Yosef. *Jewish Refugees from Poland in the Soviet Union, 1939–1946.* Jerusalem: ha-Universitah ha-Ivrit bi-Yerushalayim, ha-Makhon le-Yahadut zemanenu, 1988.

Litwin, Howard, and Elazar Leshem, "Late-Life Migration, Work Status, and Survival: The Case of Older Immigrants from the Former Soviet Union in Israel." *International Migration Review* 42, no. 4 (Winter 2008): 903–25.

Lourie, Richard. *Russia Speaks: An Oral History from the Revolution to the Present.* New York: E. Burlingame, 1991.

Lukin, Benyamin, "An-ski Ethnographic Expedition and Museum." *YIVO Encyclopedia of Jews in Eastern Europe.* Available at http://www.yivoencyclopedia.org/article. aspx/An-ski_Ethnographic_Expedition_and_Museum, accessed August 22, 2013.

Manley, Rebecca. *To the Tashkent Station: Evacuation and Survival in the Soviet Union at War.* Ithaca: Cornell University Press, 2009.

Mantovan, Daniela. *Yiddish Poets and the Soviet Union, 1917–1948.* Heidelberg: Universitätsverlag Winter, 2012.

Mccaffrey, Ruth. "The Lived Experience of Haitian Older Adults' Integration Into a Senior Center in Southeast Florida." *Journal of Transcultural Nursing* 19 (2008): 33.

Mead, George. *The Philosophy of the Present.* La Salle, IL: Open Court, 1959.

Mead, George Herbert. "The Nature of the Past." In *Essays in Honor of J. Dewey,* edited by John Coss, 235–42. New York: Henry Holt, 1929.

Meir, Natan M. *Kyiv, Jewish Metropolis: A History, 1859–1914.* Bloomington: Indiana University Press, 2010.

Merridale, Catherine. *Ivan's War: Life and Death in the Red Army, 1939–1945.* London: Macmillan, 2007.

Messana, Paola. *Soviet Communal Living: An Oral History of the Kommunalka.* New York: Palgrave Macmillan, 2011.

Mikheev, V. F. "'Leningradskoe delo' (po materialam sledstvennykh del) (chast' II)" ["'The Leningrad Affair' (on the Base of the Investigatory Files) (Part II)"]. *Noveishaia istoriia Rossii = Modern history of Russia* 1 (2013): 178.

Moskoff, William. *The Bread of Affliction: The Food Supply in the USSR During World War I.* Cambridge, UK: Cambridge University Press, 1990.

Moskoff, William. "Soviet Higher Education Policy during World War II." *Soviet Studies* 38, no. 3 (July 1986): 406–15.

Moss, Kenneth B. *Jewish Renaissance in the Russian Revolution.* Cambridge: Harvard University Press, 2009.

Murav, Harriet. *Music from a Speeding Train: Jewish Literature in Post-Revolution Russia.* Stanford: Stanford University Press, 2011.

Naimark, Norman M. *Stalin's Genocides.* Princeton: Princeton University Press, 2010.

Nathans, Benjamin. *Beyond the Pale: The Jewish Encounter with Late Imperial Russia.* Berkeley: University of California Press, 2002.

Naumov, Vladimir P., and Joshua Rubenstein. *Stalin's Secret Pogrom: The Postwar Inquisition of the Jewish Anti-Fascist Committee.* New Haven: Yale University Press, 2005.

Northrop, Douglas Taylor. *Veiled Empire: Gender & Power in Stalinist Central Asia.* Ithaca: Cornell University Press, 2004.

Ofer, Dalia, and Lenore J Weitzman, ed. *Women in the Holocaust.* New Haven: Yale University Press, 1998.

Orelick, Anelise. *The Soviet Jewish Americans.* Westport: Greenwood, 1999.

Oswald, Ingrid, and Viktor Voronkov, "The 'Public–Private' Sphere in Soviet and Post-Soviet Society: Perception and Dynamics of 'Public' and 'Private' in Contemporary Russia." *European Societies* 6, no. 1 (2004): 97–117.

Oushakine, Serguei Alex. "'Against the Cult of Things': On Soviet Productivism, Storage Economy, and Commodities with No Destination." *Russian Review* 73 (April 2014): 198–236.

Paperno, Irina. *Stories of the Soviet Experience.* Ithaca: Cornell University Press, 2009.

Parush, Iris. *Reading Jewish Women: Marginality and Modernization in Nineteenth-Century Eastern European Jewish Society.* Hanover: University Press of New England for Brandeis University Press, 2004.

Passerini, Luisa, ed. *Memory & Totalitarianism.* New Brunswick: Transaction Publishers, 2005.

Peltz, Rakhmiel. *From Immigrant to Ethnic Culture: American Yiddish in South Philadelphia.* Stanford: Stanford University Press, 1997.

Pennington, Reina. "From Chaos to the Eve of the Great Patriotic War, 1922–41." In *Russian Aviation and Air Power in the Twentieth Century*, edited by Robin Higham, John T. Greenwood, and Von Hardesty, 37–61. London: Frank Cass, 1998.

Peter Konecny, *Builders and Deserters Students, State, and Community in Leningrad, 1917–1941.* Montreal: McGill-Queen's University Press, 1999.

Petrone, Karen. *Life Has Become More Joyous, Comrades: Celebrations in the Time of Stalin.* Bloomington: Indiana University Press, 2000.

Pinchuk, Ben-Cion. *Soviet Jews in the Face of the Holocaust: A Study in the Problem of Deportation and Evacuation.* Tel Aviv: Goldstein-Goren Diaspora Research Center, 1979.

Pinkus, Benjamin. *Me-ambivalenṭiyut li-verit bilti-ketuvah: Yi´sra'el, Tsarfat vi-Yehude Tsarfat 1947–1957.* [Israel]: Mekhon Ben-Guryon le-heker Yi´sra'el, ha-Tsiyonut u-moreshet Ben-Guryon, Kiryat ´Sedeh Boker, Hotsa'at ha-sefarim shel Universitat Ben Guryon ba-Negev, 2005.

Pinkus, Benjamin. *The Jews of the Soviet Union: The History of a National Minority.* Cambridge: Cambridge University Press, 1990.

Pinkus, Benjamin. *The Soviet Government and the Jews, 1948–1967: A Documented Study.* New York: Cambridge University Press, 1984.

Pipes, Richard. *Russia Under the Bolshevik Regime.* New York: Vintage, 1995.

Pollock, Ethan. *Stalin and the Soviet Science Wars.* Princeton: Princeton University Press, 2006.

Portelli, Alessandro. *The Death of Luigi Trastulli, and Other Stories: Form and Meaning in Oral History.* Albany: State University of New York Press, 1990.

Portelli, Alexandro. *The Battle of Valle Giulia: Oral History and the Art of Dialogue.* Madison: University of Wisconsin Press, 1997,

Potemkina, Marina. "Evakuatsiia i natsional'nye otnosheniia v sovetskom tylu v gody Velikoi Otechestvennoi voiny (na materialakh Urala)." *Otechestvennaia istoriia* 3 (2002).

Propp, Vladimir. *Morphology of the Folktale.* Bloomington: Research Center, Indiana University, 1958.

Propp, Vladimir Ia., and A. N. Afanas'ev. *Morfologiia skazki.* St. Petersburg: Nauka, 1995.

Raleigh, Donald. *Soviet Baby Boomers.* Oxford and New York: Oxford University Press, 2012.

Raleigh, Donald J. *Russia's Sputnik Generation: Soviet Baby Boomers Talk about Their Lives.* Bloomington: Indiana University Press, 2006.

Ransel, David. *Village Mothers: Three Generations of Change in Russia and Tataria.* Bloomington: Indiana University Press, 2000.

Rapoport, Tamar, Edna Lomsky-Feder, and Angelika Heider. "Recollection and Relocation in Immigration: Russian-Jewish Immigrants 'Normalize' Their Anti-Semitic Experiences." *Symbolic Interaction* 25 (2002): 175–98.

Rapoport, Ya. L. *The Doctors' Plot of 1953.* Cambridge: Harvard University Press, 1991.

Redlich, Shimon. *Propaganda and Nationalism in Wartime Russia: The Jewish Antifascist Committee in the USSR, 1941–1948.* Boulder: East European Quarterly, 1982.

Redlich, Shimon. *War, Holocaust and Stalinism: A Documented Study of the Jewish Anti-Fascist Committee in the USSR.* Luxembourg: Harwood Academic Publishers, 1995.

Remennick, Larissa. "Former Soviet Jews in the New/Old Homeland: Between Integration and Separatism." In *Diasporic Homecomings: Ethnic Return Migrations of the Late 20th Century,* edited by Takeyuki Tsuda, 208–26. Stanford: Stanford University Press, 2009.

Remennick, Larissa. "Intergenerational Transfer in Israeli-Russian Immigrant Families: Parental Social Mobility and Children's Integration." *Journal of Ethnic and Migration Studies* 38, no. 10 (2012): 1533–50.

Remennick, Larissa. "The 1.5 Generation of Russian Immigrants in Israel: Between Integration and Sociocultural Retention." *Diaspora: A Journal of Transnational Studies* 12, no. 1 (Spring 2003): 39–66.

Remennick, Larissa I. *Russian Jews on Three Continents: Identity, Integration, and Conflict.* New Brunswick: Transaction Publishers, 2007.

Roberman, Sveta. "Commemorative Activities of the Great War and the Empowerment of Elderly Immigrant Soviet Veterans in Israel." *Anthropological Quarterly* 80.4 (2007): 1035–64.

Roberman, Sveta. "Fighting to Belong: Soviet WWII Veterans in Israel." *Ethos* 35, no. 4 (2007): 447–77.

Roberman, Sveta. *Sweet Burdens: Welfare and Communality among Russian Jews in Germany.* Albany: SUNY Press, 2015.

Robine, Jean-Marie. *Longevity: To the Limits and Beyond.* Berlin: Springer, 1997.

Roginsky, Dina. "Israelis in Toronto: From Stigmatization to Self-Organization." Paper presented at the annual meeting of the American Association for Jewish Studies, Toronto, December 16, 2007.

Ro'i, Yaacov. *The Struggle for Soviet Jewish Emigration, 1948–1967.* Cambridge: Cambridge University Press, 1991.

Ro'i, Yaacov. "Union of Soviet Socialist Republics." *YIVO Encyclopedia of Jews in Eastern Europe.* Accessed December 8, 2014.

Ruble, Blair A. "The Leningrad Affair and the Provincialization of Leningrad." *Russian Review* 42, no. 3 (1983): 301–20.

Samuel, Lawrence R. *The American Dream: A Cultural History.* Syracuse, NY: Syracuse University Press, 2012.

Schlesinger, Rudolf. *The Family in the U.S.S.R.* London: Routledge, 1949.

Seidman, Naomi. *The Marriage Plot: Or, How Jews Fell in Love with Love, and with Literature*. Stanford: Stanford University Press, 2016.

Sherman, Joseph, ed. *From Revolution to Repression: Soviet Yiddish Writing 1917–1952*. Nottingham: Five Leaves, 2012.

Shik, Na'ama. "Sexual Abuse of Jewish Women in Auschwitz-Birkenau." In *Brutality and Desire: War and Sexuality in Europe's Twentieth Century*, edited by Dagmar Herzog, 221–46. New York: Palgrave Macmillan, 2009.

Shlapentokh, Vladimir. *Love, Marriage, and Friendship in the Soviet Union*. New York: Praeger, 1984.

Shlapentokh, Vladimir. *Public and Private Life of the Soviet People: Changing Values in Post-Stalin Russia*. New York: Oxford University Press, 1989.

Shneer, David. *Through Soviet Jewish Eyes: Photography, War, and the Holocaust*. New Brunswick: Rutgers University Press, 2011.

Shneer, David. *Yiddish and the Creation of Soviet Jewish Culture, 1918–1930*. Cambridge: Cambridge University Press, 2004.

Shulman, Georgii. "Ne puskaete na Blizhnii Vostok, budu ezdit' na Dal'nii." *Mishpokha* 12(2), 2002, http://mishpoha.org/nomer12/a24.php, retrieved on August 21, 2014.

Shrayer, Maxim. *Leaving Russia: A Jewish Story*. Syracuse: Syracuse University Press, 2013.

Shternshis, Anna. "Between Life and Death: Why Some Soviet Jews Decided to Leave and Others to Stay in 1941." *Kritika: Exploration of Russian and Eurasian History* 15, 3 (2014): 477–504.

Shternshis, Anna. "Between the Red and Yellow Stars: Ethnic and Religious Identity of Soviet Jewish World War II Veterans in New York, Toronto, and Berlin." *Journal of Jewish Identities* 4, no. 1 (2011): 43–64.

Shternshis, Anna. "Kaddish in the Church: Perceptions of Orthodox Christianity among Moscow Elderly Jews in the Early Twenty-First Century." *Russian Review* 66, no.2 (April 2007): 273–94.

Shternshis, Anna. "Salo on Challah: Soviet Jews' Experience of Food in the 1920s–1950s." In *Jews and Their Foodways*, edited by Anat Helman. New York: Oxford University Press, 2015.

Shternshis, Anna. *Soviet and Kosher: Jewish Popular Culture in the Soviet Union, 1923–1939*. Bloomington: Indiana University Press, 2006.

Shulman, Elena. *Stalinism on the Frontier of Empire: Women and State Formation in the Soviet Far East*. New York: Cambridge University Press, 2008.

Siegel, Dina. *The Great Immigration: Russian Jews in Israel*. New York: Berghahn Books, 1998.

Simons, William B. *The Soviet Codes of Law*. The Hague: M. Nijhoff, 1984.

Singer, Wendy. *Creating Histories: Oral Narratives and the Politics of History-Making*. Delhi: Oxford University Press, 1997.

Slezkine, Yuri. *The Jewish Century*. Princeton: Princeton University Press, 2004.

Smilovitsky, Leonid. "Byelorussian Jewry and the 'Doctors'Plot.'" *East European Jewish Affairs* 27.2 (1997): 39–52.

Smith, M. B. *Property of Communists: The Urban Housing Program from Stalin to Khrushchev*. DeKalb: Northern Illinois University Press, 2010.

Stampfer, Shaul. "Patterns of Internal Jewish Migration in the Russian Empire." In *Jews and Jewish Life in Russia and the Soviet Union*, edited by Yaacov Ro'i, 28–51. London: Frank Cass, 1995.

Takemoto, Paul Howard. *Nisei Memories: My Parents Talk about the War Years*. Seattle: University of Washington Press, 2006.

Thurston, Robert W. "The Soviet Family during the Great Terror, 1935–1941." *Soviet Studies* 43, no. 3 (1991): 553–74.

Timasheff, Nicholas. *The Great Retreat: The Growth and Decline of Communism in Russia*. New York: E. P. Dutton, 1946.

Tolts, Mark. "Demography of the Contemporary Russian-Speaking Jewish Diaspora." Paper presented at the conference on the Contemporary Russian-speaking Jewish Diaspora (Harvard University, November 13–15, 2011).

Tromly, Benjamin. "The Leningrad Affair and Soviet Patronage Politics, 1949–1950." *Europe-Asia Studies* 56, no. 5 (2004): 707–29.

Tromly, Benjamin. *Making the Soviet Intelligentsia: Universities and Intellectual Life Under Stalin and Khrushchev*. New York: Cambridge University Press, 2014.

Tsivyan, Tatiana. "Iz russkogo provintsial'nogo teksta: 'tekst evakuatsii.'" *Russian Literature* 53 (2003): 127–41.

Tsuda, Takeyuki, ed. *Diasporic Homecomings: Ethnic Return Migrations of the Late 20th Century*. Stanford: Stanford University Press, 2009.

Tumarkin, Nina. *The Living & the Dead: The Rise and Fall of the Cult of World War II in Russia*. New York: Basic Books, 1994.

Valk, Anne M., and Leslie Brown. *Living with Jim Crow: African American Women and Memories of the Segregated South*. New York: Palgrave Macmillan, 2010.

Van Onselen, Charles. *The Seed Is Mine: The Life of Kas Maine, a South African Sharecropper, 1894–1985*. New York: Hill and Wang, 1996.

Vaupel, James W. "Demographic Analysis of Aging and Longevity." *American Economic Review* 88, no. 2 (May 1998): 242–47.

Veidlinger, Jeffrey. *In the Shadow of the Shtetl: Small Town Jewish Life in Soviet Ukraine*. Bloomington: Indiana University Press, 2013.

Veidlinger, Jeffrey. *Jewish Public Culture in the Late Russian Empire*. Bloomington: Indiana University Press, 2009.

Veidlinger, Jeffrey. *The Moscow State Yiddish Theater: Jewish Culture on the Soviet Stage*. Bloomington: Indiana University Press, 2000.

Vinokurova, Faina. "The Holocaust in Vinnitsa Oblast." Available at http://www.rtrfoundation.org/webart/UK-arch-d2.pdf, accessed on August 21, 2014.

Viola, Lynne. *Peasant Rebels Under Stalin*. Cambridge: Cambridge University Press, 1997.

Viola, Lynne. "Popular Resistance in the Stalinist 1930s: Soliloquy of a Devil's Advocate." *Kritika: Explorations in Russian and Eurasian History* 1, no. 1 (2000): 45–69.

Viola, Lynne. *The Role of the OGPU in Dekulakization, Mass Deportations, and Special Resettlement in 1930*. Pittsburgh: University of Pittsburgh Press, 2000.

Viola, Lynne. *The Unknown Gulag: The Lost World of Stalin's Special Settlements*. New York: Oxford University Press, 2007.

Viola, Lynne, ed. *Contending with Stalinism: Soviet Power & Popular Resistance in the 1930s*. Ithaca: Cornell University Press, 2002.

Viola, Lynne, ed. *The War Against the Peasantry, 1927–1930: The Tragedy of the Soviet Countryside*. New Haven: Yale University Press, 2005.

Walke, Anika. *Pioneers and Partisans: An Oral History of Nazi Genocide in Belorussia*. New York and Oxford: Oxford University Press, 2015.

Wells, Kathleen. *Narrative Inquiry*. New York: Oxford University Press, 2011.

Whitewood, Peter. *The Red Army and the Great Terror: Stalin's Purge of the Soviet Military.* Lawrence: University Press of Kansas, 2015.

Wood, Elizabeth A. *The Baba and the Comrade: Gender and Politics in Revolutionary Russia.* Bloomington: Indiana University Press, 1997.

Yalen, Deborah Hope. "Red Kasrilevke: Ethnographies of Economic Transformation in the Soviet Shtetl, 1917–1939." PhD diss., University of California, Berkeley, 2007.

Yurchak, Alexei. *Everything Was Forever, Until It Was No More: The Last Soviet Generation.* Princeton: Princeton University Press, 2005.

Zeltser, Arkadii. *Evrei Sovetskoi provintsii: Vitebsk i mestechki, 1917–1941.* Moscow: ROSSPEN, 2006.

Zubkova, Elena. *Obshchestvo i reformy 1945–1964.* Moscow: Rossiia molodaia, 1993.

Zubkova, Elena. *Poslevoennoe sovetskoe obshchestvo–politika i povsednevnost´, 1945–1953.* Moscow: ROSSPĖN, 2000.

Zubkova, Elena. *Russia After the War: Hopes, Illusions, and Disappointments, 1945–1957.* Armonk, NY: M. E. Sharpe, 1998.

Zuskina-Perel´man, Alla, and Sharon Blass. *The Travels of Benjamin Zuskin.* Syracuse: Syracuse University Press, 2015.

## Interviews Cited (transcripts in possession of Anna Shternshis)

1. Anna M., Moscow, June 2002.
2. Anonymous, Brighton Beach, New York, August 1999.
3. Ava T., Potsdam, June 2002.
4. Bella G., Berlin, June 2002.
5. Boris G., Toronto, May 2010.
6. Esfir A., Potsdam, June 2002.
7. David B., Moscow, 2002.
8. David S., Brooklyn, New York, February 1999.
9. David Sh., Moscow, June 2001.
10. Dora Z., Moscow, June 2001.
11. Elizaveta K., Brooklyn, August 1999.
12. Elizaveta K., Philadelphia, March 2001.
13. Elizaveta K., Potsdam, June 2002.
14. Elizaveta Z., Berlin, June 2002.
15. Etya G., Brooklyn, New York, January 1999.
16. Evgeniia B., Brooklyn, New York, May 1999.
17. Evgeniya R., Moscow, June 2001.
18. Faina D., New York, 2001.
19. Faina M., Philadelphia, 2000.
20. Fira F., Berlin, June 2002.
21. Fira G., New York, March 1999.
22. Froim B., New York, 1999.
23. Grigorii B., Berlin, June 2001.
24. Grigorii B., New York, April 1999.
25. Hasya, Philadelphia, 2001.
26. Ilya F., Berlin, June 2002.
27. Ilya R., Moscow, June 2001.
28. Ilya Sh., Moscow, June 2001.
29. Iona K., Potsdam, June 2002.
30. Izrail N., Berlin, June 2001.

31. Klara G., Berlin, June 2002.
32. Klara G., Brooklyn, New York, August 2000.
33. Klara G., Philadelphia, March 2001.
34. Klara R., Berlin, June 2002.
35. Lazar F., Moscow, June 2001.
36. Lev G., New York, August 1999.
37. Lev L., Moscow, June 2001.
38. Lilya Sh., Berlin, June 2002.
39. Lisa S., New York, May 1999.
40. Liusia G., New York, August 1999.
41. Liza R., New York, August 1999.
42. Lyubov B., Berlin, June 2002.
43. Maria M., New York, August 2001.
44. Mariya D., Berlin, June 2002.
45. Mariya K., Moscow, June 2001.
46. Mariya Kh., Toronto, 2007.
47. Mariya P. and Mikhail P., Berlin, July 2002.
48. Mariya S., Brooklyn, New York, March 1999.
49. Mariya, Toronto, 2010.
50. Maya D., Berlin, 2002.
51. Mikhail B., Potsdam, June 2002.
52. Mikhail K., Moscow, 2002.
53. Mila Ch., Brooklyn, New York, March 1999.
54. Mira G., Philadelphia, February 2001.
55. Moyshe B., Toronto, 2007.
56. Nissan K., New York, 2001.
57. Olga K., Brooklyn, New York, March 1999.
58. Olga K., Moscow, June 2001.
59. Roza K., Philadelphia, 2000.
60. Rozaliya U., Moscow, June 2001.
61. Samuil G., New York, April 1999.
62. Sara K., Toronto, June 2007.
63. Semion Sh., Brooklyn, New York, August 1999.
64. Semyon and Faina Ya., Berlin, June 2002.
65. Semyon D., Moscow, 2002.
66. Semyon F., Moscow, June 2001.
67. Sima F., Berlin, June 2002.
68. Veniamin Sh., Moscow, June 2001.
69. Vera L., Moscow, June 2002.
70. Victor Kh., New York, August 1999.
71. Vladimir Ia., Berlin, June 2002.
72. Vladimir K., Potsdam, July 2002.
73. Yakov B., Moscow, June 2001.
74. Yosef V., Berlin, June 2002.
75. Yurii K., Berlin, 2001.
76. Yurii P., Berlin, June 2002.
77. Zhenya, Toronto, 2008.

# THE OXFORD ORAL HISTORY SERIES

**J. Todd Moye,** University of North Texas
**Kathryn Nasstrom,** University of San Francisco
**Robert Perks,** The British Library
*Series Editors*

**Donald A. Ritchie**
*Senior Advisor*

# Index